Magnet and Specialized Schools of the Future

A Focus on Change

Edwin T. Merritt
James A. Beaudin
Charles R. Cassidy
Patricia A. Myler

with contributions by Donald Bodnar, Christine M. Casey,
Timothy P. Cohen, Daniel Davis, Robert Dixon, L. Gerald Dunn,
Thomas A. Fantacone, Mark S. Hesselgrave, James A. Keaney Jr.,
Julie A. Kim, LEARN, Jeffrey M. Leavenworth, Richard S. Oja,
John C. Oliveto, Marcia T. Palluzzi, Chester A. Salit, Michael E. Schrier,
Jeffrey A. Sells, Gary Thierrien, and James Waller

Published in partnership with Fletcher-Thompson, Inc.,
and the Association of School Business Officials International

SCARECROWEDUCATION
Lanham, Maryland • Toronto • Oxford
2005

Published in partnership with Fletcher-Thompson, Inc., and the
Association of School Business Officials International

Published in the United States of America by ScarecrowEducation
An imprint of The Rowman & Littlefield Publishing Group, Inc.
4501 Forbes Boulevard, Suite 200, Lanham, Maryland 20706
www.scarecroweducation.com

PO Box 317
Oxford
OX2 9RU, UK

Chapter 5, "Finding a Home: The Facilities Side of the Charter School Debate," originally appeared in
slightly different form in the November 2002 issue of *American School & University* and is republished
here with permission of PRIMEDIA Business Magazines & Media, Inc. © 2002, PRIMEDIA Business
Magazines & Media, Inc. All rights reserved.

Chapter 6, "Special Ed That's Even More Special: Designing Schools for Autistic Students" originally
appeared in slightly different form in the November 2003 issue of *American School & University* and is
republished here with permission of PRIMEDIA Business Magazines & Media, Inc. © 2003, PRIMEDIA
Business Magazines & Media, Inc. All rights reserved.

Materials reproduced in Chapter 8, "A Draft Magnet School Operations Plan," were created by LEARN,
Southeastern Connecticut's Regional Educational Service Center. Adapted and reprinted by permission.

Chapter 14, "One-Stop Shopping? The Perils and Promise of Design-Build Project Delivery," was
originally published in the April 2004 issue of *School Business Affairs*. Reprinted by permission.

British Library Cataloguing in Publication Information Available

Library of Congress Cataloging-in-Publication Data

Magnet and specialized schools of the future : a focus on change / Edwin T. Merritt . . . [et al.].
    p. cm.
    "Published in partnership with Fletcher-Thompson, Inc., and the Association of School Business
Officials International."
    Includes bibliographical references and index.
    ISBN 1-57886-180-2 (pbk. : alk. paper)
    1. Magnet school facilities—United States—Planning.   2. Magnet school facilities—United States—
Design and construction. I. Merritt, Edwin T., 1936– .
LB2818.M34   2005
373.24′1—dc22   2004012736

Contents

Part III: Issues in Specialized-School Planning, Design, and Construction

Acknowledgments

The two-year-long task of putting together this book—the most complex and wide-ranging volume to date in Fletcher-Thompson's Schools of the Future series—involved the work and assistance of many, many people, all of whom deserve our profound and heartfelt thanks.

First, we would like to express our deep gratitude to the principals of Fletcher-Thompson, Inc., for their willingness to support the series' production and their recognition of its importance. The many staff members at Fletcher-Thompson and at the firm's New Jersey subsidiary, RJF Fletcher-Thompson Architecture, LLC, who participated directly in this book's creation by contributing ideas or written text to various sections of the book have our great thanks. Over time, the entire Fletcher-Thompson Education Practice Group has become involved in this series, and all have exhibited patience and enthusiasm on the many occasions when the books have gotten in the way of revenue-producing work.

Fletcher-Thompson administrative assistants Joyce A. Saltes and Marie Fennessy provided invaluable aid and always found time to help move the project along. Crucial research assistance was provided by Katie Voelker, a summer intern at Fletcher Thompson. The firm's graphic design and marketing staff—especially Andy Krochko, Brian Russo, Jan Pasqua, Diane Kozel, and Deborah Friend—were always ready to help with the many details that go into a book's production.

This book has been made much richer by the enthusiastic participation of a number of other design firms. Special gratitude is owed to Jim Lord, Pam Smith, and Greg Anderson of KGA Architecture, Las Vegas, which designed the Advanced Technologies Academy featured on pages 51–57; to Tyler Smith and Kent McCoy of Smith Edwards Architects, Hartford, designers of the Montessori Magnet Elementary (pages 33–41); to Whit Iglehart and Holly DeYoung of Tai Soo Kim Partners, Hartford, which designed the Greater Hartford Academies building (pages 41–51); and to Jane Greenwood and Mickey Kostow of Kostow Greenwood Architects, New York City, which designed the rooftop addition to the Manhattan Comprehensive Night and Day High School (pages 70–73). Ken Baird, system engineer for Visual Communications Systems, Las Vegas, and the designer of the television broadcast system so creatively used at Las Vegas's Gilbert Magnet Elementary School (see pages 127–30), is likewise owed our sincere thanks.

The work of compiling this book took us to magnet schools and other schools of choice in cities in the Northeast and around the country, and we had the pleasure of meeting and talking with numerous educators, all of whom graciously gave us their time and generously shared their expertise. Especially helpful were Barbara Chandler Allen and Dr. Claire Gallagher of the Charter High for Architecture + Design, Philadelphia (featured on pages 57–62); Barbara Bowman of

Las Vegas's Advanced Technologies Academy, as well as two ATech seniors, Joanna DeGuzman and Cinthia Paez-Valenzuela, who served as our tour guides and made our visit to that remarkable school so enlightening and enjoyable; Glenn Cooper, C. J. Curry, and other members of the administration of Las Vegas's Desert Pines High School, home of the Academy of Information Technology magnet program; Tim Dearman and Cathy McCaffrey of the Gilbert Magnet Elementary, Las Vegas; Gus Penna, of Connecticut's Capitol Region Education Council; Timothy Nee, principal of the Montessori Magnet Elementary, Hartford; Howard J. Thiery and Dr. Herbert "Doc" Sheppard, directors, respectively, of the Greater Hartford Academy of Math and Science and the Greater Hartford Academy of the Arts; and Stanley Teitel, principal of New York City's Stuyvesant High. Teachers at all these schools were incredibly gracious—allowing us to interrupt their classes, taking time out to discuss their experiences with us, and inviting us, in many cases, to witness the learning process firsthand.

Thanks also go to Doreen Marvin of LEARN, the regional educational service agency of southeast Connecticut, who was instrumental in securing permission for us to use the sample operations plan that appears on pages 137–46. Fern Eisgrub, magnet program director for the Yonkers (New York) Public Schools, merits special mention; she spent a day with us touring two of that city's magnet schools and sharing her wisdom—born of long experience—about magnet education. Whether credited or not, her thoughts deeply inform this book's pages.

Two chapters originally published as magazine articles likewise benefited enormously from the participation of concerned educators and school business officials. Chapter 5, "Finding a Home," is enriched by the insights of Rex Shaw, director, and Ernest Villany, treasurer, of the Teaneck (New Jersey) Community Charter School; Michael Duggan, executive director of the Domus Foundation, which operates Stamford, Connecticut's Trailblazers Academy; and Charles Knoph, business manager for the Unity Charter School in Morristown, New Jersey. Chapter 6, "Special Ed That's Even More Special," could not have been written without the assistance of two deeply committed autism educators: Thomas Parvenski, director of the River Street School in Windsor, Connecticut, and David Holmes, who heads Princeton, New Jersey's Eden Institute.

Finally, we are greatly indebted to the faith in our endeavor so consistently demonstrated by the editorial staff at ScarecrowEducation, and by the Association of School Business Officials, which has so generously lent its name to the Schools of the Future publication project.

Preface

For this, the fourth volume in Fletcher-Thompson's Schools of the Future series, we decided to take on the task of outlining future directions for those public schools that, more than any other, are changing the face of American pre-K–12 education. Specialized public schools—and especially magnet schools—are, we believe, the crucible in which some of the most promising new approaches to education are today being forged and tested. In a system that cries out for change, these are the places where change is really happening.

The job of creating guidelines for such schools' planning, design, and construction is, however, a daunting one, for two related reasons. First, magnet and other "schools of choice" are very much an experiment in progress. Second, these schools represent a breathtaking diversity—not just of pedagogical approaches but also of thematic focuses, student populations served, and yes, facility types. Early on in this project's life, we recognized that it would be hard enough even to describe that portion of the American public-education landscape that these schools now occupy, much less to predict the future course of the schools-of-choice movement or to recommend school-design strategies to help bolster its chances of success. While writing this book, we always remained aware that our work—in both its descriptive and prescriptive senses—would necessarily be incomplete. Still, we forged ahead, convinced that a book like this, no matter what its deficiencies, is sorely needed.

The Schools of the Future series is an unusual venture. Most books on architectural design, whether the design of schools or other building types, are written by designers and for designers. In undertaking this series, we decided to do something different: to create guidebooks aimed at a lay audience composed of all the other people involved in the school planning, design, and construction process.

Our firm's long experience in designing public school buildings throughout the Northeast persuaded us of the need for such a series. After all, architects play only a limited role in school planning and design, and a great deal of the decision-making power rests with the other stakeholders in a school construction project—superintendents, boards of education, building committees, state and local school-system administrators, and (in the best cases) faculty, parents, other concerned citizens, and schoolchildren themselves. All too often, however, the nondesigners who play such a crucial role in facility-related decision-making are thrown into the process without a clear notion of the many, many factors that will influence a facility's short- and long-term viability. It was our idea, in developing this series, to give them a leg up on all the issues they'll confront.

It has also been our idea to help all the people involved in school construction projects of whatever type to navigate the rather stormy seas of change through which American public education is now voyaging. We don't, of course, pretend to be able to prophesy the future. What we do know, though, is that charting a reasonable course through these waters demands some awareness of the trends currently influencing education, as well as those likely to affect it in the years to come. In times of swift and inexorable change, a truly visionary, future-oriented approach is needed to ensure that the school buildings we create today—at an enormous expense of money and effort—will serve our communities well for years to come. Understandably but unfortunately, that much-needed visionary approach is too often scuttled as decision-makers scramble to deal with all the details involved in bringing a school construction project to completion.

Throughout this volume—as in the other volumes in this series—we reiterate the need to *always* keep the future in focus while working through every school construction–related decision, whether it pertains to the specifics of learning technologies, furniture, and equipment or to the larger questions of information-technology infrastructure, spatial configuration, long-term sustainability, or even the "delivery method" by which a school will be designed and built.

We likewise repeatedly stress our conviction that, for a school to be successful, curricular planning must proceed hand-in-hand with facility design. That conviction only grew stronger as we researched the present book—visiting magnet and other specialized schools, familiarizing ourselves with the current literature, and engaging in discussions with our firm's design staff, educators from around the country, and architects from other firms involved in cutting-edge school-facility design. New approaches to learning require new kinds of learning environments. If we aren't going to sell our children short, we greatly need to perform a thoroughgoing reassessment of how school buildings come into being, of how they're designed, and—yes—even of their purpose and function in the life of our communities and our country.

That's a far-ranging goal. It's our hope that *Magnet and Specialized Schools of the Future: A Focus on Change* makes a contribution to its realization.

Introduction

Think About It *Today*

Edwin T. Merritt, Ed.D.

THE NEED FOR A PRAGMATIC, FUTURIST APPROACH TO SCHOOL PLANNING AND DESIGN

We can't stop the future from happening. We're moving into it, every moment of our lives. The future belongs to us, but more than that, it belongs to *our children*. These are simple, inarguable truths. So why is the future so often ignored—or given very short shrift—in school planning and design? I can think of several, related reasons.

First of all, it can be difficult to think about the future. Not only is the future unpredictable, but getting even a limited grasp on the kinds of developments the future might bring requires us to know something about the many trends and forces that are shaping human life right now. That's quite a large field—and so it's no wonder that people feel intimidated before they even begin. Understanding and solving *today's* problems seems challenging enough. Who has the time or energy to think about the future?

Second, thinking about the future can be . . . well, it can be a little scary. We Americans are in love with technology; we're thrilled by scientific and technical advances, and we're very quick to welcome the latest innovations—whether they're new features on our cellphones or new gizmos in the doctor's office. But that pleasure is just one facet of what we feel toward technology. Technical advances also frustrate, concern, and—yes—frighten us. The complexity of this emotion is perfectly reasonable. "Technology" doesn't just mean cellphones and MRIs; it means cloning and genetically modified food and sophisticated weapons systems and corporate Big Brothers reading your mind every time you make a credit-card purchase. No wonder our feelings are so mixed—and no wonder that, when asked to think about the future, we so often take refuge in the Scarlett O'Hara syndrome: "I'll think about it *tomorrow.*"

Third, planning for the future can seem expensive, or financially risky. We sometimes feel that people who want to talk to us about the future are trying to sell us a bill of goods, trying to get us to shell out for costly things that we may never really need—or that will become obsolete before we ever get around to learning how to use them. This kind of fear—that if we think about the future, we'll be taken for a ride—grows more intense during a time of economic instability, when every financial outlay has to be carefully justified.

Finally, thinking about the future can seem impractical. For hundreds—perhaps thousands—of years, people have been making predictions about the future that simply haven't come true, or that have come true in ways so very different from what the prophets imagined that it more or less amounts to the same thing. The actual year 1984 didn't look at all like the world predicted in George Orwell's 1949 novel. Y2K was a well-publicized bust, and the year 2001—the setting for Stanley Kubrick's 1968 *Space Odyssey*—passed without any earthling actually engaging in interplanetary travel. If you'd gone to the "Futurama" exhibit at the 1939 New York World's Fair, you'd have seen the world of 1960 as envisioned by the automakers at General Motors; their vision got some things right—the freeways, the highway cloverleafs—but it also got a lot wrong (the GM folks neglected to mention the rush-hour traffic jams, or the flight to the suburbs that would wreak havoc on our cities). Because so little of what I or anyone has to say about the future may come true anyway—or may "come true" in a way so different from what we envision—why bother to listen?

So, since thinking about the future is so hard, so scary, and so difficult to justify economically, let's not rush right into it here. Instead, let's approach the matter "through the back door," spending a little time thinking about the past and the present—particularly as they relate to the ways we've educated (and continue to educate) our children and to the school buildings we send them to, expecting them to learn.

BACKWARD-LOOKING EDUCATION?

As someone once said, "The past is prologue," and there's no better way to get a handle on the importance of thinking about the future when planning new schools than to examine how well the school facilities built over the past half-century have accommodated the "future." (The future, that is, that's already passed or passing.)

Let's be clear: I'm *not* talking about school buildings that are in bad shape, physically (though there are lots of those, obviously, and there's a crying need for a program of national scope to repair, upgrade, and in many cases replace deteriorating school facilities). I'm talking about well-maintained schools in affluent school districts. How well have such facilities responded to the great changes that have occurred—technologically and otherwise—in American education over, say, the past 20 years? How well have they adapted to social, economic, and other changes impacting education?

The short answer is: *not* very well.

Let's begin with the very simplest sort of example. The *New York Times* has reported on a number of Connecticut public high schools that were forced to restrict the privilege of driving to school to seniors, leaving junior-year drivers grumbling about the indignity—the "uncoolness"—of having to return to taking the bus to and from school each day (Gross 2003). The reason for this harsh new restriction: there's no room for all the cars. This, obviously, is more a social than an educational problem per se, and it's obviously a problem that could only afflict an extremely wealthy society, but it points to something noteworthy. All over the country, high school parking lots are groaning, bursting at the seams from an onslaught of private vehicles—a crisis (of sorts) that these schools' planners and designers never imagined. Snarled traffic has become the norm even at many suburban elementary and middle schools, as parents have increasingly taken to dropping their children off and picking them up rather than relying on the school bus. *Could* yesterday's school planners have anticipated this situation, and taken steps to alleviate it? Perhaps not, but it's certainly an interesting question.

So let's turn our attention to another current space-related issue, one that bears more directly on the educational experience itself: books. Printed books are physical objects—they take up space. Today, school media centers (which in the days before the "information revolution" used to be known as *libraries*) are, with rare exceptions, designed to store many, many books. They have lots of bookshelves, lots of what librarians call "stack space." So what's wrong with that? We want our schoolchildren to have access to lots of information, right? Doesn't that mean lots of books (and lots of space to store them)?

Well, not quite. Few people seriously doubt that books—printed books—have great value, or that the technology of the printed book, which has been with us ever since Gutenberg, will remain a useful technology for years and years to come. The issue is that, over the past few decades, books—and for that matter, other printed information sources, like magazines and newspapers—have been supplemented by a wide range of other technologies for conveying and accessing text-based information. *Electronic* technologies.

We all know this. We use these technologies every day. And we know that for many purposes, electronic technologies are superior to books as repositories of information. Which is better: a multivolume printed encyclopedia or an online encyclopedia? The "real" encyclopedia takes up several feet of shelf space and gathers dust when it's not being used. It can be physically damaged, and each of its volumes can be used by only one reader at a time. What's more, the pace of advance in scientific and technical fields is so rapid that a printed reference work like this is almost guaranteed to be out of date in certain important respects even before the ink is dry. And obsolescence doesn't just apply to the scientific and technical information such a work contains. Geographical information becomes quickly obsolete (an encyclopedia published in 2002 would have named Saddam Hussein as the president of Iraq). History in all its dimensions—artistic, biographical, cultural, political—continues to unfold, which means that information on the arts, people, governments, and so on all needs to be constantly updated.

A virtual encyclopedia, unlike its tangible, physical cousin, has none of these drawbacks. It takes up no storage space—or not, at least, at the point of access. Its "pages" can't get dog-eared (or cut out); it has no spine to break. It can be used by multiple researchers simultaneously. It can be rapidly and continuously updated. What's more, it can be searched—*mined* might be the better word—for information in a much more thorough, much more creative way than a printed reference work. It can be interactive. And as if all that weren't enough to convince us of its superiority, subscribing to such an online reference is likely to be vastly cheaper than having to replace that heavy, hardbound, printed set every couple of years.

As I say, we all know this. Students today are very much in the habit of taking advantage of electronic resources like the online encyclopedia I've just described (and many, many other such resources besides). Why is it, then, that we're still designing media centers to accommodate lots and lots and lots of printed materials? Why are we still dedicating all that valuable, expensive square footage to storage space that, as the years go on, will be less and less necessary?

We all recognize that schools designed even a decade or two ago have in many cases adapted only very uncomfortably to the technological revolution that has so recently transformed virtually every aspect of education. We're all familiar with learning spaces—including media centers—into which computers and other electronic technologies have been squeezed, in ways that are not very ergonomic or aesthetically satisfying and, most important, in ways that inhibit rather than enhance flexibility. So why do we still design and build new school facilities in ways that probably won't serve future purposes very well?

One reason, certainly, is that we are creatures of habit. We often have trouble seeing the changes that *are* taking place—that *have already* taken place—much less those that lie ahead. We often can't see that solutions to our problems are right at our fingertips.

Let's stay on the subject of printed books for a moment. In December 2002, the *New York Times* carried a story about parents in California and elsewhere around the country who were raising Cain about the weight of all the textbooks their children were being forced to carry to and from school each day (Dillon 2002). Textbooks have gotten bigger and bigger, heavier and heavier: the story tells of one mother who weighed her daughter's textbook-stuffed backpack, which came in at 28 pounds. Another mother reported that her son's daily textbook burden amounted to 42 pounds. In districts that have eliminated lockers because of concerns about weapons and drugs, the burden on schoolchildren's backs is even greater, since they must lug the books around with them all day long. Backpacks, it seems, are *literally* bursting at the seams; parents were not only concerned about the long-term health effects for their children from carrying all this weight, but also angry about the cost of having to replace torn backpacks every few months.

The story mentioned several proposed solutions to the problem: make textbooks lighter; divide them up into multiple smaller volumes; issue students two sets of books—one for use in school, the other for use at home; allow students to bring wheeled packs to school; bring back school lockers. What's so interesting here is that the *best* possible solution appears never to have crossed the minds of those parents, educators, and legislators who were interviewed for the story: *Why not just eliminate printed textbooks entirely and replace them with electronic books or other, web-based products?* The technology for solving the problem already exists—indeed, *has* existed for a long time. Why not use it?

Granted, there are economic interests at stake here. The publishing companies that produce printed textbooks would have to come up with alternative electronic products. Textbook printers and distributors would no doubt suffer a sharp decline in business. School districts would have to take steps to ensure that each schoolchild could access electronic resources at home. And so on. But changing our basic ways of doing things always has some economic consequences, and in this case it's hard to see how those consequences, as a whole, would be worse than the consequences of what we're now doing—which is virtually guaranteeing that a whole generation of children grows up with musculoskeletal problems resulting from lugging all that weight around.

Now, let's turn our attention away from that old-fashioned technology—paper and ink—and back to "current" technology (i.e., the computer). Why have I put those quotation marks around "current"? Because—as we're all aware—computer and computer-related technologies change so quickly that it's very dangerous to describe something as "current." The almost brand-new iMac on which this is being written has a storage capacity of 80 gigabytes—a capacity that would have been unimaginable in a home computer just a few short years ago. What's more, it's networked, wirelessly, to another home computer and a remote printer. It's perpetually connected to the Internet via cable TV, and access to the Web is virtually instantaneous. Wow, huh?

Well, as you and I know, such a home setup is hardly unusual these days. And if you're reading this five or even two years hence, you're probably not thinking, "Wow!" You're probably thinking, "Gee, what a puny little machine. And what a primitive little network!"

I'm hardly trying to brag about how "wired" (or "wirelessly wired"?) I am. The point I'm working toward is that—knowing all we do about the rapidity of change in the arena of computer technology—we continue to design schools for *today's* technology (or even yesterday's), not tomorrow's. Of course, some new schools have been designed in technologically savvy, future-oriented ways, but plenty of others are based on the "state-of-the-art" designs of five or even ten years ago. Face it: Hard-wired computer stations and dedicated computer labs—no matter how well integrated into an overall design—begin to look positively antique in an era when students are carrying cellphones that let them take and send photos to one another instantly and PDAs that enable them to connect wirelessly, effortlessly, and oh-so-portably to the Internet.

In fact, we're not even fully exploiting the *wired* technologies that we have. In many cases, high school science-lab suites are still being designed in ways that don't realize the space- and cost-saving possibilities conferred by virtual laboratory environments—which are now quite sophisticated, highly interactive, and every bit as good for teaching the experimental method, especially in the lower high school grades, as their "real life" equivalents. And, with some notable exceptions, American school systems are certainly not fully utilizing the existing distance-learning and teleconferencing technologies that allow schools, districts, regions, and even statewide systems to share resources more effectively, cutting costs and (probably) enabling space reductions in individual schools.

It isn't at all difficult to imagine the space-related implications of a situation in which all of a school's students (and faculty, and staff) have immediate, personal, wireless, fully portable access to a full range of electronic information resources. This kind of situation—and we're not very far from getting there—would eliminate the need for the various sorts of dedicated computer spaces that are still being designed and built into new schools today.

Parking lots. Printed books. Information technology. So far, I haven't even touched on the core aspects of the educational experience—the curriculum itself, the instructional methods used, socialization dynamics, the ways schools are organized (and the ways they make decisions)—or on how these central aspects of education, as they exist today, do or do not relate to today's and tomorrow's realities.

This past year, I read an intriguing little book (you see, I do appreciate the value of paper-and-ink technology!) called *Tomorrow Now: Envisioning the Next Fifty Years* (2002), by futurist Bruce Sterling. Let's listen to Sterling's trenchant take on contemporary American education and its relevance to the world outside the schoolhouse. "My older daughter," Sterling writes,

> is a student in high school. . . . [S]he lives in harsh paramilitary constraint. She has a dress code. She fills out permission forms and tardy slips, stands in lines, eats in a vast barracks mess room. She comes and goes at the jangle of a bell, surrounded by hall monitors. . . . My child leads a narrow, tough, archaic working life. Though she isn't paid for her efforts, she'd do pretty well as a gung-ho forties-era Rosie the Riveter. . . .
>
> Today's schoolchildren are held to grueling 19th-century standards. Today's successful adults learn constantly, endlessly developing skills and moving from temporary phase to phase, much like preschoolers. Children are in training for stable roles in large, paternalistic bureaucracies. These enterprises no longer exist for their parents. . . .
>
> Today's young students are being civilized for an older civilization than their own. . . .
>
> It's no coincidence that my daughter is appalled by her schoolwork but thrilled by the

Internet. Loathing her official school assignments, she spends hours tracking down arcana on the Net, in patient orgies of pop-culture research. (pp. 42–44)

Certainly Sterling is exaggerating for effect, and he's generalizing from his own child's experience—or his impression of it—to make claims about the experience of all schoolchildren in America today. As an educator, I know that American education gets a lot right, and that conditions in many schools aren't nearly so harsh or so "archaic" as Sterling would have us believe. But even so, the overall point he's making has some real validity. The enforced routines his daughter is made to follow in school are backward looking; they have precious little to do with the world outside school—or with the workworld she'll ultimately enter. That workworld's values include an extremely high degree of flexibility, intensive teamwork, the ability to think and act effectively "on your feet" and in "nonlinear" modes. That workworld, and its valued employees, are *protean*—constantly changing, constantly shifting, constantly *adapting*—and nothing could be further from the inflexible, regimented routines that Sterling's daughter has to endure.

It's clear that that backward-looking approach to education *has* to change.

A CRITICAL JUNCTURE

American public education has reached a critical juncture. The trouble is, the situation is confusing, and no one really knows which of several directions we'll eventually end up moving in. It's likely, in fact, that we'll continue moving in several different directions simultaneously. Let me give some examples.

On one hand, a concern for diminishing performance in reading, math, and science skills is leading us, as a nation, toward greater standardization in curriculum, with an emphasis on evaluating every schoolchild's performance—and that of every school and school district—through standardized testing. This approach, epitomized in the No Child Left Behind Act passed by Congress and championed by the Bush administration, has its virtues—it demonstrates real concern for academic excellence—and it has many advocates. (Along with many—increasingly vociferous—critics.)

At the same time that there's this push toward standardized curriculums and standardized testing, however, there's a movement in what seems to be the opposite direction: toward highly exploratory, individualized (and individually directed) learning. There are, for example, teachers, parents, and students across the country who are railing against the practice of "teaching to the test," which, in their view, sucks the life (and a great deal of the value) out of the educational experience. There's the gathering strength of the middle school movement, which has always emphasized a highly exploratory, highly interactive educational experience for young adolescents. There's the fact that advances in learning and information technologies make it possible, as never before, to individualize curriculums while making sure that each student's performance matches or exceeds standards. (I'm talking here about sophisticated "data warehousing" or "data mining" systems that enable a student's performance to be plotted against schoolwide, districtwide, statewide, and national standards as well as against that student's own past record. Such systems foster the development of individualized curriculums that closely attend to students' academic strengths and weaknesses.)

Then there's the growing importance in American education of what's called "multiple intelligences" theory, which emphasizes that children have different gifts, different inherent abilities, and which stresses the need to recognize these differences when designing curriculums and instructional methods. The multiple-intelligences movement, with its emphasis on adapting educational technique to the ways in which children actually learn, dovetails with another trend—that of applying the lessons of neurological science to instructional methods and even to curriculum itself. MIT professor and popular science writer Steven Pinker, whose books describing how the brain works have been bestsellers, is, like futurist Bruce Sterling, very concerned about our schools' failure to adequately prepare children for life outside the classroom. In a *New York Times* op-ed piece (Pinker 2003), he takes American schools to task not only for teaching the "wrong" subjects (he thinks all students should receive basic instruction in economics and statistics, for example), but for teaching *in the wrong way*—that is, by neglecting to apply what science has learned about human cognition to what goes on in the classroom. (The connection between neurology and education is one to which I'll return below.)

Finally—and perhaps most important—there's the unstoppable movement toward greater choice in American public education: the growing number of magnet schools, charter schools, and other "alternative" (theme-based and specialized) schools that are offering parents real alternatives in how their children will be educated. That movement, of course, is the subject of the present volume in the "Schools of the Future" series.

What's so interesting about this current, conflicted situation—in which "standardization" vies with "experimentation"—is that there *are* ways of making these competing, seemingly divergent approaches come together. One of the ironies of this critical juncture is that some "alternative" schools—magnets, charters, and others—whose instructional methods, curricular approaches, and modes of organization are anything but "standard" may offer the greatest hope of improving students' performance according to standard measures. Magnets, charters, and other specialized schools—highly attentive to the needs of individual schoolchildren and specific populations—stand, in many ways, at the cutting edge of American public education. Alternative schools' potential to transform American education for the better is being increasingly recognized: in February 2003, for example, the Bill and Melinda Gates Foundation—which is turning into one of the most important "movers and shakers" on the American educational scene—gave a grant totaling $31 million to fund the startup of 1,000 new alternative schools across the country (Winter 2003).

Not all such schools are successful, of course, and the jury is still out regarding whether the charter school movement will live up to its proponents' promise to revolutionize learning, but it is clear that the best magnet, charter, and other specialized schools are doing something that too many "traditional" schools are failing to achieve: they're actually preparing their students for the world—including the workworld—outside the school doors while at the same time ensuring that they "measure up" academically.

FUTURE SCHOOLING—*AND* THE FUTURE SCHOOL

At this point, you may be asking: "What does any of this have to do with the school buildings—the physical places—in which we educate our children?" The short answer is: *plenty.*

I've described a present-day situation that is, at best, confusing, and I've begun outlining a future in which, it seems, the only certain thing is change. Given these realities, it's pretty clear that the most important, overriding principle in school design should be flexibility. If a learning space is likely to be used for the traditional, "stand and deliver" instruction best suited for preparing students for standardized tests *and* for more exploratory forms of learning combining large- and small-group interaction and individual research, then that learning space must be flexible to succeed in both its purposes. If, as seems certain, new learning, information, and other technologies are going to continue coming "online"—and if, as also seems certain, these technologies will quickly be adopted by public schools—then it is absolutely essential that schools' learning spaces and infrastructure be designed to flexibly accommodate them.

When you look at the future this way—focusing on the inevitability of change and, therefore, on the need to flexibly accommodate it—"futurism" turns out not to be a flight of imaginative fancy but rather a very pragmatic approach.

Keeping that in mind, let's take a look at some of the other changes that the future is likely to bring to American education. Some changes, of course, are likely to be expansions or extrapolations of current trends. Because educators increasingly recognize that the performing arts are great tools for building leadership capabilities and fostering the kinds of interpersonal dynamics that enhance teamwork and democratic decision-making, schools of the future are likely to contain a greater variety of (technologically sophisticated) performance spaces, or spaces that can easily be adapted for performing-arts purposes. As everyone grows increasingly conscious of the impact of the physical environment on learning, the indoor-air and acoustical environments of school buildings are likely to be of higher and higher quality. As the manifold benefits of environmental/sustainable, or "green," design become clearer, multiple aspects of a school's interior and exterior environments are likely to be shaped with green-design principles in mind—covering everything from energy efficiency, to natural daylighting, to recyclable building materials, to indoor environmental quality. And as concern grows over increasing rates of childhood obesity, the wholesale retooling of school food programs, with an eye toward balanced nutrition, becomes inevitable. When compared with upcoming technology-based changes, however, these sorts of developments appear tame and relatively uncontroversial. We don't have any trouble envisioning them; in fact, we welcome them optimistically and with open arms.

We need to keep that openness and optimism handy when looking at some of the technological advances that lie ahead. Some of the developments discussed below, if and when they are proposed or implemented, are likely to be highly controversial and sure to set off heated debates. But because technology continues to develop so rapidly, I think it's high time that those debates begin, so the technology-based changes that are introduced into public education result from truly democratic decision-making involving American society at large.

If we don't think about these things now, we're *not* being pragmatic. We run the risk of letting the future determine us, rather than vice versa.

HUMAN/COMPUTER INTERACTIVITY

Even as we prepare this book, the media tell us of successful human-brain chip implants that help disabled people by restoring or simulating sensory abilities, enabling them to function better and more completely by supplementing the brain's power with computer power. It's easy to imagine this kind of technology being more widely applied—for instance, in the form of remedial reading or math chips implanted in the brains of students with certain kinds of learning disabilities. Such an application would, I think, represent a marriage of education and neurological science like that which Steven Pinker proposes. (And who knows? Such chips might eventually enable ordinary human beings to communicate "telepathically" by directing their thoughts at others.)

In a similar vein, voice-activated technologies—in which spoken commands generate computer responses—are a reality today, assisting people with disabilities, those who suffer from repetitive stress injuries, and people who must keep their hands free for nonkeyboard tasks. It strikes me that such technologies naturally lend themselves to educational uses, and that, far from merely "responding" to spoken commands, computers—with whom students will communicate wirelessly—may actually play a role in directing the educational process.

For instance, when the full range of personal data on each student is "warehoused" on school and family servers, the computer will "know" enough about the student to respond to questions such as, "What question *should* I have asked?" The answer will control the direction the student takes. As this kind of artificial intelligence advances, it's interesting to speculate about the kinds of answers computers might give to philosophical or spiritual questions. Will the home system give the same kinds of answers as those provided by the school computer? How will school systems deal with church-state questions, and how will parental rights be protected? We don't know the answers to these questions. In fact, we don't even know whether they're the *right* questions—but we can predict with some certainty that this kind of high-level human-computer interactivity will set off some heated debates.

BIOTECHNICAL AND GENETIC TECHNOLOGIES

Interactive technologies like those just described may be supplemented by biotechnical and genetic technologies that enhance mental and physical performance. I can certainly envision the day—perhaps not too distant—when genetic blueprints of each student are available to educators (and their computer "assistants") to help them determine students' inherent strengths and weaknesses and to design individualized educational programs on that basis. I can even foresee educational prescriptions—for both mental and physical activity—being regularly updated (perhaps even daily) through ongoing analyses, conducted in school-based labs, of students' blood chemistry. A changing regimen of dietary supplements and drug therapies would be prescribed to modify and control the changes in students' biochemistry and to prepare students for optimum educational experiences. (If nutritional programs were individualized, you can just imagine how the cafeteria environment might be altered!)

In such a scenario, computers would be involved not only in prescribing dietary/pharmaceutical regimens but in monitoring each student's well-being and measuring and assessing the progress he or she makes. As information was collected, the computer would make the necessary adjustments to the prescription, and teacher/facilitators would monitor the computer-student interaction and intervene when appropriate. "Guidance counseling" would come to include mental capacity mapping, sense acuity diagnostics, and the monitoring of brain and overall physical development informed by an intimately detailed understanding of the student's genetic makeup.

The facility-related impacts of these trends are likely to be extensive—involving, for example, the expansion of today's nurse's suites into small-scale, comprehensive diagnostic and treatment centers, and the transformation of physical education spaces into banks of individual workstations equipped with smart machines that use genetic and biochemical data to help individual students maximize physical performance.

Let's not underestimate the importance or scope of the changes that will be wrought by advances in biotechnical and genetic-engineering technologies. Futurist Bruce Sterling devotes a chapter of *Tomorrow Now* to the coming biotech revolution. "Biotech is by no means tomorrow's only major technology," he writes, but "if it survives and flourishes, it will become the most powerful" (pp. 5–6). So, in thinking about schools of the future, let's try to think about what a school in which educational and biomedical functions are intertwined might look like.

We're making a mistake if we don't at least try to anticipate such changes. Schools designed 30, 20, or even a dozen years ago didn't anticipate the explosion in social, support, and technical services that are, today, commonplace features of the educational environment—everything from ESL labs, to planning and placement teams (PPTs), to on-site social workers, to IT support. The result? A situation in which such services are squeezed—uncomfortably—into facilities not designed to accommodate them.

SECURITY, SCHEDULING, AND ENVIRONMENT

Security technology is currently being revolutionized by biometric devices, which "read" and store handprint, fingerprint, and retinal patterns—or scan and remember human faces—and that permit or disallow access based on whether a person's biometric attributes match those in the security database. Inevitably, biometrics will come to be used in school security systems, providing a much higher level of access control than is possible with the card-access and other, similar systems in widespread use today.

These technologies will reinforce the attitude that the school community is a family, supported by the school's safety and security system. All the members of the community will be connected to one another, and, in effect, the community will protect itself. "Bubbles of caring" will invisibly surround school facilities so that security personnel will be alerted instantly when a problem arises. The technology for this networkable system—in which security is based on individual alert buttons worn by all staff and students—already exists and has been implemented at some colleges.

That "bubble of caring" will embrace scheduling as well. It's more than conceivable that the standard school day will become a thing of the past. As learning programs are increasingly individualized, it will become less and less necessary for all students to arrive at and depart from school grounds at the same times each day. With computerized scheduling and navigational systems in place, school bus routes could be highly individualized, with students being picked up from home, delivered to school, and then taken back home or to after-school activities as their individual schedules require. (In fact, such a system could make sure that the efficiency of a fleet of buses is maximized, potentially leading to reductions in the number of buses needed to serve a school's student population.) Moreover, if students were required to wear or carry chips connecting them to the global positioning system (GPS), their whereabouts could be constantly tracked and monitored. (Another option would be to surgically implant such chips—making it impossible to lose a student or for a student to elude authority—but this sort of procedure would surely be greeted by outright hostility by some members of the public, making its introduction controversial, to say the least!)

In the school building itself, computers will control the interior environment—not just to modulate comfort conditions as necessary, but also to alter aesthetic characteristics of the environment. We can foresee a day when the colors of walls, floors, and ceilings; images projected on walls; and the amount and quality of light in interior spaces are all controlled by computers, which will change the colors, images, and light as changing educational and recreational activities warrant. On a gloomy day, a ray of artificial (though natural-looking) "sunlight" might stream through the atrium skylight; the mood of a dismal winter afternoon might be enlivened through the projection of a lush lawn onto the floor adjacent to a wall showing a virtual waterfall.

And technology is likely to alter the school environment in another way. Throughout the Schools of the Future series, we often speak of the trend—in all public school facilities—toward increased after-hours use of the school building by the larger community. Pursuing that trend further, we can envision a time when educational facilities become even more tightly interwoven with the overall governmental and institutional life of the community. As data resources and support services become ever more intertwined (and instantly, virtually accessible), and as land for municipal construction projects becomes ever more costly (and less readily available), a time may come when it makes a great deal of sense to consolidate many or all municipal functions—governmental, recreational, health, and educational—on a single campus.

THE SCHOOL AS "LABORATORY"

Whether any of the particular changes discussed in the preceding sections are ever implemented, it's clear that technology will continue to radically transform the educational experience. One of the most sweepingly important aspects of this transformation will be that education—at all levels, from preschool on—will become increasingly experimental and laboratory-like. Not only will students be in increasingly constant virtual communication with electronic resources, but the seamless interplay between computers and their human users will enable an educational approach that is individualized, problem-solving-oriented, and "experimental" in the best sense of the word. This will be true in all schools—but some magnet, charter, and other alternative schools are even now on the cutting edge of this transformation.

No longer will experimentation be confined to the science lab. Instead, a school building's learning spaces will become all-purpose laboratories in which hands-on and virtual experimentation of many different, interdisciplinary sorts can be carried on. Students—employing personal digital assistants (PDAs) that combine MP3, DVD, cellphone, and laptop computer functions in a single device—will communicate with electronic resources containing vast amounts of information. Wall-mounted interactive whiteboards will replace conventional blackboards/whiteboards in classrooms and other learning spaces, making even the traditional, lecture-style format a much more interactive experience. Through empirical experiments and heuristic thinking, students will continually be testing the truth and viability of their parents' and teachers' assertions and creatively evaluating the workability and wisdom of schools' organizational structures.

Experimentation, of course, is an ongoing, never-ending process. It involves dialog, the back-and-forth of argument and counterargument, the openness and flexibility required to change one's mind and alter one's direction. It involves interaction—and interactivity is the foundation of a healthy democratic society. Advances in learning and information technologies don't mean very much—they aren't very valuable—unless they support and extend our ability to work together to find solutions to the challenges besetting us. Education doesn't mean very much—it isn't very valuable—unless it prepares our children for the life that awaits them outside the school's doors.

This, finally, is the earmark of the school building of the future: that it not only enables students to learn interactively, but that it actually nurtures the dynamics of creative, positive, solutions-oriented interaction. It does this in all sorts of ways, from incorporating interactive technological resources into every dimension of learning; to articulating space in ways that enhance human-computer, one-on-one, small-group, and large-group interaction and democratic decision-making; to ensuring that the environment enhances rather than impedes learning.

*   *   *

Does all this sound scary? Change always is at least a little scary, and designing facilities to flexibly accommodate change while ensuring that change is for the better is scarily daunting.

But let's not be frightened. To respond effectively to the changes the future may bring, we must ourselves be willing to change our thinking, our strategies, and our priorities. This is a potentially endless task, and one that we—as designers, educators, parents, and citizens—should welcome. Let us, together, begin thinking about the future *now*.

1

MAGNET AND OTHER SPECIALIZED SCHOOLS: THE BASICS

"School Choice" and the Planning and Design of Specialized Schools

Choice: For well over a decade, this deceptively simple word has been the most important, oft-used, and contentious buzzword in American education. Without a doubt, American public school systems are moving, ever more rapidly, toward a situation in which students and their parents are offered a wide array of school choices, at every grade level. Unfortunately, the phrase *school choice* covers so much territory and can be used to denote so many different things that it's impossible to neatly summarize its meaning. And because the purposes to which the term can be put are sometimes in direct conflict, it's just as impossible to come down "in favor of" or "against" school choice—unless you know just what *kind* of choice is being proposed.

This book, like the other books in the Schools of the Future series, is about the planning and design of truly future-oriented public school facilities. Its purpose is to help the stakeholders in a school construction project—who include educators, parents, school administrators, government officials, and other community members—to understand and deal effectively with the many factors that affect the success of a school planning and design process. It is not—or not primarily—a book of educational theory, but trends in educational theory and practice do have a significant influence on school design. This is nowhere truer than in the design of specialized schools.

WHY FOCUS ON SPECIALIZED SCHOOLS?

Why devote an entire book to the planning and design of magnet and other specialized schools? For the simple reason that we believe the various movements to expand school choice represent a cutting edge in American education. We agree with educators Robert D. Barr and William H. Parrett when they write that magnet, charter, and other alternative schools have "disproved the traditional idea that all schools must be alike and all teachers and students must teach and learn in the same manner" (1997, p. 6).

Especially (but not solely) in the nation's big cities, schools of choice are obviously offering educators, parents, and schoolchildren an increasingly broad range of options for combating the ongoing crises in American education, including low academic performance, high dropout rates, school violence, poor preparation for the world of work, and so on. Where given the chance to exercise choice, American families are certainly demonstrating enthusiasm for the option. In Minnesota, for example, which began adopting school choice laws in the mid-1980s, nearly 18 percent of the state's 850,000 public school students were enrolled in a choice program of one sort or another during the 2001–2002 school year (*Star Tribune* 2002). Though scientific data are just beginning to come in, it does appear that some magnet, charter, and alternative schools are indeed raising standardized test scores, improving student morale and achievement, and in the case of magnet schools, successfully addressing problems of racial and economic imbalance in heavily minority urban districts.[1] Some of the good effects of alternative schools are difficult to gauge in terms of educational outcome but are nonetheless impressive: at Philadelphia's Charter School for Architecture + Design (CHAD), for example, daily attendance rates top 95 percent, while the average is 63 percent at the city's comprehensive public high schools. (For more on CHAD, see pages 57–62.)

Part of our enthusiasm for specialized schools—especially magnets—is economic. Numerous reports suggest that, given its investment in education, the United States is not getting a decent return compared with the performance of other nations. Granted, spending on education varies widely from state to state (and even, unfortunately, from locale to locale within a given state). Granted, too, that the economic downturn of recent years has pinched—sometimes severely—educational budgets all over the country. But even so, the United States spends more public and private money to educate a student than any other country. Obviously, change is desperately needed, and we believe that the kind of change represented by many magnet school programs has the best chance of producing higher levels of academic performance in a way that, potentially at least, can be cost effective.

Although the main focus of this book is magnet schools, we also believe that the innovative educational approaches exemplified in all sorts of specialized schools—not just magnets but also some charters and alternative schools—are opening the door to a new era of freedom in the conception, planning, and design of school facilities. Changing instructional methods and curriculums invite a thoroughgoing reexamination of the school building itself—its size, shape, siting, organization, purpose—and of the learning spaces it contains. As designers, we welcome this new freedom to explore, and we strongly believe that innovations engaged in by schools of choice will inevitably have an impact on all of America's public schools—not just on the way learning happens, but on the look and, more important, the function of school facilities. It's therefore to be hoped that no matter which kind of "specialized" school you may be involved in creating—whether it be a magnet school, a charter, or any of the numerous kinds of alternative schools that public school systems are currently experimenting with—you will find some helpful guidance in these pages.

Unfortunately, the cutting edge embodied by the various schools-of-choice movements is also sometimes a "bleeding edge." This is most readily apparent in the case of charter schools. As its proponents are quick to point out, the charter school movement has registered many successes, but it's also true that many charters have failed, and that facility-related issues are implicated in at least some of these failures. (For a quick overview of the kinds of facilities-related issues that charters typically face, see Chapter 5, "Finding a Home: The Facilities Side of the Charter School Debate.") The potential for failure has to be taken *very seriously* by those who are bringing any sort of alternative or specialized school into being, and guarding against failure involves fully addressing facilities-related issues and ensuring that they play an *essential* part in the process of creating a new school of choice.

It's our view that such issues are all too often accorded a secondary status by those who develop plans for new magnet, charter, and other alternative schools. For example, Barr and Parrett's otherwise comprehensive guide to the creation of schools of choice, *How to Create Alternative, Magnet, and Charter Schools That Work*, cited above, contains no more than a couple of vague paragraphs on facilities issues, and most of the current literature on magnet and charter schools all but ignores the critical role that facilities play in these schools' success or failure.[2] Part of this book's purpose is to begin to address this deficiency.

PARSING "SCHOOLS OF CHOICE"

As we say above, *school choice* covers an incredibly wide range of alternatives to conventional public education—everything from vouchers that parents can use to pay for or to offset the cost of private schooling; to magnet and charter schools of many different kinds; to alternative or specialized schools created to address specific social problems or serve special-needs populations; to home schooling, in which parents oversee their children's education; to online, or "virtual," schools whose students, though they work from home, interact via their computers with professional educators (see White 2003). The diversity of alternative schools and approaches to schooling—already astonishing—continues to increase with every passing year.

Because this book is about school planning and design, we naturally concentrate our attention on just a few of these approaches—mostly on magnet schools and, to a limited extent, charter schools and alternative/specialized public schools. But to say "just a few" is misleading, since each of these categories includes a very diverse range of institutions. For example, and without attempting to be comprehensive:

- *Magnet schools* include schools of every grade configuration. They encompass schools that differ from conventional schools in instructional approach (e.g., Montessori schools, "basic skills" schools), schools whose curriculums are career-oriented (performing arts schools, high-technology academies, etc.), and schools for special-needs populations. Most magnet schools are intradistrict magnets, but some are interdistrict, bringing together students from different (urban and suburban) school districts. Some magnets are self-contained schools; others function as school-within-a-school magnet programs, or "academies."
- *Charter schools*, like magnets, include schools of every grade level, but the specific missions of charter schools are, if anything, even more varied than those of magnet schools. Like charter schools themselves, charter school themes are all over the map: in St. Paul, Minnesota, the High School for Recording Arts takes hip-hop music as its point of departure (it's even nicknamed "Hip Hop High"), and in Las Vegas, Nevada, tennis star Andre Agassi recently founded a charter college-preparatory academy named after him that offers—you guessed it—intensive tennis instruction. Because legislation enabling charter schools differs—sometimes markedly—from state to state, charters can differ in purpose and character depending on where they are located. Some charters are large and well funded (sometimes partly supported by contributions from local industries, professional groups, or other community organizations); others are small, shoestring operations. Some have complex, state-of-the-art facilities; others operate from storefronts; still others are

"schools without walls." There are charters that function as online academies and possess little or nothing in the way of permanent facilities.

- *Alternative and specialized public schools* address an extremely wide range of purposes that usually have to do with a specific social problem (high schools for teenage mothers and mothers-to-be) or serve a specific special-needs population (e.g., schools for autistic children). There are—to choose just a few examples—alternative/specialized schools for emotionally/behaviorally troubled youth (sometimes these are "transitional" schools whose aim is to teach students to cope with, and to return them to, the conventional school environment); for gay and lesbian youth who are uncomfortable or endangered within the conventional high school environment; for talented and gifted children; and for at-risk high schoolers who are more than likely to drop out of an ordinary, comprehensive high school.

This list doesn't include a number of types of public schools that have long had a place in many—especially big-city—districts and whose curriculums revolve around a certain theme or focus: namely, vocational-technical high schools and competitive high schools that offer an advanced program in a particular area of study to gifted students (who must take an entrance examination to gain admission). Chapter 2, "Specialized Schools: Twelve Exemplary Projects," features one future-oriented, New Jersey vo-tech school—distinctive in part because it's located on the campus of a local community college. We do not make more than passing mention, however, of competitive theme-based high schools—epitomized by four famous New York City schools: Brooklyn Technical High School, the Bronx High School of Science, Stuyvesant High School, and Fiorello H. LaGuardia High School of Music and Art and Performing Art. The restricted admissions policies of such schools run counter to the educational philosophy of the charter school movement and of most (not all) magnet schools, and for the most part, these schools occupy older facilities inappropriate for a discussion of schools of the future. Even New York City's most renowned competitive high school, Stuyvesant—which moved to its present, lower Manhattan location in 1992—has a facility that is technology-poor and relatively inflexible when compared to many of the schools featured in this book.

PLANNING AND DESIGN ISSUES—COMMONALITIES

What do all these highly diverse schools have in common, and what are the key characteristics that set them apart from other, more conventional public schools? Perhaps the most important thing they share is their particularity. They're all highly individualized schools for highly individualized populations. From a planning and design standpoint, that's extremely important. Good school design is usually specific in the sense that designers are responding, to the best of their ability, to the needs of a specific community or specific program. But that general rule is even more true in the case of specialized schools (e.g., a high school for teenage mothers must include day-care facilities; a performing arts magnet must contain a variety of rehearsal and performance spaces). Much of our focus in this book concerns the need to be extremely attentive to this particularity when planning and designing alternative/specialized schools, and the book's second chapter, which features a number of "exemplary projects," does little more than hint at the great diversity of specialized schools now in existence.

A second characteristic shared by many (not all) of these schools is that they are *urban* schools. Magnets, especially, are predominantly an urban phenomenon, since among their primary reasons for being are the desire to address racial/economic imbalances in heavily minority school districts (which are usually urban districts) and the need to improve and equalize educational opportunity for minority schoolchildren. This attribute, too, is critically important to planning and design, since a host of facilities-related issues (including, for example, siting and security issues) can differ markedly depending on whether a school is in an urban or suburban setting. For the past half-century, the predominant model for school planning and design in this country has been a suburban one, but magnets (as well as some charters and alternative/specialized schools) significantly alter that picture.

A third characteristic that sets these schools apart from conventional public schools is that new magnet, charter, and alternative schools are often housed in existing buildings—sometimes older schools, sometimes buildings originally constructed for other purposes. Few occupy new, purpose-built structures, due to the tight capital budgets and the generally small size of these institutions, as well as the lack of suitable sites for new school buildings in densely built areas. Obviously, this characteristic brings issues of renovation and adaptive reuse to the fore—as well as the prior question concerning how to select an appropriate building. (A few of the schools featured in Chapter 2 occupy preexisting buildings; specific issues raised by these buildings' adaptation/renovation are raised there.)

A fourth characteristic shared by many magnet, charter, and alternative schools is that they are, relatively speaking, *smaller* than their traditional counterparts. Small size—a high school that serves 200 or 300 students, say, rather than the several thousand who attend a comprehensive high school—does impose certain constraints on design. It may be harder, for example, to justify the incorporation of numerous amenities into a small facility, where cost-effective economies of scale just don't apply. At the same time, however, we believe that smaller schools can free up designers' hands and lead to new ways of envisioning a school's relation to other educational institutions and the surrounding community.

The fifth characteristic is that magnets and charters (especially) often have relatively uncertain funding streams over the long haul. From a design point of view, this uncertainty can be critically important. The school's long-term financial viability may be directly tied to how energy efficient and easily maintainable its facility is.

Finally, magnet, charter, and many alternative schools are unlike conventional public schools in that their populations are self-selecting. In the conventional model of public education, students are simply assigned to neighborhood elementary schools, local middle schools, and comprehensive high schools on the basis of where they live. (Place of residence is the determining factor even when kids are involuntarily bused to another neighborhood to achieve court-mandated desegregation.) But parents must intentionally decide to send their children to magnets, charters, and some alternative schools. This is a big difference, because it means that these schools must appeal to an audience of potential attendees and their families. Though a great deal has been written about how such schools can make themselves attractive to potential enrollees—and even about how to mount effective public relations campaigns to ensure that enrollment targets are met—we find it curious that good facility design is almost never mentioned as a factor that might help convince parents and students to choose a magnet, charter, or alternative school. (Several of the projects featured in Chapter 2 stand as exceptions.)

When it comes to their appeal to parents and students, many schools of choice have a lot to recommend them. Career-based magnet schools can offer an educational experience that's much more relevant to the world of work than what conventional comprehensive secondary schools typically provide. Charters are often free to operate outside the rules and regulations with which conventional public schools must comply—and which may in some cases have a stifling effect on teaching and learning. Alternative schools can offer a degree of individualized attention that at-risk kids may sorely need. For the most part, all these schools possess intensely committed administrators and faculty, and many go out of their way to nurture a degree of parental and community involvement that's too often lacking in conventional public schools. What's more, available data suggest that many magnet, charter, and alternative schools are succeeding in their mission to help children thrive academically.

Given all these pluses, no parent should be dissuaded from sending his or her child to a school of choice because its facility is less than adequate. In fact, having a well-designed facility—one that accommodates and fosters the school's mission—*should be* among the selling points that any magnet, charter, or alternative school can proudly use in attracting parents and students to its program.

NOTES

1. See Barr and Parrett 1997, especially pp. 12–16; Brooks et al. 1999, esp. chs. 2 and 3; Gormley 2003. Data on charters' success are more mixed; see, for example, Herszenhorn 2004.

2. There are exceptions. For example, on its website, the Charter Friends National Network publishes a thorough study of charter schools facility financing (CFNN 1999), but even this otherwise comprehensive document does not cover planning or design issues per se.

Specialized Schools: Twelve Exemplary Projects

The 12 school projects featured in this chapter are exemplary in several different senses. Many represent a careful, creative, and coherent response to a particular set of design challenges. Several employ technology in ways appropriate to the schools' particular mission and budget. A few illustrate the wisdom of sharing facilities with other institutions. Three of the selected projects reveal how designers overcome challenges inherent in adapting older buildings to today's educational purposes. And one—Philadelphia's Charter High for Architecture + Design—is remarkable not so much for its current facility but for the "visioning" process the school is undergoing as it plans a move to a new site.

Of course, it's impossible within the scope of a single book to present a comprehensive survey of current architectural trends in magnet/specialized school design. Knowing this, we decided to present a range of projects that, in their diversity, could at least hint at the incredible variety of specialized schools being created across the United States today.

PROJECT #1: A PROPOSED HIGH-TECH MAGNET ACADEMY
By L. Gerald Dunn, R.A.

This project is a proposal for the Academy of Information Technology and Engineering in Stamford, Connecticut, for grades 9–12, designed by Fletcher-Thompson, Inc. Key issues are:

- "Outside the box" design
- Transparency/visibility
- Workplace-like learning environments
- Flexibility for easy reconfiguration
- Exposed building services
- Energy efficiency/environmental sustainability
- Integrating natural and technological worlds

In inviting a small group of architecture firms to compete for the job of designing its new Academy of Information Technology and Engineering (AITE), the Stamford, Connecticut, school district made it very clear that they wanted the participating designers to think "outside the box." Fletcher-Thompson, Inc.'s proposed design does just that. For this magnet high school, projected

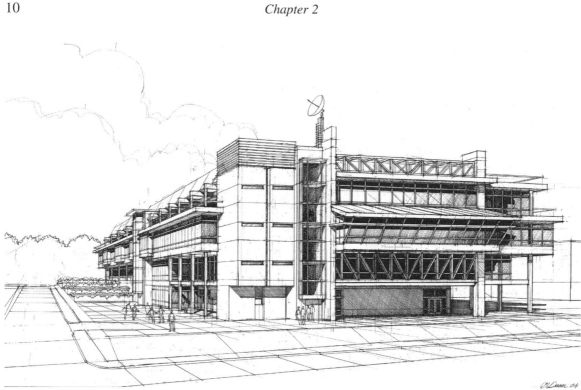

Figure 2.1.1. This perspective view of the proposed AITE facility shows the eastern end of the building, where the second-floor media center cantilevers out beyond the structural frame. *Rendering by Fletcher-Thompson, Inc.*

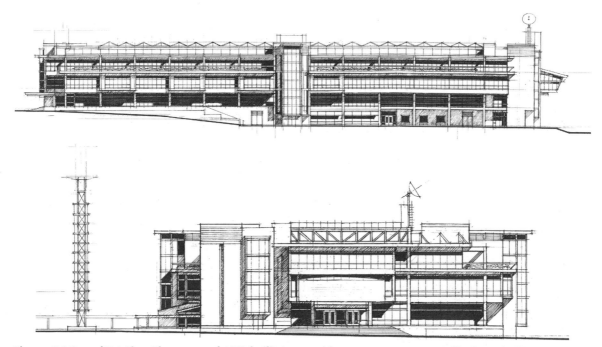

Figures 2.1.2a and 2.1.2b. The proposed AITE facility's resemblance to contemporary office/R&D facilities is clearly visible in these elevations of the south (top) and west (bottom) sides of the building. *Drawings by Fletcher-Thompson, Inc.*

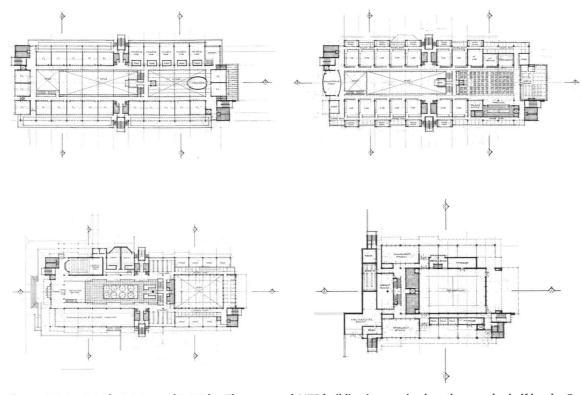

Figures 2.1.3a, 2.1.3b, 2.1.3c, and 2.1.3d. The proposed AITE building is organized on three-and-a-half levels. On the topmost (third) floor (at top, above), classrooms and science labs surround the open light courts; the egg-shaped seminar room, suspended above the second-floor café, is visible toward the right of the plan. The second floor—the heart of the building—houses a variety of lab spaces, "think tanks," and individual study pods, as well as an elliptical presentation room (left side of second-floor plan), the media center (right side), and the school's café/plaza (right of center). The first floor features a spacious exhibition gallery just inside the main entrance (at the left), a variety of music instruction and performance spaces, and clusters of individual study pods; the central garden court is accessible from this level. Athletic facilities are located on the half-level ground floor (bottom), making it easy to zone off the rest of the building during after-hours use. *Drawings by Fletcher-Thompson, Inc.*

to serve a population of 600 to 650 students, Fletcher-Thompson created a conceptual plan that incorporates late-breaking trends in office and R&D workplace design and demonstrates a multidimensional commitment to environmental sustainability. The "high concept" at work in the proposed AITE design is a high-tech, loft-type building married to an inner garden that enriches and inspires the educational experience by creating a "biotechnic" environment that synthesizes the natural and human-made worlds.

The proposed 110,000 square-foot facility—which because of its sloping site is four stories at its western end and three stories on the east—is organized around two interior "light courts." These glass-roofed, open spaces penetrate the building vertically, suffusing the entire building with natural light. The courts, coupled with an extremely liberal use of interior glazing, create an interior possessing the highest possible degree of transparency. In this visually hyper-connected environment, students will be energized by their awareness of all the activity occurring around them. The light courts also serve an energy-conserving purpose, acting as a temperature-regulating "pendulum" that helps warm the building during colder months and cool it down on warmer days.

Transparency and Flexibility

The transparency of the proposed AITE facility is so great that, from nearly any point on the exterior, an observer will be able to see straight through the building to the other side. Stamford-area corporations participating in the school's sponsorship have pointed to the need to acquaint public school students, early on, with the look and feel of the workplace—and transparency is an essential strategy in much contemporary office design. Eliminating visual barriers between work-spaces has been shown to break down hierarchies, foster communication, and increase productivity, and similar rationales are at work in this magnet school design.

Visual connections within the AITE building will stimulate community interaction, even as views of the outside world and sky provided by exterior windows and skylights maintain users' awareness of the shifting patterns of sunlight and the gradual change of seasons. (This sensory connection with the natural environment has been shown to improve people's sense of well-being and hence to spur achievement in both workplace and educational settings.) Glare and heat buildup—the downsides of natural daylighting—will be controlled through a number of coordinated strategies, including overhangs, louvers, and the specification of heat-absorbent glass at appropriate places on the exterior. The amount of light entering the interior courts will be adjusted by sets of computer-operated Roman shades that automatically change positions over the course of the day. Classrooms and other spaces will be outfitted with blinds and shades so that occupants can control the light entering interior spaces from the courts.

The proposed AITE facility's interior is intensely *internally reflexive*—its constituent parts tied together in ongoing visual interaction. That interactivity is underscored by the organization of interior space, the fundamental flexibility of space conferred by easily movable walls and services, and the decision to leave building-service components and conduits—for power, telecom, and HVAC—exposed and accessible throughout the interior.

"Declension" of Space. The arrangement of interior space in the proposed AITE building is dictated by the desire to maximize the mutual accessibility of different kinds and sizes of learning spaces and thus facilitate transitions from one sort of learning experience to another. Architects sometimes speak of the "declension" of space, by which we mean the organization of interactions among spaces of differing scale. In configuring school buildings, architects define the interplay between individual learning spaces, small-group spaces, spaces in which large-group instruction occurs, and those even larger spaces in which a significant segment of the overall community can gather and interact.

The organizational principles at work in the proposed AITE facility can most easily be seen on the second floor (see accompanying floor plans), where perimeter corridors outside lab spaces (for group instruction and project production) are lined with workstation-type "pods" (for individual study) and punctuated at regular intervals by "think tanks," where small groups can gather for brainstorming sessions or other project-specific work. This kind of spatial interaction resembles that of many contemporary offices, where workstations are grouped around smaller, think tank–type conference rooms while full-size conference rooms accommodate larger groups. The plan likewise evokes present-day R&D facilities, where labs are adjacent to breakout spaces for small-group interaction as well as to offices or workstations where researchers can engage in individual tasks.

At either end of the second floor are shared spaces accommodating larger groups: on the east, the media center; on the west, a sizable, elliptically shaped space where students can present their projects and have them critiqued by faculty members and peers. Also on the second floor is the school's café/plaza. This central gathering/socializing spot is connected, physically and visually, to upper and lower floors by the central vertical circulation area just outside its entrance and by the open space of the interior garden courtyard beyond. (The vertical circulation area, visible just to the left of the café on the second floor plan, consists of twin stairways, a glass-enclosed elevator, and a suspended bridge linking the northern and southern halves of the building.)

A Rational, Easily Manipulable Structure. The overall organization of the proposed AITE facility is extremely simple and rational. Stationary elements such as toilets and stairways are placed at the building's corners and midway along its north and south sides. But within the building's repetitive steel frame—consisting of a series of 30-by-40-foot bays—virtually everything else is movable. The floors are service plates; the light, infill walls are much like the easily reconfigurable walls of a contemporary office. In fact, the building can "move outside" its structural frame, as it does on the second floor, where the media center cantilevers beyond the perimeter—putting it "outside the box" in a literal sense. Even the exterior cladding is flexible: the glass-and-metal panels that cover the building are prefabricated and self-insulated, designed to snap on and off the frame—meaning that the building's shape, dimensions, and look could change over time.

Exposed Services. Exposing the system components and conduits for basic building services—power and telecommunications pathways, mechanical-system ductwork—doesn't just enhance flexibility; it also serves a heuristic purpose, making the building's "inner workings" visually accessible to students and thus familiarizing them with the circuits and nodes of a living, breathing, "thinking" modern building. That's of special importance in a magnet school like AITE, where studies will focus on information technology and engineering. The building's "brain"—the IT Tech Center—will be similarly exposed to view, occupying a glass-walled room that juts out over the garden court, making it a focal point of the entire interior. (The central position of this room, which will contain the school's main server and workspace for IT staff, can be seen on the second floor plan, where it appears just to the right of the stairwell outside the cafeteria entrance.)

Environmental Sustainability

The sense of well-being fostered by an abundance of natural light and visual connections to the exterior environment is but one of the ways the proposed AITE facility epitomizes green-design principles. Another—just as important—is the building's energy efficiency. That's conferred, in part, by the solar panels on its roof, which will generate a portion of the power used by the building. But it's also a function of the tempering role played by the central garden/plaza. Skylit from above, this greenhouse-type space will act as a "heat sink" in winter, accumulating warm air that, as it rises, will enter the mechanical system to be distributed throughout the building. During warmer months, the central open space will do just the reverse: flushed with cooler air during nighttime hours, the space will help cool the building throughout the day.

Other Notable Features

A few other aspects of the proposed AITE building deserve mention:

- *Community use of athletics facilities.* The academic program—accounting for 90 percent of the overall space—is contained in the upper three levels. The athletic fitness program, whose facilities will be open to community users before and after school hours, is located on the lower half-level—an arrangement that allows the academic areas to be easily zoned off and thus protected against unauthorized entry.

- *Exhibition/gallery space.* On the first floor, immediately inside the entry at the building's western end, is a large gallery space that will be devoted to shows of student work and other exhibits. Celebrating the achievements of the AITE community, this space also evokes the design of many contemporary corporate headquarters—where exhibit space displaying current projects and products often greets visitors on arrival.

- *Music/TV production.* Beyond its thematic focus on the IT and engineering disciplines, AITE will provide a comprehensive curriculum similar to that of a conventional Connecticut high school—including fine arts education. At AITE, the fine arts curriculum will focus on music and visual media, with an emphasis on their integration in video and audio broadcast and in film. The proposed design includes a complement of music instruction/rehearsal rooms, as well as a screening room/recital hall/auditorium on the first floor. Hands-on instruction in TV broadcast and film production technologies will occur in a suite of TV lab and production rooms on the north side of the second floor. A reprographics production studio is also located here, adjacent to the café/plaza.

- *Communications tower.* AITE will share the site of an existing middle school. Because it will be located behind the other school, it will not be clearly visible from the street—but its presence will be announced by a separate, high communications tower (visible in the west elevation; see accompanying drawing). The tower will be used by the school and will be commercially available to communications companies, because of the shortage of such facilities in Stamford.

A Rational, Human, and *Poetic* Building

As we've emphasized, the proposed AITE facility's plan is simple and highly rational—as befits an environment geared to high-tech education. But the building is also extremely human. The central, planted garden court, for example, provides a quiet, contemplative counterpoint to the beehive-like activity surrounding it. The café is a far cry from the factory-like high school cafeterias of yesterday; here, students can wander through the food-service area, choosing from among many options offered at deli-style counters. A coffee kiosk will be open throughout school hours, giving students a place to engage in informal conversation while taking a break—just as would happen in a contemporary office. And, as in any office, each student will have his or her own workplace—one of the study pods scattered throughout the building. That, certainly, is testimony to the importance that AITE's planners accord the individual's needs.

Finally, Fletcher-Thompson's conceptual design for AITE incorporates a whimsical touch of poetry—the egg-shaped seminar room, accessible from the third floor and suspended in the open space above the school's cafeteria. This unusual conference room—loft-like and quite literally aloft—will be shared by the social science and humanities classes meeting on the third floor. Its shape might be thought of as a metaphor for interdisciplinary cross-fertilization; its aircraft-like appearance, conferred by an aluminum skin and a Plexiglas "nose cone" window overlooking the atria, serves as a symbol for the flight of the intellect engaged in exploring knowledge.

PROJECT #2: AN ARTS MAGNET ELEMENTARY SCHOOL
By Chester A. Salit, AIA

This project is the Rotella Magnet Elementary School in Waterbury, Connecticut, for grades pre-K–5, designed by Fletcher-Thompson, Inc. It was completed in 2000. Key issues are:

• Specialized visual arts/performance spaces
• Community use
• Accommodating vehicular traffic
• Interior circulation patterns
• Controlling life-cycle costs

Figure 2.2.1.   On a fair-weather day, kids enjoy reading in the courtyard at the Rotella school. *Photograph by Elliott Kaufman Photography.*

Figure 2.2.2.   The lobby space at the Rotella school flows around the curving wall of the adjacent auditorium. *Photograph by Elliott Kaufman Photography.*

Figure 2.2.3. Rotella's media center extends into the central courtyard. *Photograph by Elliott Kaufman Photography.*

At the Rotella Magnet Elementary School in Waterbury, Connecticut, arts education isn't just an "add-on." Instead, the arts—visual and performing—are integrated into every aspect of this inter-district magnet's curriculum. To support the school's educational focus, the building incorporates several arts-related spaces that go far beyond what one would usually find in an elementary school, including a comprehensive visual-arts instruction suite and a 650-seat auditorium/theater whose quality equals or betters that of typical high school auditoriums.

Community involvement in the life of the school was an especially important goal of the Waterbury Board of Education, which initiated the Rotella Magnet. (The cost of the building was fully funded through the state of Connecticut's interdistrict magnet school program.) To foster community participation, the theater is available for use by community groups, and the school includes a large (1,200 square foot) community room, with an office space and kitchenette, that can be used for meetings and other gatherings of community members, even during school hours. As always, opening a school building to community use necessitates separating the core, shared areas from the academic portion of the facility. At Rotella, that's accomplished by grouping the shared spaces around the school's main lobby. The media center—an extensive suite of spaces that include the library proper, a computer lab, and a TV broadcast studio—separates the building's public area from the classroom wing behind.

Figure 2.2.4.   The Rotella school's floor plan groups core, common spaces around the lobby (left), segregating them from the academic wing (right). This arrangement allows academic areas to be "zoned off" during after-hours use by community groups. *Drawing by Fletcher-Thompson, Inc.*

The lobby—whose curving form follows the curved back wall of the adjoining auditorium—serves a number of purposes. It's the arrival point for students entering the building, it's where audiences gather before and after events in the auditorium, and it's a gallery space for the display of student artwork. The lobby is strongly linear in character—the result of a site constraint that made it necessary to separate the bus queuing area from other vehicular traffic on the site, including the parent drop-off area. Conceiving the lobby as an "interior street" and placing an entrance door at either end of this broad, high-ceilinged space made it possible for all children, whether arriving by bus or being dropped off by their parents, to assemble in a single place at the beginning of the school day—a much better solution than having two remote assembly areas.

Circulation patterns were important in the school's interior as well. To avoid dead-end corri-

Figure 2.2.5. At the Rotella school, red metal roofs evoke images of the farm buildings that dot this area of west-central Connecticut. *Photograph by Elliott Kaufman Photography.*

dors, designers fashioned the classroom wing to arc around a central courtyard space. The media center juts into this plaza, which features a gazebo and which classes can use for outdoor learning during fair weather.

One feature of the Rotella Magnet's mechanical-system design merits special mention. Often, to save on a school's construction costs, air-handling units and other mechanical equipment are roof-mounted. This may appear to be the cheapest solution but may actually add significantly to a building's long-term, life-cycle costs for two reasons: roof-mounted equipment is relatively inaccessible and therefore more difficult to maintain and repair than equipment placed at ground level, and the flat roofs required for roof-mounted equipment may be more prone to weather damage and leaks than are sloping roofs. (This is especially true in regions with snowy winters, like this area of west-central Connecticut.) To ease maintenance and reduce life-cycle costs, Rotella's mechanical equipment was located in protected, enclosed penthouses accessible from inside the building. This decision allowed for sloped roofs across the building. Besides minimizing leaks, these rooflines became a signature element in the school's design. The red metal roofs, with standing seams, recall the rooflines of barns and farm buildings—and thus hearken back to this now-suburbanized area's agricultural past.

PROJECT #3: A MAGNET ELEMENTARY, HOUSED IN AN EXISTING SCHOOL BUILDING
By Timothy P. Cohen

This project is a Regional Multi-Cultural Magnet School in New London, Connecticut, for grades pre-K–6, designed by Fletcher-Thompson, Inc. It was completed in 2003. Key issues are:

- Renovation and addition to Victorian-era school building
- Urban setting
- Site and zoning restrictions

By 1996, the Regional Multi-Cultural Magnet School had occupied its 1870s-vintage building in New London, Connecticut's Post Hill neighborhood for several years. That's when Fletcher-Thompson, Inc., was called in to study the school's need for renovated and expanded facilities. It took a total of seven years to win approval for a much-needed addition to the school and to design and construct that facility as well as perform the full-scale renovation of the existing building. This logistically complex project underscores many of the challenges involved in renovating older

Figure 2.3.1. In this computer-generated exterior view of the Multi-Cultural Magnet, the new addition appears in the right foreground. *Image: Fletcher-Thompson, Inc.*

Figure 2.3.2. The original, 1870s-era building appears at the left of this computer-generated view of the Multi-Cultural Magnet's exterior. Using modern materials, the designers recreated the patterns of the building's original multicolored slate roof. *Image: Fletcher-Thompson, Inc.*

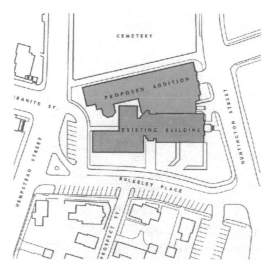

Figure 2.3.3. This simplified site plan, developed early in the project, shows the relation between the Multi-Cultural Magnet's original building and the addition. *Drawing by Fletcher-Thompson, Inc.*

school buildings for today's educational purposes and in siting new educational facilities in densely built urban areas. But it also illustrates the aesthetic rewards of reusing architecturally significant structures from past eras as homes for contemporary magnet schools.

A Historical Building

The existing Neo-Gothic-style building on the Regional Multi-Cultural Magnet's thoroughly revamped urban site—which opened in the fall of 2003—has a long and, in recent decades, somewhat unusual history. The structure, built in 1871 as the Bulkeley School for Boys (originally a privately funded public school), is a gem of early American public school architecture. The building, added onto twice during the early 20th century, remained in use as a public school until the late 1960s, when it was abandoned. It sat empty for several years, until being acquired by the Mohegan Indian tribe, which converted it for use as administrative offices for the tribe's business enterprises. (The Mohegan tribe demolished one of the earlier additions and erected a 60-car parking garage on the lot.) Then, in the late 1980s, the building once again changed hands, again becoming a school—the home for the newly formed Multi-Cultural Magnet.

By the mid-1990s, the staff, faculty, and students of the Multi-Cultural Magnet had grown to appreciate—even to love—the quirkily elegant 19th-century building that housed their school. They wanted to stay—but they'd become painfully aware of the building's inadequacies: classroom space was extremely tight; administrative functions were, for the most part, crammed into a series of improvised spaces on the building's below-grade-level ground floor; and accessibility for disabled students was problematic, to say the least (just one of the ways in which the building didn't comply with current codes). The obvious solution would couple a thoroughgoing renovation of the old building with the addition of a new structure housing classrooms and some of the school's common spaces.

Site Constraints

That "obvious" solution, however, took a long time to realize. For one thing, the school's 1.4-acre site—which included the original 1871 building, the one remaining addition, and the parking garage—was extremely constricted. For a new building to be built, something would have to go. Working with the City of New London and with the Connecticut Historical Commission (the building is listed on the commission's registry of historic places), Fletcher-Thompson architects determined that the remaining 1930s-era addition could be demolished without violating landmark regulations or damaging the aesthetic integrity of the 1871 building.

The architects and Multi-Cultural Magnet administrators also sought to eliminate the parking garage, hoping to rely on curbside parking for school staff and visitors. The City of New London, however, maintained that this would violate zoning regulations, so it denied the request. Regarding bus queuing, it was eventually decided that the only practical option would be to have buses queue on the street outside the school's main entrance, despite the impediment to other vehicular traffic during morning arrival and afternoon departure times. (For more on accommodating student drop-off and pick-up on constricted urban sites, see Chapter 10, "Site Design and Landscape Architecture for Urban Magnet Schools.")

Adding to the project's complexity were zoning setback requirements for new construction (a particularly challenging issue here, in that the school's site was bordered on three sides by city streets). The problem was solved by a building lot coverage waiver. Another difficulty involved the antipathy voiced by a few of the school's neighbors regarding the proposed expansion. One neighbor sued to prevent the project, contending that the expanded school would be too big for the site, forcing teachers to use a nearby public park (in lieu of an on-site playground) for the students' recreation—a practice that the neighbor insisted would harm the park. The suit was ultimately resolved through arbitration, and the building's lot coverage was reduced slightly to enlarge the on-site play area. Today, the Multi-Cultural Magnet does indeed use the nearby park for some recreational activities; however, far from damaging the park, the presence of the schoolchildren and their teachers and the school's participation in the park's maintenance have rejuvenated this public greenspace, which had formerly been a haven for drug dealers. (This is just one of the ways in which the school has served as an anchor for the overall revitalization of this run-down area.)

Building Design

Once the zoning and related matters were resolved, work on planning and designing the renovation and addition began in earnest. In reconfiguring the school, Fletcher-Thompson architects decided to locate the majority of the classroom spaces in the new building (the old building never lent itself well to the standardized classroom spaces of contemporary schools). The old building would continue to house a few classrooms but would mostly be used for administrative offices and common learning spaces such as the media center and art and music rooms. To enable the fullest utilization of the cramped site, the designers decided to extend the upper two floors of the new building over the parking garage. To comply with codes requiring that primary-grade students have immediate access to the outside, all pre-K–2 classrooms were located on the ground floors of the old and new buildings.

In renovating the 1871 building, the designers strove to maintain its much-admired "quirky" character—and they decided to carry over some of that same quirkiness into the design of the new building. Part of their research involved studying historical photographs of the old structure to determine what it had originally looked like. These photos revealed that the building had once had a polychrome slate roof; during renovation, that look was reproduced through the use of Fiberglas shingles that mimic the original multicolored slate.

For the old building's interior, it was decided to allow the original brick load-bearing walls to remain in place—and to allow these walls to dictate the spatial configuration. When exposed, these brick walls were quite beautiful, and their presence led to some idiosyncratic design decisions: for example, despite its acoustical disadvantage, a brick wall in what would become the school's music room was left exposed. Ordinarily, such a wall—in such a space—would be covered by sheetrock for easier maintenance, but in this case it was decided to let aesthetics trump practical considerations.

Use of Existing Elements

Wherever possible, the old building's ornamentation was preserved, restored, or reused in a new context. This effort to maintain the school's original architectural spirit is seen most clearly in the redeployment of a series of stained-glass windows that had decorated the exterior of the demolished 1930s-era addition. The windows—allegories of academic themes such as "Chemistry," "Poetry," "Mathematics," and so on—were cleaned and redistributed throughout the two-building complex. Some were used on the exterior of the addition; others, backlit and set above display cases, now ornament new interior walls.

Several aspects of the 1871 building's renovation exemplify the kinds of problems that might be encountered in any renovation of a school building of this vintage. The need, for example, to locate components of a new mechanical system in this building's attic space raised some thorny challenges. The hand-hewn timber beams supporting the roof had to be carefully analyzed to ensure that the structure could bear the additional weight of the air-handling units that would now occupy the attic, and some ingenuity was required to devise ways of threading ductwork around and through the maze of beams cluttering this space. The effort to maintain the character of the glazing proved troublesome from a budgetary perspective, in that the double-hung windows chosen to replace the 1871 building's windows—and to recreate the old building's original look—were much more expensive than the kind of windows that would ordinarily be used in new school construction today. Also, the need to introduce above-ceiling infrastructure into the classrooms and other spaces on the building's ground level created very low ceiling heights—no higher than seven and a half feet in some places. (That staff found this solution acceptable is a testimony to their fondness for the building—and to the fact that they had grown used to working in its already-constrained spaces.)

Old and New Together

Though the materials used in the new building could not replicate the grand masonry-and-stone fabric of the old—and though this new facility, it was felt, should not attempt to strictly mimic the 1871 structure—the new building does employ an array of materials that are much richer than those typically used in contemporary school buildings. The two buildings are joined by a glass-enclosed lobby—a "transparent" space that connects the structures to one another while preserving their separate identities. In a design approved by the state historical commission, the exterior facades of the two buildings remain exposed and visible inside the lobby—and the buildings "talk to" one another across this space.

That conversation continues inside the new building. For example, something of the old building's pleasant idiosyncrasy is recaptured on the new building's fourth floor. To reduce the apparent mass and height of the new structure, this top story is fashioned as a dormered attic space tucked under a sloping roof. The roof's angles lend an interesting character to the ceilings in the classrooms directly beneath, and wooden benches nested inside the dormer spaces provide a note of old-fashioned elegance and comfort.

Highlighting Cultural Diversity

The Multi-Cultural Magnet's program—which emphasizes the incorporation of resources from a diversity of cultures and ethnic groups into every aspect of the curriculum—influenced the facility's design in a number of ways. Signage, for example, is in English, Spanish, and braille throughout. And because the school's mission stresses the importance of neighborhoods in preserving and transmitting ethnic pride, the school's interiors evoke residential streetscapes—with each classroom entrance modeled as a housefront (including a window with window box beside each classroom's door). In one case, the school's mission necessitated a significant change to the original plan for the revamped, expanded facility. That plan had called for the school to be equipped with a warming kitchen only; meals would be prepared off site and brought to the school each day. But that would have curtailed the school's ability to provide a variety of lunches—with each menu based on a different ethnic cuisine—for students to enjoy and learn from. Recognizing the importance of this aspect of the school's program, the state permitted the school to have its own full-service kitchen.

PROJECTS #4–5: MAGNETS FOR CHILDREN OF WORKING PARENTS
By Jeffrey A. Sells, AIA

These projects are the 6 to 6 Magnet Elementary School and Thurgood Marshall Magnet Middle School in Bridgeport, Connecticut, for pre-K–5 (elementary) and 6–8 (middle), designed by Fletcher-Thompson, Inc. The elementary school was completed in 1994 and the middle school in 2003. Key issues are:

* Renovation of existing school building
* Accommodating before- and after-hours programs
* Expansion of program to middle-school grades
* Constrained site

For many working families—both single-parent and two-parent households—the typical school day isn't long enough. If children don't arrive at school till 8:00 or 8:30 in the morning and must leave at 3:00 in the afternoon, there may still be several hours, before and after school, when their parents are unavailable to supervise or care for them. The problem of what to do with the kids isn't an easy one to solve for many lower- and even middle-income families. It's not safe to let children fend for themselves during the nonschool hours when parents are at work, and good day-care programs may be unaffordable or simply unavailable. Bridgeport, Connecticut's interdistrict 6 to 6 Magnet Elementary School was founded to help address this pressing social need.

The 6 to 6 Magnet, which opened in 1994, is run by Cooperative Educational Services (CES), one of six regional educational agencies that provide special services to Connecticut's public schools. (Another such agency, the Capitol Region Education Council, operates the Montessori Magnet Elementary and the Greater Hartford Academies discussed on pages 33–41 and 41–51, respectively.) Besides offering an innovative school program, the 6 to 6 Magnet Elementary School provides day care for preschoolers, before- and after-school activities for K–5 students, and an optional, extended school year to help parents whose work schedules are disrupted by lengthy school vacations. (The school charges fees for some of its preschool, day-care, and extended-schedule services.)

The 6 to 6 program proved so successful that in 2001, CES decided to continue such services through the middle-school grades as well. For the first two years, middle-school classes were housed in portable classrooms, but in the fall of 2003, CES dedicated the new Thurgood Marshall Magnet Middle School, which is adjacent to the 6 to 6 Elementary and offers similar before- and

Figure 2.4.1.   The 6 to 6 Magnet Elementary School's designers added a number of playful (but functional) elements to the original structure—cladding them in "Playskool"-colored ceramic tiles, and thereby transforming a dull, corporate-looking building into a child-friendly setting. *Photograph by Lampel Photography.*

after-school programs for children in grades 6–8. Both schools draw students from the city of Bridgeport and four surrounding suburban districts. Admission is by lottery, though siblings of children who already attend the schools are given priority.

Fletcher-Thompson designed both facilities—the first a gut renovation of an existing middle school and the second new construction. (Both buildings are located on Bridgeport's John F. Kennedy public school campus, which is also home to two other K–8 magnet schools as well as a shared common building housing a swimming pool, gym, auditorium, and health-care suite, and other support spaces.)

A Full-Scale Renovation

The building now occupied by the 6 to 6 Elementary Magnet was originally built in the 1970s, and in some ways epitomized the reductive and impersonal school architecture of that era. Corridors ran along the building's perimeter; the interior classroom spaces were windowless, and the whole building had an intimidating, "corporate" look inappropriate to a learning environment for young children. The gut renovation permitted the interior configuration to be reversed: classrooms

Figure 2.4.2. Note the wealth of storage space in this classroom at the elementary school—which also functions as a before- and after-hours play and learning environment. *Photograph by Lampel Photography.*

(with windows) now line the perimeter. Beyond reconfiguring the interior, the designers added a number of functional but visually playful architectural elements—in vibrant "Playskool"-colored ceramic tile—to the exterior, giving the building a more child-friendly character and distinguishing the school from the neighboring schools on the JFK campus. A new, red-tiled entry-lobby "house," a blue-clad elevator tower, and a yellow fire stair—all external to the main building—rendered the existing building much less intimidating and also helped minimize costly structural work.

At the center of the existing building, a large, concrete-clad mechanical riser was demolished to create a skylit, glass-walled atrium, bringing natural light and a view of the sky into the heart of the classroom building. A palette of primary colors was used throughout the transformed structure—including bright red window mullions for all exterior glazing. Around the exterior, new small-scale view windows were placed at child-accessible height.

The school's special mission was accommodated architecturally through the provision of several highly flexible, smaller-than-classroom spaces that could be used for a variety of purposes before and after the normal school day. Some of the school's basic learning spaces, however, were planned to perform double duty, serving as classrooms during the school day and as activities rooms in the early morning and late afternoon. These rooms were provided with extra storage space so that classwork could be hidden away during before- and after-school hours and the toys and other materials used during activities periods could be securely stashed while school was in session. In effect, the entire facility was envisioned as a child-care/child-development facility before and after school hours, and the design had to assist in facilitating that daily transformation.

A 6 to 6 Middle School

The Thurgood Marshall Magnet Middle School, which continues the 6 to 6 program through the middle school years, occupies a brand-new structure connected to the preschool/elementary building. In planning the new middle school, designers faced a major hurdle: the John F. Kennedy campus was already crowded with school buildings, and only one relatively small corner of the site was available for new construction. Although this unbuilt portion of the campus had the advantage of being very near the 6 to 6 Elementary Magnet, a service drive and parking lot separated it from the existing facility. This was a problem, since educators and designers alike believed it was essential to physically link the two facilities—not just to provide psychological continuity (though that was important) but to permit children in the higher elementary grades to easily access some of the new building's common areas, including its media center. The problem was solved through an overhead, enclosed pedestrian bridge that joins the elementary school to the middle school.

The new building's site was constrained in another way as well. Its relative narrowness meant that the middle school would have to have a strongly linear expression. That, and a relatively Spartan budget, necessitated a single, double-loaded, classroom corridor plan. That's not usually the preferred configuration for a middle school whose student body is divided into grade-level teams, as is Thurgood Marshall's: its target population of 180 will be split into three teams of 60 students each. Designers compensated for their inability to cluster each team's learning spaces by arranging them in groups of three—each consisting of two classrooms and a science lab—along the corridor and placing an alcove (with team identification and display area) at the front of each team's area. Classrooms double as activities rooms for before- and after-school programs.

The classroom corridor is on the building's second floor, as is the media center, which is situated at the end of the building nearest the 6 to 6 Elementary School. In this location, it can easily be reached by elementary school students, who cross over via the pedestrian bridge. At the other end of the building is the school's main entry and lobby, a circular, two-story rotunda, which is lit from above by natural light and visually enlivened by two commissioned works of art by Connecticut sculptors. The rotunda lobby provides convenient access to a gymnasium and a 300-seat auditorium, and—with doors on both the street and campus sides—is monitored by the immediately adjacent first-floor administrative offices. The first floor also houses other shared common spaces, including a music room, cafeteria (with a protected outdoor seating area for fair-weather dining), art room, consumer science room, tech-ed room, and a variety of staff and building-support spaces. Several of these spaces are also used by community groups, and the arrangement—classrooms above, common spaces below—allows the academic areas to be easily locked off whenever community groups make after-hours use of the building.

The "magnetism" of the 6 to 6 elementary and middle schools isn't just a matter of the special before- and after-school and extended-schedule programs that the schools provide. Each school also has a focus, or theme. At the 6 to 6 Elementary, the curricular focus is on science

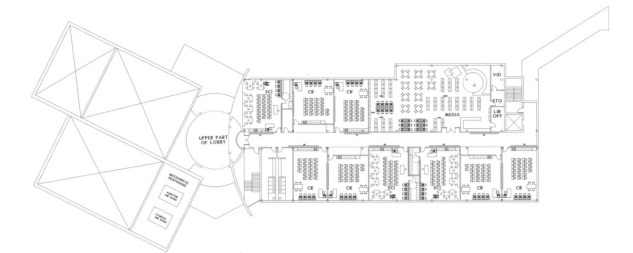

UPPER FLOOR PLAN

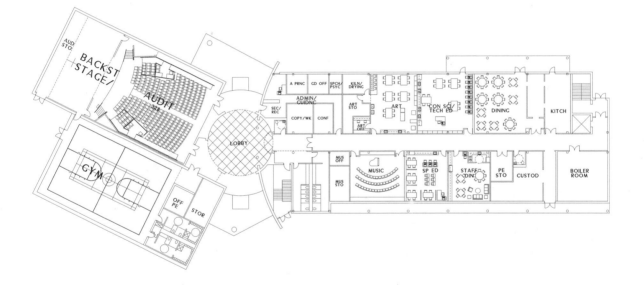

LOWER FLOOR PLAN

Figures 2.5.3a and 2.5.3b.   The upper floor of the Thurgood Marshall Magnet Middle School (top) houses classrooms as well as the media center, which is located adjacent to the pedestrian bridge connecting Thurgood Marshall to the elementary school. Common spaces are located on the lower level (bottom). The school's strongly linear arrangement was dictated by its narrow site. *Drawings by Fletcher-Thompson, Inc.*

Figure 2.5.4. The architectural focus at the Thurgood Marshall school is the rotunda-like atrium, visible in this view of the school's main entryway. The tiled wall (center) recalls the ceramic-clad elements of the neighboring elementary school. *Photograph by Fletcher-Thompson, Inc.*

Figure 2.5.5.   Thurgood Marshall Magnet Middle features a 300-seat auditorium, accessible from the rotunda. *Photograph by Fletcher-Thompson, Inc.*

and social studies, and in-school learning is enhanced through frequent field trips to local cultural institutions as well as businesses, factories, and farms in the Bridgeport area. At Thurgood Marshall, the emphasis is on instilling social responsibility—a fitting theme for a school named after the first African American justice of the U.S. Supreme Court.

AN INNER-CITY MAGNET SCHOOL CAMPUS

Hartford, Connecticut's Learning Corridor represents one of the most innovative and far-reaching implementations of the magnet school concept in the country. By bringing together four separate public magnet schools—the Montessori Magnet Elementary, the Hartford Magnet Middle School, the Greater Hartford Academy of Math and Science, and the Greater Hartford Academy of the Arts—it underscores the idea that magnet education can be comprehensive in scope, reaching children from prekindergarten years through high school. By also incorporating facilities—a Commons Building, the Theater of the Performing Arts—that are shared by the entire campus, it demonstrates the value of using economies of scale to avoid unnecessary duplication of services. And by transforming a brownfield site—the former location of a city bus garage—into a vibrant greenspace surrounded by a series of architecturally dynamic buildings, the Learning Corridor illustrates that magnet schools can play a significant role in the revitalization of blighted inner-city neighborhoods.

Located in the Frog Hollow area of Hartford's south side, the Learning Corridor is the brainchild of Evan Dobell, the former president of Trinity University, whose campus abuts the Learning Corridor on the west. The idea of developing a brand-new magnet school campus sprang from the college administration's recognition of two related realities. First, there was the acknowledgment that Trinity—one of New England's premier private universities—ought to be doing more to serve its neighborhood, which was burdened by a set of interlocking problems including crime, deteriorating housing stock, poorly performing schools, and a low homeownership rate—the whole catalog of stresses that afflict some urban neighborhoods. Second, Trinity's administrators recognized that the university's enrollment was falling—in part because of the declining fortunes of the neighborhood. Taking measures to help revitalize the neighborhood would very likely benefit the college as well.

To get the project off the ground, Trinity joined forces with a consortium of southside Hartford institutions known as SINA—Southside Institutions Neighborhood Alliance—whose members include nearby Hartford Hospital, the Institute of Living (Hartford Hospital's mental health network, whose campus is directly across Washington Street from the Learning Corridor), Connecticut Children's Medical Center, and Connecticut Public Television and Radio. Also taking part in the Learning Corridor's planning were the State of Connecticut, the City of Hartford, and the Capitol Region Educational Council (CREC), a regional educational service agency that assists public school districts throughout central Connecticut. (CREC operates all the Learning Corridor's interdistrict magnets.) Funders of the project included a host of corporate, foundation, and individual donors.

Work on the project began in 1996, with the Hartford-based architecture firm of Tai Soo Kim Partners (TSKP) drawing up a master plan for the new, 16-acre campus. For the actual design of the Learning Corridor's schools and other facilities, TSKP joined forces with three other local firms. This "Hartford team" consisted of TSKP (which designed the building housing the Greater Hartford Academies of Math and Science and the Arts, as well as the campus's theater building and parking garage; see pages 41–51, Smith Edwards Architects (responsible for the Montessori Magnet Elementary; see pages 33–41, Clarke/Tomaccio (the Magnet Middle School and the Commons building, which houses a dining room and kitchen, gym, multimedia room, community organizations' offices, and a regional center for training Montessori teachers), and Jeter, Cook & Jepson, which managed the project and coordinated the design team's work. Construction costs for the project totaled about $110 million; total square footage of all the Learning Corridor's facilities is about 400,000 square feet.

The Learning Corridor's schools opened in 2000, and by any measure the project has been a stunning success. The schools' magnet programs have proved extremely popular with parents and students from the Frog Hollow neighborhood, the larger city of Hartford, and outlying suburban districts alike—realizing the Learning Corridor's mission of reducing racial/economic isolation and nurturing truly diverse educational environments. One of the schools—the Montessori Magnet—has won a prestigious architectural award. Together, all the buildings—along with the central quadrangle they surround—have aided in the transformation of the neighborhood, leading to increases in homeownership and rising property values. In the words of the *Hartford Courant*, the Learning Corridor "is a model for ailing metropolitan areas that suffer the ills of deteriorating urban schools" (Kay 2003). It's a new paradigm that cities across the country might do well to consider emulating.

PROJECT #6: A MONTESSORI MAGNET ELEMENTARY SCHOOL
By James Waller

This project is the Montessori Magnet School in Hartford, Connecticut, for ages 3 through 12, designed by Smith Edwards Architects. It was completed in 2002. Key issues are:

- Translating educational method into built form
- The "houses and garden" concept
- Child-scaled environments
- Landscaping
- Natural daylighting

"If childhood is a journey, let us see to it that the child does not travel by night": Tyler Smith and Kent McCoy, designers of the Montessori Magnet School at Hartford, Connecticut's Learning Corridor, are fond of quoting this aphorism from Aldo van Eyck. Van Eyck (1918–1999), a Dutch modernist architect famous for (among other things) the design of more than 700 playgrounds, undoubtedly meant his remark to be taken figuratively and literally—and this "let there be light" approach to school design is beautifully realized in both the figurative and literal senses at the Montessori Magnet.

The school's striking design—which won a 2002 award from the Connecticut chapter of the American Institute of Architects—is one that will appeal to children of all ages. The colorful stylized "housefronts" that line the building's inner facade—facing the Learning Corridor's quadrangle—are extremely eye-catching. They're the first thing a visitor to this magnet-school complex notices, and the impression they make—of an environment that's adventurous yet comfortable and humanistic—is one that lasts.

Educational Method Into Built Form

The chief challenge faced by the architects—both on staff at the Hartford-based firm of Smith Edwards Architects—was to devise a design that, as a whole and in all its many parts, would carefully and creatively respond to the unique pedagogical approach of a Montessori school. The Montessori method, developed during the early 20th century by Italian physician and educator Maria Montessori (1870–1952), focuses on the needs and abilities of the individual child, encour-

Figure 2.6.1.   **The Montessori Magnet's curving classroom wing (with "housefronts" facing the courtyard garden) is clearly visible in this aerial view. A copper-clad barrel-vaulted roof (left foreground) covers the school's gymnasium. To the right of the gym are skylit art and music rooms (center foreground) and the multipurpose room (just above the art and music rooms in this view).** *Photograph courtesy Smith Edwards Architects.*

aging each child's inherent love of learning and guiding children through an increasingly complex, exploratory engagement with the physical, social, and intellectual worlds in which they live. Maria Montessori—who, as a pediatrician, was a close and skilled observer of children—outlined a series of developmental stages that, she said, every child travels through on his or her journey toward adulthood. These stages are three- to four-year-long cycles of transformation, and Montessori classrooms therefore typically group children together by age ranges rather than arbitrarily imposed grades. (The Hartford Montessori school has "primary" classes for children ages 3–6, "lower elementary" classes for ages 6–9, and "upper elementary" classes for ages 9–12.)

Montessori pedagogical method also places great emphasis on practical life, including the home arts: schoolchildren eat their meals from real china, use real metal cutlery, and wipe their lips with real fabric napkins. The school as house (or *home*) is a central theme of Montessori education, as epitomized by the school that Maria Montessori herself founded in Rome in 1907—and which she called the *Casa dei Bambini* ("Children's House"). Moreover, Montessori classrooms typically have a distinctive look conferred by the special teaching tools developed by Montessori educators over nearly a century of practice. These tools—many of them fashioned from wood and other natural materials—have a simple, elegant, richly textural character.

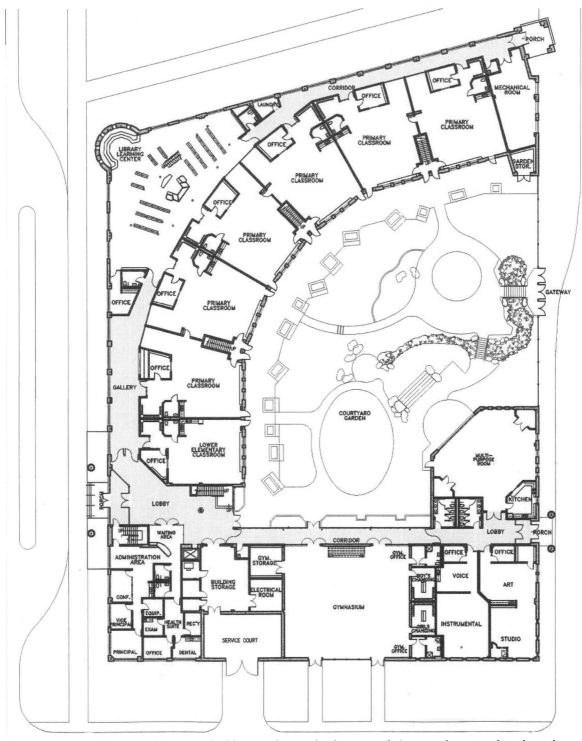

Figure 2.6.2. The Montessori Magnet's building nearly completely surrounds its central courtyard garden, whose meandering pathways are outlined on this first-floor plan. (On its eastern side, the courtyard is separated from the quadrangle beyond by a wrought-iron gated fence.) *Courtesy Smith Edwards Architects.*

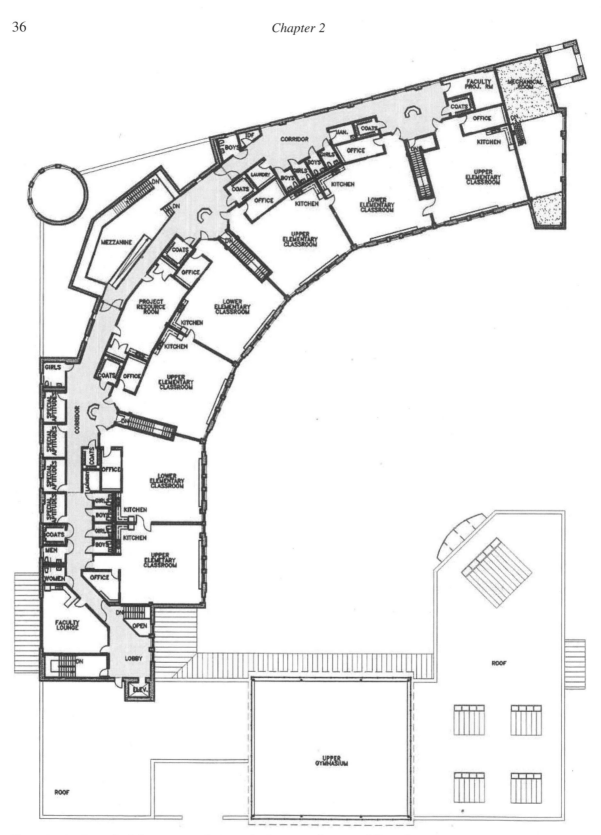

Figure 2.6.3.   In each of the Montessori Magnet's "houses," the second-floor classroom is connected by stairs to the first-floor classroom below. A technology area (top left) occupies a mezzanine overlooking the media center. *Courtesy Smith Edwards Architects.*

Figure 2.6.4. The polygonal "nodes" that dot the Montessori Magnet's classroom-wing corridors serve a number of purposes. Their tackable surfaces make them kiosks for the display of announcements and artwork. But they're also informal study and play spaces. *Photograph © 2001 by Robert Benson; used by permission.*

Montessori schools have long been a feature on the American educational landscape, but until comparatively recently virtually all Montessori schools in the United States were small, private institutions whose high tuition put them out of the reach of most poor and minority families—somewhat ironic, since Maria Montessori's own school was founded to serve the underprivileged children of one of Rome's poorest districts. The face of American Montessori education has, however, begun to change with the adoption of the Montessori method by public magnet schools (especially magnet elementaries) whose mission, in part, is to reduce racial and economic isolation. That's certainly true of the Hartford Montessori Magnet, an interdistrict magnet that during the 2003–2004 school year enrolled about 295 children from the city of Hartford and 15 nearby suburban districts; about 50 percent of its students are African American, 25 percent Latino, and 25 percent white.[1]

So how to design a Montessori school? The architects realized that the first thing they had to do was inform themselves about Montessori pedagogy. Their research included holding a day-and-a-half-long "charrette" (architect-talk for an intensive work session) with a group of experienced Montessori teachers. The basic concept for the school's design emerged out of that session: one

Figure 2.6.5. The whole interior of the Montessori Magnet Elementary is infused with natural daylight. Natural lighting is used to particularly dramatic effect in the media center's semicylindrical storytelling area, which is lit by a domed skylight. Note the small, child-height windows that punctuate the wall just above the amphitheater-style risers. *Photograph © 2001 by Robert Benson; used by permission.*

of the teachers, making reference to Maria Montessori's own Casa dei Bambini, said that, ideally, a Montessori school should resemble "houses surrounding a garden."

Houses and Garden

The designers conceived the main, academic wing of the school as a series of two-story "houses"—a little village, really—gently curving around a courtyard garden. In each house, a primary or lower elementary classroom occupies the first floor; the floor above is an upper elementary classroom. In each case, the two rooms—upper and lower—are connected by an interior stair. And the resemblance to a house doesn't end there: each of the primary/lower elementary classrooms has its own toilet room, kitchen, and sleeping area (an alcove, or nook, in which cots can be set up when needed; when cots are folded away, the area can serve as an additional learning space). Upper-floor classrooms also have kitchens, and each house has a front door, giving it direct access to the garden—which is both a playscape and an outdoor classroom. (For more on the garden, see below.)

The classrooms on each level are connected by a corridor reached through their "back doors." (See the accompanying floorplans.) This corridor, which follows the curve of the classroom-houses, opens up at its midpoint into a spacious Learning Center, with a library on the ground-floor level and a technology area (with computer workstations) on a mezzanine above. The hallway's exterior windows look onto Broad Street, which marks the Learning Corridor's western boundary, as well as onto an open, paved area that separates the Montessori Magnet from the adjacent Hartford Magnet Middle School. On these sides, the exterior walls are masonry—dark brown brick enlivened by a confetti-like scattering of tiles whose rainbow colors repeat those used on the housefronts facing the courtyard. The school's official entrance is on the Broad Street side, but the actual main entrance is at the quadrangle end of the building's other wing, which houses several shared, core spaces (gym, art and music rooms, and a multipurpose room) and which encloses the courtyard garden on its southern side.

Inside the building, finishes and architectural detailing are, in the designers' words, "simple and elemental"—the overall visual effect is more subdued than what one would find at many other contemporary elementary schools. Bright colors are used, but very sparingly, and much of the millwork (cabinetry and window and door frames) is executed in soothing, light-colored, natural maple. The principle guiding the design of the interior, as well as the selection of furniture and finishes throughout, was to complement the elegant and simply designed Montessori tools that students use in their work. As Principal Timothy J. Nee puts it, "Natural finishes were used so that children would be drawn to the [Montessori] materials, not distracted from them."

The shapes of windows and other architectural elements also echo the Montessori materials' geometries—producing an extraordinarily harmonious environment—not at all "precious," but gracious, coherent, and fluid. Among the most interesting elements of the school's interior architecture are the high-sided polygonal nodes that sit in the corridors just outside the classroom doors. These serve numerous purposes: places for children to pull on boots, sit and chat, and engage in impromptu play. Their exterior surfaces are covered in tackable linoleum, so they also function as kiosks for displaying artwork and announcements (see figure 2.6.4).

The Montessori method's emphasis on the home arts had several design implications. Meals are served family style in classrooms, which meant that each classroom had to be outfitted with a kitchen, which in each case includes a heavy-duty dishwasher that meets state health codes. (Most of the components of breakfasts and lunches are prepared in the kitchen of the Learning Corridor's Commons building, then delivered to the Montessori Magnet, but they may be warmed up in the classroom and embellished by breads or cookies that the children participate in baking.) The Montessori Magnet also has a laundry room where students wash and dry table linens—a feature that, it goes without saying, one would not find at a typical elementary school.

Child-Scaled Environments

Inside and out, the Montessori Magnet is scaled for the accessibility and comfort of the children who attend school there. The sills of the first-floor classroom windows, for example, are low enough so that even the smallest child can enjoy the view of the garden outside.

Furniture, too, is scaled for children's bodies, as are plumbing fixtures. Child-scaling the toilets and sinks imposed a bit of a challenge because heights of toilet and sink rims are specified by state building codes—requiring the designers to obtain variances for these smaller-than-usual fixtures.

Even the school's one large assembly space—the multipurpose room—is child-scaled. The sills of its main windows are low enough to allow children, no matter how tall they are, to see the courtyard garden beyond, and the room's side walls have inset windows of varying heights. (Inset windows of differing heights are also used in the music and art rooms; in fact, every room in the building has at least one window through which even the youngest, smallest students can easily peer.) Designed for large-group learning activities, the multipurpose room also plays host to parent gatherings and other events, but its size isn't so grand as to overwhelm a child.

The school has no need for a full-scale auditorium; should such a space be required for a special event, there's one just across the Learning Corridor's quad, in the theater building adjacent to the Greater Hartford Academy of the Arts (see pages 50–51). The presence on campus of a 650-seat theater that can be used whenever needed by any of the Learning Corridor's four schools is just one way in which the complex, through economy of scale, avoids unnecessary duplication of resources. The library in the Commons building, which is shared by the Hartford Magnet Middle and both of the Greater Hartford academies, is another.

Landscape for Play and Learning

Aside from its colorful, "housefronted" classroom wing, the Montessori Magnet's most distinctive and charming feature is the courtyard garden. It would be fair to say that this outdoor space—equally an environment for play and for learning—is the focal point of the entire design. Enclosed on three-and-a-half sides by the building, the courtyard is further protected by a gated fence that separates it from one of the complex's interior roads and the quadrangle just beyond. (For more active play, Montessori Magnet class-groups can leave their school's grounds and cross over to the quad, which besides a wide-open lawn contains a large playground.) As architects Smith and McCoy describe the garden space—which was designed by Phil Barlow of the TO Design landscape architecture firm—it is meant to "provide mobility within a safe area. The perimeter is secured, but there's a free-range environment within."

The garden is used in every season. ("There is no such thing as bad weather, only inappropriate clothing," is a basic principle of Montessori education, and the school's use of its outdoor space embodies that philosophy.) It represents, in microcosm, a complete ecosystem: a watercourse (dry unless it rains) meanders through it, beds are planted with wildflowers and seagrass, and there's even a small sandy, desert-like environment. For play and exploration there are bridges and pathways (including a tricycle track) and seating areas, and for outdoor study there are 14 above-ground planters—one for each of the school's classrooms—in which children can grow flowers, herbs, or fresh vegetables.

Natural Light

Many educators and school designers pay lip service to the positive effects of natural daylighting on schoolchildren's moods, receptivity to learning, and academic performance, and yet it's not at all uncommon for school interiors—even in brand-new facilities—to be mostly artificially lit. (It isn't even uncommon for new school buildings to have windowless classrooms—a decision that's too often justified by the weak argument that "kids get distracted if they can look outside.") By contrast, the designers of the Montessori Magnet fully embraced the philosophy of natural daylighting—producing an interior environment that's among the most cheerfully light-suffused that the authors of this book have ever seen.

Windows are everywhere—at a variety of heights and in a variety of forms. Besides those already mentioned, there are windows alongside the interior classroom doors, along the garden wall of the corridor that runs from the quad-side entrance to the building's lobby, and along the outer walls of the classroom-wing corridors. (There are even small, low-set windows in the walls between the first-floor classrooms' napping alcoves and the corridor behind—allowing just a little light to flow through in both directions.) Natural light is used to particularly dramatic effect in the school's Learning Center, where the semicircular storytelling area is illuminated from above by a dome-shaped skylight as well as from the sides by a series of tiny inset windows (see figure 2.6.5).

Just as the light they provide enlivens the interior environment, the windows—their different shapes, and heights, and dimensions—enliven the building's architecture, inside and out. That's especially true on the facades facing Broad Street and the middle school, where the upper-story windows are of a triangularly pedimented shape that echoes that of the housefronts on the other side of the building—even as they simultaneously recall the arched windows of the Neo-Gothic buildings on the campus of Trinity University to the west.

Perhaps the most remarkable visual effect occurs in the faculty room just above the school's Broad Street entrance. That room is lit by a large triangular window that, without it's being planned, perfectly frames the Neo-Gothic spire of Trinity University's chapel. This kind of serendipity seems just right—almost as if the spirit of Maria Montessori (and perhaps that of Aldo van Eyck) had a guiding hand in the design of this very special school.

PROJECT #7: A SHARED FACILITY FOR HIGH SCHOOL MAGNET PROGRAMS
By James Waller

This project is the Greater Hartford Academy of Math and Science and Greater Hartford Academy of the Arts in Hartford, Connecticut, for grades 9–12 (half-day programs), designed by Tai Soo Kim Partners. The schools were completed in 2000. Key issues are:

- Architectural integration of science and arts programs
- Responsiveness to architectural character of surrounding streets
- Collaboration in programming and design
- R&D-type science education environment
- Accommodation of multidimensional arts curriculum
- Professional-caliber theater

What do the arts and sciences have in common? On the campus of Hartford, Connecticut's Learning Corridor, these divergent fields of study share a single facility. "It was like putting together the right brain and the left brain," says architect Whit Iglehart about the decision to house both the Greater Hartford Academy of Math and Science and the Greater Hartford Academy of the Arts in one building.

Iglehart, who was managing principal of the team at the Hartford-based architecture firm of Tai Soo Kim Partners that designed the building, explains that opportunities for creative cross-

Figure 2.7.1.   Washington Street is a main commercial-institutional thoroughfare of Hartford's south side. The Washington Street facades of the Theater of the Performing Arts (left) and the Greater Hartford Academy of the Arts (right)—a mix of white block, glazing, and colonnades—have an appropriate "cultural" look. *Photograph by Timothy Hursley.*

Figure 2.7.2. A broad pedestrian plaza connects the theater and the Arts Academy wing of the Greater Hartford Academies building—and provides a dramatic entrance to the Learning Corridor's quadrangle beyond. *Photograph © 2001 by Robert Benson; used by permission.*

disciplinary interchange are incorporated into the facility's design. Though each of the schools occupies its own wing of the building, the academies share a light-filled, two-story central entrance lobby, and the two wings partly enclose a common courtyard. Just off the lobby is a 115-seat auditorium that serves as a recital hall for the Arts Academy and as a lecture hall for the Academy of Math and Science. Branching right and left from the lobby on both floors, the corridors that face the courtyard feature a continuous bench along the window walls and a display area opposite—resulting in a place where Arts students and their peers from the Math and Science program can casually meet and interact.

Internally, the facility links these very different constituencies and provides each with its own distinctive and appropriate learning environment. Externally, the Greater Hartford Academies (GHA) building and the adjacent Theater of the Performing Arts—which serves as the Arts Academy's main performance venue—accomplish a similar feat, in that the structures respond architecturally to two very different urban streetscapes while providing a coherent visual anchor for the Learning Corridor campus as a whole.

Figure 2.7.3. The Math and Science Academy wing of the GHA building (left foreground) is distinguished from the Arts Academy wing by its red-brick cladding. *Photograph © 2001 by Robert Benson; used by permission.*

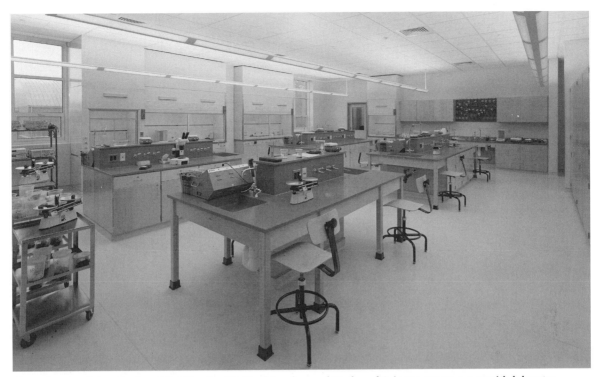

Figure 2.7.4. Laboratories at the Greater Hartford Academy of Math and Science are on a par with labs at a contemporary R&D facility. *Photograph © 2001 by Robert Benson; used by permission.*

Together, the GHA and theater buildings occupy the northeastern corner of the Learning Corridor site, at the intersection of Vernon Street—a residential side street—and Washington Street, which is one of Hartford's main institutional and commercial thoroughfares. The facades of the GHA building combine red-brick masonry, white ground face block, and glass, but the Vernon Street facade is expressed mostly in brick, while the larger white block dominates the Washington Street facade—which is topped by a curving, metal roof-structure that, in designer Iglehart's words, "makes a large-scale gesture toward" the plaza that separates the academic building from the theater. The theater building's skin—combining the white-block cladding, extensive glazing, and a ground-floor colonnade on the plaza side—intensifies the sense of vitality and larger scale, as befits a building intended to be a cultural venue in the neighborhood.

The plaza space that cuts diagonally between the GHA building and the theater is one of the campus's main pedestrian entrance points. The plaza's diagonal thrust visually extends the line of Retreat Avenue, which enters the Vernon and Washington Streets intersection from the northeast, catercorner to the Learning Corridor campus. As one enters the plaza, the GHA building stretches out on the right, but on this side—which faces the campus quadrangle—the building is more clearly divided into two sections: the white-block-clad Arts wing and the mostly red-brick-and-glass-faced Math and Science wing. Here, too, there's continuity in diversity: the brick walls of the Math and Science wing provide a visual bridge to the brick-clad Commons Building just beyond.

This melding of continuity and diversity isn't just an architectural matter; the two institutions that share the Greater Hartford Academies building are both like *and* unlike one another. The schools, for example, share a number of organizational similarities. Both are under the aegis of the Capitol Region Educational Council (CREC), the regional educational-service agency that op-

Figure 2.7.5. **The recital hall at the Arts Academy doubles as a lecture hall for the Math and Science Academy. Its location adjacent to the building's main lobby makes it easily accessible to both schools.** *Photograph © 2001 by Robert Benson; used by permission.*

erates all four of the Learning Corridor's interdistrict magnets (see also the Montessori Magnet Elementary School described in the preceding section). Both offer half-day programs[2] for high schoolers from Hartford and a large number of surrounding districts. (During the 2003–2004 year, the Math and Science Academy enrolled 228 students from 20-plus districts; the Arts Academy's 385 students hailed from 53 different districts.)

But the schools have distinct cultures and very different histories: The Academy of the Arts, founded in 1985, is the oldest interdistrict magnet program in Hartford, and its program—which offers professional-caliber training in the performing, literary, and visual arts—was flourishing and nationally recognized long before the school's move to the new Learning Corridor facility. By contrast, the Academy of Math and Science—which was founded specifically *for* the Learning Corridor—came into being at the same time that the GHA facility was being planned and designed. The Arts Academy's programmatic requirements were well established; those for the Math and Science Academy were formulated by a group of educators who closely collaborated with the design team.

Figure 2.7.6. The metal-clad roof structure of the Arts Academy—evocative of the curved eaves of Asian buildings—is a signature element of the GHA building's design. Here, it is seen through the windows of the theater lobby's mezzanine. *Photograph by Charles R. Cassidy.*

The Academy of Math and Science

The Math and Science Academy presented architects with much more freedom than is usual in the design of a public school. To develop a program for the new school, the architects and the Learning Corridor's sponsors brought together a committee of senior science-department faculty from high schools around Connecticut. As Iglehart recalls, the committee's members were given a simple but far-reaching charge: "We want you to *dream*," they were told. Dream they did, but this kind of dreaming required a lot of legwork.

In the visioning process it undertook, the committee enlisted the help and advice of the National Consortium for Specialized Secondary Schools of Mathematics, Science, and Technology (NCSSSMST)—a national alliance of 80 specialized high schools and high school programs. Architects and committee members traveled around the United States visiting other math and science–themed schools, from New York City's Stuyvesant High to the Kalamazoo Area Mathematics and Science Center in Kalamazoo, Michigan. Program and design evolved hand in hand, and the building that resulted resembles a state-of-the-art R&D facility as much as it does a high school.

Design proceeded from committee members' shared conviction that scientific exploration typically crosses disciplinary boundaries. To facilitate an interdisciplinary approach—and to nur-

Figure 2.7.7. In the theater's lobby, the second-floor mezzanine defines a central open space shaped—appropriately—like the case of a grand piano. *Photograph © 2001 by Robert Benson; used by permission.*

Figure 2.7.8. The Arts Academy uses the Learning Corridor's stunning, professional-caliber theater for its Broadway-style musical productions. The other Learning Corridor schools can book it when they're in need of a full-size auditorium for special events. *Photograph by Timothy Hursley.*

ture a collegial atmosphere in which interaction is encouraged—designers rejected the typical configuration in which corridors are merely hallways through which students move from one self-contained classroom or laboratory space to another. Instead, the Math and Science Academy's corridors are conceived as "science suites" that integrate classroom and out-of-classroom learning. Along these extra-wide corridors, laboratories are paired; the front doors of each pair of labs open onto a shared breakout area. The corridors are lined with workstations, and the breakout spaces and workstations alike are wired for data so that students—each of whom is given a laptop computer—can pursue individual and small-group work whenever and wherever they please.

Ongoing informal interaction between students and faculty is facilitated by situating faculty offices directly adjacent to the corridor. As in many of today's R&D facilities, the spatial layout increases the possibility that researchers (in this case, students and faculty) will regularly "run into" each other—the idea being that creativity is spurred by casual meetings and exchange of ideas. Throughout the lab areas, cross-disciplinary interchange is further highlighted by the inventive use of interior glazing: labs aren't visually shuttered off; instead, a series of interior windows connects lab spaces with one another and with the corridor workspaces.

The Academy of Math and Science boasts a panoply of specialized labs and scientific equipment that far surpasses what an ordinary comprehensive high school—even one in an extremely affluent district—could possibly offer. Specialized research spaces include, for example, a cell culture lab, a laser lab, a robotics/electronics lab, and a molecular genetics lab. Research equipment includes gas chromatographs and DNA sequencers. (Some of the school's sophisticated equipment has been donated by corporate partners/sponsors.) There are also mathematics classrooms, a faculty research lab, a greenhouse, and a number of project rooms in which students can pursue independent work.

The academy's relationship with nearby Trinity University—which spearheaded the development of the Learning Corridor (see pages 31–33)—has been a dynamic one. In 1999, while construction of the GHA building was under way, Trinity inaugurated a pilot Academy of Math and Science program that brought together 80 students from 12 "charter districts." These high schoolers—who studied forensic science and river ecology in the pilot program—became the "seed students" for the new academy. Today, Trinity and the academy sometimes cosponsor educational programs in which college and high school students work together, as peers, on cross-disciplinary topics. There's even some movement of faculty between the two institutions; for example, one Trinity math professor recently took a yearlong sabbatical, using his time off to teach at the Academy of Math and Science.

Arts Academy

The Greater Hartford Academy of the Arts isn't just the longest-lived interdistrict magnet program in Hartford; it's also one of the premier high school arts programs in the country. Begun in a Hartford church in 1985, the school moved to a retrofitted funeral home for a few years before coming to the Learning Corridor in the fall of 2000. The relocation to the new facility has enabled it to expand its program: previously limited to about 170 students, the academy now enrolls almost 400. The academy's faculty is a mix of full-time, permanent "core" instructors and a much larger group of arts-world professionals who may teach one or two courses per term and whose role is similar to that played by "artists in residence" at a college or university.

The academy offers concentrated courses of study in seven fields—creative writing, dance, film and TV, instrumental and vocal music, theater, theater design and production, and visual arts—and the facility's learning spaces reflect the variety of the school's curriculum. The Arts wing of the GHA building includes music, dance, and art studios; the recital hall (discussed above); a "living room" space for creative writing seminars; and a special multidisciplinary space dubbed the "paintry and poeting" room, where students work on projects that cross the boundary between the visual and literary arts. The Arts Academy's program actually extends across three Learning Corridor buildings: its TV and film production facilities are housed in the adjacent Commons Building, and the theater building (discussed below) is, of course, the locus for courses in theater and theater design/production.

Theater of the Performing Arts

The theater building—also designed by Tai Soo Kim Partners—serves as a point of connection for all of the Learning Corridor's schools, as well as between the Learning Corridor and Hartford's

Frog Hollow neighborhood. All the schools make at least occasional use of the building's 650-seat proscenium theater for large assemblies, and both the main theater and black-box theater are available for rental by community theater companies and other groups. But the building's primary purpose is to provide venues for the theatrical productions mounted by students of the Greater Hartford Academy of the Arts. These productions—whether lavish, Broadway-style musical comedies or intimately scaled dramatic works—are all of a professional caliber, and the school's shows draw audiences from all over the Hartford region.

The theater building was designed to accommodate these productions' requirements. In the words of architect Iglehart, the main, 650-seat house is "better than anything you'd find in a typical high school, though perhaps not as good as the Bushnell." But if the theater isn't quite as well equipped as Hartford's famed Bushnell Center for the Performing Arts, it certainly doesn't fall too far short. It features, among other things, a full stagehouse and fly space, sophisticated lighting and sound systems, and backstage workshops and dressing rooms. The black-box theater—located behind the main auditorium—is also professionally equipped and accommodates audiences of up to 150 people.

The design of the building's two-story lobby—which fronts on the plaza at the corner of Washington and Vernon Streets—is exhilarating. This capacious, largely glass-enclosed space features a wraparound mezzanine whose undulating line defines a central void that's shaped—appropriately and wittily—like the case of a concert grand piano. Besides serving as a pretheater and intermission gathering place, the lobby also provides a dramatic gallery space for shows of student and faculty artwork, and it's roomy and comfortable enough to double as an informal learning space. (A yoga class was using the lobby's carpeted downstairs area on the afternoon that compilers of this book visited the building.) And the architectural drama isn't reserved for the interior: at the building's northeastern corner, directly above the main entrance, rises a narrow, glass-walled "campanile"—a modern, stylized take on a Renaissance bell tower. It's a fitting signpost for the renaissance of this inner-city neighborhood that the Learning Corridor has helped inspire.

PROJECT #8: A PURPOSE-BUILT, TECHNOLOGY-THEMED, MAGNET HIGH SCHOOL
By James Waller

This project is the Advanced Technologies Academy in Las Vegas, Nevada, for grades 9–12, designed by KGA Architecture. The original building was completed in 1994, the gymnasium was finished in 1998, and an addition was built in 2002. Key issues are:

- Visioning process
- IT connectivity
- Facility as showpiece
- Flexible design
- Master planning and expandability

At Las Vegas's Advanced Technologies Academy, they seem to do everything right. The magnet high school—which was selected as a 2003 Blue Ribbon School under the U.S. Department of

Figure 2.8.1. ATech's spacious, skylit media center, positioned near the school's main entrance, was a major drawing card, enticing parents to enroll their children at the new magnet school. *Photograph by Opulence Studios.*

Figure 2.8.2. The skylit interior courtyard/atrium in ATech's new wing deftly melds angles and curves into a harmonious whole. Locker areas—visible at the lower left—line the atrium's ground floor. *Photograph by Opulence Studios.*

Education's No Child Left Behind initiative—has a multidimensional program geared toward preparing its students for further study and careers in seven sectors of the high-tech economy: business and finance, computer graphic design, computer science, law-related education, systems technology support, information technology, and pre-engineering. But just reading about the program—as impressive as it is—can't prepare you for the sky-high level of enthusiasm and commitment on the part of students, faculty, and administrators that a visit to the school reveals.

To tour the school—dubbed "ATech" by those who study and teach there—is to witness an educational program that is enviable in its relevance and rigor. Besides which, it looks as if students and teachers are having a great deal of productive fun. The two compilers of this book who visited the academy in the fall of 2003 were immediately infected by the excitement. In a systems technology support "immersion lab," we saw students working on projects that would prepare them for certification exams administered by major computer manufacturers. In a business writing class, we were treated to student-produced audiovisual presentations that were remarkable for their wit and professionalism. A CADD (computer-assisted drafting and design) instructor proudly told us of the student design competitions (sponsored by the American Institute of Architects and other organizations) that ATech kids had won. And a pre-engineering teacher boasted—justifiably—that his students regularly tackled problems and issues that were far more advanced than what he, himself, had encountered in *college* engineering courses.

Moreover, our tour of the facility was made all the more informative—in the sense of allowing us to get a real idea of the *life* of the school—by the fact that our tour guides were ATech students: two seniors who were poised, articulate, and immensely knowledgeable about their school. Of all the many magnet and charter schools we visited while preparing this book, it was only at ATech that students served as our primary guides. It's a great idea—demonstrating, among other things, the faith that ATech has in its students' abilities. As we say, at ATech, they seem to do everything right.

The Visioning Process/Architectural Objectives

When the Advanced Technologies Academy opened in 1994, it was the first purpose-built magnet school in Las Vegas. The Clark County School District of Nevada—to which Greater Las Vegas Valley schools belong—had initiated a magnet school program a few years earlier, but its first magnets were developed along the school-within-a-school model or were housed in existing facilities. According to KGA Architecture, which served as the design firm for the original building and the two additions that have been made to the campus since 1994, the architect wasn't brought on board until a visioning committee composed of local educators and planners—and spearheaded by Michael Kinnaird, a forward-thinking educator who was ATech's first principal—had spent six months considering how best to approach the project.

Among other things, the committee's members made visits to other state-of-the-art schools throughout the region to get a firsthand look at what others were doing. Having done its homework, the committee presented the selected architecture firm—the Las Vegas–based KGA—with a proposed curriculum, a list of classes the building would house, a projected student population (of 750—a figure that would eventually rise), a budget, and some essential objectives. Those objectives, which were quite novel in the early 1990s, included the following:

- *Connectivity:* The vision committee insisted that students be able to access their own work files from any computer in the building—*and* that they be able to connect to any other of the school's computers. Though these goals sound ho-hum today (when we take networking, Internet access, and even wireless communications for granted), they were groundbreaking at the time, and they illustrate the wisdom of thinking seriously about the future when planning a new school facility.
- *School as Showpiece:* The visionary members of the planning committee also recognized that they might face a genuine challenge in persuading students from all over the Greater Las Vegas Valley area to consider attending the school. After all, the school would be located in a section of central Las Vegas that was rather far removed—geographically, culturally, and economically—from "The Strip" so familiar to visitors to the city as well as from this burgeoning area's more affluent suburbs. ATech was, in fact, the first new school construction project to be undertaken in its inner-city neighborhood in many years. But it wasn't just the character of the neighborhood that was potentially problematic. The long commutes needed to get to and from the school were likely to prove a hurdle to meeting

enrollment targets in this far-flung desert community. Moreover, students attending ATech would, at least for the new school's first few years, have to give up some of the perks of attending an ordinary comprehensive high school—for example, athletics programs. To help ensure that the school would exert enough "magnetism" on parents and students from all over the district, designers were charged with creating a facility that would truly be a showpiece. It wouldn't just "wow" visitors—it would also *show* them, in an immediately visible way, the brand-new, future-oriented kind of education that ATech's students would receive.

The first of these objectives—connectivity—was architecturally addressed in a way that, given the state of information-technology art in the early 1990s, made a great deal of functional sense. As a brochure produced by KGA Architecture at the time of the original building's completion puts it, "All classrooms are located within the two-story section of the building to shorten both computer connections and student circulation." In other words, the main academic area of the building would be *compact*, in part to facilitate the installation and functioning of the computer network that would serve as the school's lifeline. A series of infrastructure closets containing repeaters, hubs, and other necessary equipment was distributed at regular intervals throughout the two-story academic section of the building to restrict distances between the branches of the school's "technology tree"—a strategy that, at the time, was necessary to ensure network functionality. Of course, network technology has improved by leaps and bounds in the decade since ATech first opened, and many of these closets are no longer needed for their original purpose. That doesn't mean those spaces go to waste, however: today, they provide the school with additional storage capacity.

The second goal—that of creating a showpiece that would sell the school to prospective students and their parents—was realized by making many of the school's high-tech spaces immediately and clearly *visible* to the parents and prospective students who would tour the school before committing to enrolling there. KGA compares ATech's situation during this early part of its history to that faced by many private schools, which must "show their wares" to hook prospective attendees. What was, at the time, the school's main server was prominently displayed in a glass-encased room in the media center just off the main lobby. The distance-learning center in the media center—also adjacent to the lobby—was likewise showcased. These days, when such technologies have become much more familiar (and when ATech's track record of success serves as the school's main drawing card), the importance of this "wow factor" has diminished, but the strategies clearly demonstrate the savvy of using a magnet's facility to spur enrollment—a point that's emphasized elsewhere in this book.

Flexible, Program-Driven Design

What first strikes the visitor to the school today is the visual power of its overall design. As KGA makes clear, the architectural team that, in the early 1990s, set out to design this cutting-edge building did not approach the job with preconceived notions about how the building should look. The design emerged from the program—especially from the two overarching objectives discussed above. Form definitely followed function, but the building's forms, exterior and interior, are nevertheless striking. KGA Architecture says that one concept guiding the architects during the early stages of design was that of a ship—a ship breaking the waves as it cuts its way into the future. Though abstracted, that conception survives in the ATech complex's present exterior appearance, in which broad sweeps of champagne-colored "tiled" surfaces (the "tiles" are actually hybrid stucco panels) are syncopated with a variety of angular and trapezoidal elements. The idiom throughout the building is definitely modern; unlike many magnets, ATech unapologetically *looks* like a school of the future.

Exterior glazing is minimal—mostly achieved through ribbons of glass blocks that band the building's facades, their apparently darker color contrasting with the pale stucco panels and heightening the visual rhythm. The decision to use glass block—and to allow natural light to penetrate corridors while many of the school's learning spaces are windowless—was dictated by the need to balance the human occupants' need for light with high technology's aversion to natural light (a particularly important consideration given Las Vegas's relentless sunshine). ATech's media center is suffused with natural light that enters through clerestory windows and a light-monitor-equipped ceiling system.

Classroom spaces at ATech are somewhat larger than is typical at most Clark County high schools. The aim of this oversizing—to maximize flexibility—certainly appears to have worked. As the program has evolved, some classrooms have taken on the character of offices (with individual workstations/cubicles lining the room's perimeter). Others—for example, the room in which network repair and maintenance is taught—have become working laboratories for hands-on exploration of hardware. The ability to flexibly and easily reconfigure space in classrooms is enhanced by a simple innovation incorporated into the original classroom design: the main storage closets in each classroom are concealed between the whiteboard wall at the front of the class, with the sliding whiteboard panels serving as the closets' doors. It's an elegant solution to classroom clutter, and it limits the need for additional case pieces for storage, which are notoriously difficult to move from place to place.

Master Planning and Expandability

Flexibility is built in at the macro as well as the micro level. The original planning process included a master plan for ATech's campus, also devised by KGA Architecture, which allowed for expansions of the original building and the addition of other structures as funds would become available. And addition and expansion were, in fact, in the cards: the need for a gym (so that students could more easily accomplish the physical education requirements for high school graduation in Nevada) quickly became apparent, so the separate building containing the gym was the first element to be added, in 1998. Moreover, within a year of its inauguration, ATech had met its enrollment targets, and demand for admission (which requires that the student pass an entrance exam) soon exceeded supply.

Expanding the program to serve a larger number of eligible Las Vegas–area students, however, necessitated expanding the building. In September 2002, the school opened its new academic wing, which, besides providing extra classrooms, includes additional science labs, a TV studio, a fully outfitted auditorium, and a second lobby—a dramatic (and welcoming) gathering space from which stairs rise to the second-floor mezzanine overlooking it. The expansion has permitted enrollment to rise to around 1,000. (Even so, ATech's population remains well below that of comprehensive high schools in Clark County, whose average student populations hover around 2,700.)

The master plan, by the way, foresees the ultimate addition of yet another academic wing to the main building. With ATech's record of success, it seems certain that that expansion, too, will eventually happen.

PROJECT #9: A DESIGN-THEMED CHARTER HIGH SCHOOL
By James Waller

This project is the Charter High for Architecture + Design (CHAD) in Philadelphia, Pennsylvania, for grades 9–12. Key issues are:

- Galleries/display space for student work
- Charter school facilities challenges
- Visioning process

Philadelphia's CHAD is the brainchild of a visionary and socially engaged group of architects. This high-performing and highly unusual charter school is a Legacy Project of the Philadelphia

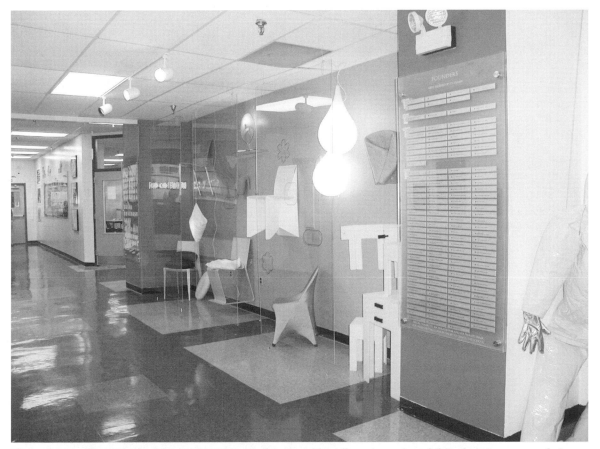

Figure 2.9.1. The main corridor at CHAD serves as a changing gallery space. An exhibit of contemporary chair design was up when this photograph was taken. *Photograph by Barbara Chandler Allen; courtesy CHAD.*

Figure 2.9.2.   Visitors to CHAD are immediately greeted by a display of high-tech design. In this photo of CHAD's reception area, principal Gregory Amiriantz stands next to a computer station where visitors can view videos made by CHAD students. *Photograph by Barbara Chandler Allen; courtesy CHAD.*

chapter of the American Institute of Architects (AIA). Each year, the AIA chapter in the city where the national organization holds its national convention is asked to create something of value for its community. Wanting to present Philadelphia with a gift of enduring worth—and in the process take a step toward correcting racial imbalance in the design professions, where minorities are severely underrepresented—the Philadelphia AIA chapter spearheaded the founding of CHAD. The school opened in the fall of 1999, in advance of the 2000 AIA convention hosted by Philadelphia.

Five years after its creation, CHAD is flourishing. During the 2003–2004 school year, the school was serving almost 370 students who hailed from 49 different zip codes throughout Philadelphia and, in a few cases, suburban areas outside the city limits. (Pennsylvania's charter school legislation permits students to cross school-district lines to attend a charter school.) Many of CHAD's students—77 percent of whom are African American—come from extremely low-performing inner-city schools. Although under Pennsylvania's charter statute CHAD cannot impose any kind of admissions criteria beyond state residency, the school makes a special effort to attract students who are "visual learners." These are kids who have demonstrated some interest or talent in the visual arts, though most have never received any formal art training. They arrive at CHAD with widely differing academic skill levels (some entering ninth graders, for example, read on a third-grade level). It's no understatement to say that for the vast majority of them, their years at CHAD will be a life-transforming experience.

The stats clearly bear this out. Whereas the average daily attendance at Philadelphia public high schools hovers around 63 percent (dropping to the 40–50 percent range at some the city's poorest-performing high schools), CHAD's daily attendance rate is a phenomenal 95+ percent. Student scores on standardized language-arts and math tests have been shown to rise by as much as 17 or 18 percent over the course of CHAD's four-year program. Eighty-two percent of the members of CHAD's 2002 graduating class went on to some form of higher education, and a number of CHAD graduates have made it into top design schools like the Rhode Island School of Design and the Pratt Institute—especially impressive achievements when one considers that college isn't even on the conceptual horizon for most students when they first come to CHAD.

CHAD takes alternative education seriously. The strength of its unique educational program—in which the problem-solving methods commonly used by designers are, to the greatest extent possible, applied across all areas of the curriculum—and its undeniable record of success have earned it the endorsement of numerous professional groups, including American General Contractors, the American Institute of Graphic Arts, the Industrial Designers Society of America, the National Organization of Minority Architects, and the Organization of Black Designers, as well as the financial support of dozens of corporate partners.

Still, CHAD is very much a work in progress—with emphasis on the word *progress*. The school struggles with a facility that, despite numerous praiseworthy features, is too cramped to accommodate CHAD's program, and whose small size limits the school's ability to grow. Change is needed, and to spur and guide that change, CHAD undertook a comprehensive visioning process during the 2003–2004 school year.

School as Art Gallery

CHAD's difference from other schools is immediately evident—visible even before one enters the front door. The school occupies a large portion of the first floor of an early-20th-century office building in downtown Philadelphia, just half a block from Independence Hall. Walking past its entrance, an ordinary pedestrian might think he or she is passing an art gallery. And it's not just that the school's logo—which appears on several windows as well as the main door—is a carefully crafted example of contemporary graphic design. What one sees when peering into the front-door vestibule *is* a bona fide work of art: an eye-popping mural by American modernist master Sol Lewitt. Enthusiastic about CHAD's mission, Lewitt contributed plans for the work to the school; the mural's panels—bright yellow, blue, and coral stripes arranged in starburst and cross-hatch patterns against contrasting, boldly colored backgrounds—were executed by CHAD students, faculty, and staff.

This vibrant, collaborative work certainly makes for a stunning entryway, but just beyond the front door is something—or, rather, an *absence* of something—that is just as stunning. CHAD's entrance has no turnstile or other security apparatus—virtually unheard of in a big-city public school. CHAD's students come here in part to escape the violence that's endemic at so many public high schools—and they are expected to treat the building, their fellow students, and the school's staff and faculty with care and respect. (And they do: much of CHAD's interior is scuffed and has an appropriately lived-in look, but nowhere are its walls scarred by graffiti or other vandalism.)

The "art gallery" feel of the place extends well beyond the front door. The wall opposite the receptionist's station and the corridor immediately beyond are, in fact, gallery spaces, featuring student work as well as changing exhibitions from the Cooper-Hewitt National Design Museum in New York City, with which CHAD has established collaborative arrangements. (CHAD faculty travel to New York for summer staff-development programs; the school plays host to portions of Cooper-Hewitt exhibitions once they've ended their New York runs.)

Just off the lobby is another noteworthy space: a small office where prospective students and their parents are interviewed by CHAD staff. Originally a drab, lackluster room, this office was recently remade by a CHAD graduate who's now in college, studying design. It was his conviction that parents and would-be students need to be made aware—up front, and in a visually unambiguous way—just what kind of place CHAD is. Armed with a small budget for furniture purchases (from Ikea), a couple of buckets of paint, and his own discerning designer's eye, this former student, volunteering his time, transformed this little meeting room into a knockout example of contemporary workplace design.

The school-as-gallery theme continues throughout the facility. Some corridor walls are lined with Homasote—a paper-based wallboard favored by architects because it's a perfect tackboard surface—and student-produced work is everywhere on proud display. (These displays are constantly changing, and three times a year CHAD puts on special, schoolwide shows of student work.) With so much to show—student work as well as examples of contemporary design contributed or lent by others—display space is at a premium, so one CHAD student dreamed up a way of creating more. The rows of student lockers that line several corridors are interrupted, now and again, by small glass-fronted showcases—each inset in a space from which a locker has been removed. It's an ingenious solution—one that relieves the lockers' visual monotony while increasing the number of places where work can be put on view.

Facilities-Related Challenges

This vital, celebratory approach to the use of space cannot, however, overcome the very real facilities-related challenges that CHAD faces. The school has, to put it bluntly, maxed-out its facility. Given the overall space constraints, CHAD's floorplan is well conceived: a loop corridor connects most of the school's learning spaces, branching off at the western end to connect with a large, airy, high-ceilinged space that serves as a computer lab. But throughout the facility, space is *very* tight. Classrooms and studio spaces are small and relatively inflexible, the single faculty room is tiny, storage space is virtually nonexistent, the cafeteria is uncomfortably cramped, and there is no room for "amenities" that most other schools take for granted. There is, for example, no media center/library—a lack that CHAD compensates for by having its students use a nearby branch of the Philadelphia Public Library. (For more on charter schools' use of local institutions for spaces and resources that the schools themselves cannot provide, see Chapter 5, "Finding a Home: The Facilities Side of the Charter School Debate.")

A visitor to the school can't help but be impressed by how fully and well CHAD exploits the space it has, but it's also obvious that it desperately needs more. And it's not just space that CHAD's in need of: furniture and equipment are often inadequate to or inappropriate for the school's programmatic needs. To take just one example, the cafeteria must double as a large-group gathering space/auditorium, but it takes hours to set up or break down the folding tables on which students eat their meals. It's obvious that a more flexible furniture system would greatly enhance this space's usefulness. Some furniture problems have been overcome by CHAD's can-do resourcefulness. For example, the large worktables in one of the design studios are "homemade": a group of students designed them, fashioning them from doors and lumber purchased at a local home-improvement outlet. These tables are serviceable and—yes—handsome, but not all of the school's furniture and equipment needs can be met so readily or cheaply.

Though CHAD administrators are understandably reluctant to revisit problems the school encountered during its earliest days, the facilities-related difficulties that CHAD endured during its first few weeks of existence are worth mentioning here for the chastening example they might provide to other founders and would-be founders of charter schools. When CHAD first opened in the fall of 1999, it did so *before* the interior of its leased space had been completely constructed. For three weeks, the brand-new school's administrators, board, teachers, and students tried to make a go of it (though a few teachers quit in frustration), but the situation—in which there was no real, physical separation between classes—soon proved impossibly chaotic, and the school was forced to close down. That could have been disastrous, especially for what was a rather high-profile undertaking. As it turned out, CHAD rose to the challenge—quickly devising and implementing an emergency plan that permitted the space to be completely built out and the school to reopen its doors after a several-week hiatus. Nevertheless, CHAD's rocky start underscores the importance of paying scrupulous attention to facilities issues, including scheduling, during a charter's planning phase. (As Chapter 5 makes clear, the early facilities-related difficulties that CHAD overcame are far from uncommon among startup charters.)

Visioning a New CHAD

The school's early history demonstrates that CHAD is good at solving problems. Now, its staff, faculty, board, and students, as well as a committed band of "CHADvocates" (design professionals from Philadelphia and elsewhere who've made the school's long-term success their cause), are grappling with the need to find new quarters for the school—and to ensure that CHAD's new home, wherever and whatever it might be, will flexibly and appropriately serve the school's dynamic program over the years ahead. One of the issues that CHAD must address is its need for a larger student body—a critical mass that would bring in the additional funding required to allow the school to provide a greater variety of shared, common resources. According to CHAD's director of development, Barbara Chandler Allen, the target population is a little less than 500—not too large, but well beyond the capacity of CHAD's current facility.

At the time of this writing, the process of visioning a new CHAD had just begun, and it is unclear whether the charter will eventually occupy a renovated school building (there had been some discussion with the Philadelphia Board of Education about the possibility of CHAD's leasing—for a dollar a year—one of its older, now abandoned properties) or whether CHAD might find the wherewithal to construct its own new, purpose-built facility. But CHAD wasn't waiting around for that issue to be resolved to begin the planning process in earnest.

In October 2003, CHAD held its first visioning meeting, which was facilitated by design gurus from IDEO, a high-profile, west coast–based firm that specializes in helping a very wide range of companies and organizations think through and creatively address their design challenges—whether those challenges concern a new product or a workplace reconfiguration. People representing the entire CHAD community—not just those who would use the new facility but some CHAD parents, some members of CHAD's board, and a sprinkling of interested Philadelphia designers as well—attended the evening-long brainstorming session. Participants were guided through the process by IDEO's head of environments, Fred Dust, who employed IDEO's trademark "Deep Dive" technique to get people's creative juices flowing. (IDEO, whose founder David Kelley is a CHAD honorary trustee, contributed its services.)

According to Dr. Claire Gallagher, CHAD's curriculum supervisor and one of the session's participants, by evening's end everybody was busy sketching out their concepts for CHAD's new home. Moreover, faculty participants from across the disciplines were learning something about incorporating problem-solution design techniques into their instructional approach. The CHAD students who attended were among the most enthusiastic visionaries—recognizing that they, too, would play an essential role in design. Given CHAD's dedication to instilling in its students not only solutions-oriented design methods but also an experience-engendered love of the design process, that makes perfect sense.

PROJECT #10: A MAGNET SCHOOL WITHIN A SCHOOL
By Michael Schrier and Mark S. Hesselgrave, AIA

This project is the Center for Global Studies at the Brien McMahon High School in Norwalk, Connecticut, for grades 9–12, designed by Fletcher-Thompson, Inc. The scheduled completion is December 2004 for the addition and December 2005 for a renovation of the existing high school. Key issues are:

- Magnet component's integration into, and separation from, the larger school
- Achieving a distinctive magnet school identity
- Renovation and addition to 1950s school building

The Center for Global Studies (CGS) is the first magnet school in Connecticut to be integrated into a comprehensive high school. Brien McMahon High School is a typical urban high school, with students from a wide range of cultural and economic backgrounds. Thus, while students at the center study cultural diversity on a global scale, they experience local cultural diversity in their daily life at school.

The CGS magnet provides students from southern Fairfield County high schools with an opportunity to study Japanese and Chinese culture through courses in language, literature, and history. The core curriculum includes Japanese language study with beginner, intermediate, and advanced levels. The comparative Asian and Western literature course includes translated works of mythology, poetry, short stories, novels, and films. Students are also required to produce essays of various types throughout the school year. A course in Japanese and Chinese history explores social, political, and economic dynamics that are significant to the global community. Courses required by students' home schools are met in the magnet school and McMahon's mainstream classes. Students out of district can participate in all extracurricular activities.

Figure 2.10.1. At the Brien McMahon High School, the separate identity of the Center for Global Studies magnet program is preserved partly through spatial organization. CGS's dedicated learning spaces appear at the upper right of this first-floor plan. *Drawing by Fletcher-Thompson, Inc.*

The McMahon High School is now undergoing a thorough renovation and expansion, slated for completion in late 2005. The Center for Global Studies has existed for a several years as a part of the high school, though on a smaller scale and with a more limited program than it will ultimately have. As the Center for Japanese Studies, the magnet occupied three classrooms at the pre-renovated McMahon School. When the current construction project is finished, facilities for the expanded magnet program will be part of a new 120,000 square foot addition adjacent to the renovated high school building. Yet when the renovation of Brien McMahon was first considered, its continued affiliation with the magnet school had not been decided.

The McMahon renovation project began with a programming phase. Program and cost data were compiled independently for the high school and the magnet school. Although day-to-day interaction with Brien McMahon's diverse culture is integral to the CGS mission, the project team wished to demonstrate the benefits of maintaining the school-within-a-school relationship. Therefore, there followed a feasibility phase during which designers and school officials studied the possibility of relocating the magnet program to its own, separate facility. The team not only compared the cost of building a new, stand-alone magnet to that of integrating it into the renovated and expanded comprehensive high school, but they also debated the benefits and disadvantages to students of a small, stand-alone school versus letting the magnet remain within the larger school. The selected school-within-a-school option—in which the magnet program will serve 300 students out of an overall projected student population of about 1,700—not only proved lower in cost than the alternative, but it will also enable the magnet's students to take advantage of all the facilities, programs, and extracurricular activities that usually only a large high school can offer.[3]

Creating and Preserving the Magnet's Identity

The greatest challenge for the school-within-a-school approach to magnet education is the risk that the magnet will not be able to create or maintain its own, distinct identity within the larger school. Addressing this challenge is partly a programmatic, organizational matter. In the reconfigured Mc-Mahon School, magnet program students will take some of their courses in the comprehensive high school, but students in the regular program will not be permitted to enroll in CGS courses, nor will they be able to use spaces dedicated to the magnet program. The challenge also has architectural implications: the magnet program must possess a somewhat distinctive character. At Mc-Mahon, the CGS identity will be preserved (1) by locating the magnet component on its own floor in the new addition, separate from the comprehensive school's other learning spaces, and (2) by giving the magnet its own separate, distinctive entry. Finally, the instructional model of the magnet school is substantively different from that of the high school, and the center's facilities must reflect that difference.

The size, configuration, and outfitting of learning spaces within the magnet component will differ from those in the comprehensive high school. The instructional model in the center calls for small, cooperative, multiage classes, but also classes that work in concert on special projects. This requires flexible instructional spaces and furnishings that are easily adaptable to changing needs. Consequently, the magnet's classrooms will be substantially larger than those in McMahon: about 1,200 square feet versus an average of 750 square feet per classroom. This additional space is required for several related reasons. Because the magnet's curriculum focuses on so many different aspects of each of the cultures studied, classrooms must be large and flexible enough to accommodate several different kinds of activities. Also, because the magnet's pedagogical approach emphasizes teamwork and group learning experiences, the spaces must be large enough to allow different activities to be pursued by several different groups simultaneously. (The teacher in this approach serves as a facilitator, floating from one group to another.) In addition, the number and variety of projects undertaken by each class necessitate a greater-than-usual amount of storage space.

The magnet's learning spaces are also distinctive in terms of their configuration and adjacencies. Each of the program's areas of concentration is assigned two rooms: a classroom and a lab. (The rooms are similar in size but outfitted differently.) In addition, each area of concentration possesses a special "project room." The three project rooms are clustered together in the center of the magnet program's floor; demountable walls separating them can be easily moved, allowing the spaces to be opened up to form a single large project room suitable for large-group activities or cross-cultural learning experiences, bringing together students and faculty from two or all three curricular areas. The CGS magnet also has a dedicated multipurpose space for group instruction and community events; appropriately called the Community Room, it is equipped with stage, dressing rooms, and audiovisual equipment. Because CGS is affiliated with schools in other countries, technology for distance learning is included in all learning spaces. The magnet also contains a teaching kitchen, enabling students to explore the cuisines of the cultures they study.

Renovating a 1950s School Building

The new addition housing the magnet component is but one aspect of construction work at the McMahon High School, which involves the like-new renovation of an existing 1950s-era school building. Although this portion of the job does not directly bear on the magnet school, it is worth discussing briefly here, since the project's designers faced challenges that would likely be encountered in other full-scale renovations of mid-20th-century school buildings.

The building was long overdue for a complete overhaul. Classrooms, for example, were quite small by today's standards, averaging only 660 square feet. In fact, space throughout the facility was much more tightly constricted than would be permitted by today's building codes: alcoves at the door to each classroom, for example, were too narrow for ADA compliance (they would not permit a wheelchair-bound student to enter unassisted), and stairways throughout the building were undersized by today's standards. Moreover, changes made to the building's interior during the school's early years had, in some cases, made the learning spaces even more uncomfortably tight: some classrooms had been subdivided with wall panels that, upon investigation, were found to contain asbestos. Taken together, these issues and others necessitated a gut renovation of the facility. The classroom dividers weren't the only place that asbestos was discovered: when exterior walls were opened, they were found to contain a waterproofing mastic with asbestos. Abatement requirements were so extensive that it was decided to remove and replace virtually the whole of the building's skin—a necessity that the original renovation plan had not anticipated.

The interior would be gutted, and large portions of the building's skin would be removed, but designers were still faced with the fact that the "bones" of the building—its basic structural components—were Mid-century Modern. The architects therefore developed a design vocabulary for both the renovated structure and the new addition that would respect the original architecture's spirit. They determined, for example, that the building should not be "dressed up" with extraneous architectural elements that would conflict with the 1950s-era building's cleanly functional lines. At the same time, however, they wanted the building to appear less monolithic than before.

The solution involved changing the window expression on the facades of the building's classroom wings; originally, these two-story facades were articulated as simple, alternating horizontal bands of masonry and ribbon windows. By contrast, the classroom-wing facades of the renovated building employ a repeated, punched-window expression on the first floor and a modulated ribbon-window expression on the floor above. This change, as well as the addition of glass-encased stairwells and other circulation elements visible from the building's exterior, give new rhythm and life to what had been a static, monolithic structure.

PROJECT #11: A VO-TECH HIGH SCHOOL ON A
COMMUNITY COLLEGE CAMPUS
By Thomas A. Fantacone, AIA

This project is the Middlesex County Academy for Science, Mathematics, and Engineering Technologies in Edison, New Jersey, for grades 9–12, designed by Rothe-Johnson-Fantacone Architecture (now RJF Fletcher-Thompson). The school was completed in 2000. Key issues are:

- High school/college synergy
- Visibility/transparency
- Building as teaching tool

Vo-tech high schools aren't what they used to be—they're better. In many places throughout the country, vocational-technical programs have been reconceptualized so that they are no longer "dumping grounds" for kids perceived to be academically disinclined. Now, forward-looking vo-tech programs offer gifted high school students rigorous, high-level preparation for 21st-century jobs.

In New Jersey, where there are 21 countywide vocational and technical districts, vo-tech schools function much like interdistrict magnets, bringing together students from multiple public school districts within each county. In 2003, 25,000 New Jersey students were enrolled in these schools of choice. One of the most innovative is the Middlesex County Academy for Science, Mathematics, and Engineering Technologies, located on the Edison campus of Middlesex County College, a two-year community college.

Figure 2.11.1. Machine Age design is evoked by the steel structure supporting the canopy over the front entry to the Middlesex Academy. *Photograph by George Shagawart Photography.*

Figure 2.11.2. **Though its extensive exterior glazing gives Middlesex Academy a Modernist feel, the brick cladding harmonizes the building with the other, collegiate-style structures on the Middlesex County College campus.** *Photograph by George Shagawart Photography.*

Situating the vo-tech high school's building on the community college campus enables a dynamic synergy between secondary and higher education: Middlesex Academy juniors and seniors can enroll in college-level courses (and in some cases earn college credit for their work). The high school's facility needs are reduced because its approximately 125 students can take advantage of existing amenities on the campus, such as the library and gymnasium.

The two-story, 30,000 square foot Middlesex Academy building was specifically designed for students pursuing studies in electronics, computer engineering, civil engineering, and mechanical engineering. The school's industrial/technological focus is announced by the main entryway, set in a glazed wall capped by an open steel gable that updates Machine Age design. Although the exterior is otherwise traditional in character—its collegiate red-brick facades harmonizing with the other buildings on campus—the interior strongly reiterates the industrial/technological aesthetic: Directly inside the entry, a series of television monitors continuously display cable news programming, and furniture and finishes throughout the building carry through the high-tech theme. The VCT flooring used in the school's corridors, for example, resembles stamped metal, and the overall look of the interior matches that of a contemporary research and development facility.

As in an R&D facility, visibility and interactivity are critical design values. All the learning and support spaces encircle a central, skylit commons area, where students can congregate and

Figure 2.11.3. **Middlesex Academy's central commons area is surrounded by a curving mezzanine leading to second-floor classrooms and labs.** *Photograph by George Shagawart Photography.*

work informally, where schoolwide assemblies are held, and where ninth and tenth graders eat their brown-bag lunches. (Students in the upper grades may eat lunch in the college's cafeteria.) The liberal use of interior glazing throughout the building heightens the atmosphere of transparency and connectivity—between classroom and classroom, and between learning spaces and common areas.

On the academy building's second floor, English, social studies, and math classrooms are paired. Set between each pair of rooms is a small, wedge-shaped, shared computer lab, where students can immediately apply classroom learning to the virtual environment. The second-floor chemistry and biology labs are also paired and share a prep room. This economical use of space also increases interaction between students and between disciplines.

Visual access extends to the fabric of the building: exposed ceilings reveal steel beams, raceways, and ductwork, permitting the building itself to become a teaching tool—an especially apt design strategy for a school that prepares some of its students for careers in the building design profession. Lighting throughout the building is indirect to highlight the facility's structure, and

Figure 2.11.4. Transparency and visual connectedness are hallmarks of Middlesex Academy's design. In this view of the commons taken from the second-floor mezzanine, note the interior glazing (upper left) that connects classroom space with the corridor, as well as the glass-walled elevator shaft (right background). *Photograph by George Shagawart Photography.*

Figure 2.11.5.   This lab/classroom's large windows afford pleasing views of the Middlesex County College campus. *Photograph by George Shagawart Photography.*

even the elevator has glazed walls so that students can view the mechanical apparatus inside the shaft.

PROJECT #12: A ROOFTOP ADDITION TO A SPECIALIZED URBAN HIGH SCHOOL
By James Waller

This project is a Manhattan Comprehensive Night and Day High School in New York City for ages 17–21, designed by Kostow Greenwood Architects, PC, for the New York City School Construction Authority. The addition was completed in 2003. Key issues are:

- Addition to century-old, historically significant structure
- Accessibility

In a city filled with specialized high schools of numerous sorts (magnet schools, competitive science- and performance-themed highs, schools for special-needs populations), the Manhattan Com-

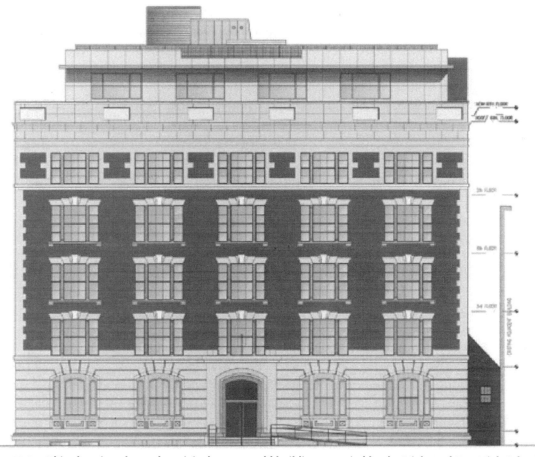

Figure 2.12.1. **This elevation shows the original, century-old building occupied by the Night and Day High School, with the new addition perched on top.** *Courtesy Kostow Greenwood Architects.*

prehensive Night and Day High School stands out as one of New York's most remarkable educational institutions. Dubbed "Last Chance High" by the *New York Times* (Lewin 2003), the Night and Day High School has an astounding track record of success serving students who, for a wide variety of reasons, cannot make it in a conventional high school setting.

Many of Night and Day's students are too old to remain in or be admitted to other city high schools. Most are recent immigrants with poor English-language skills. Many work full- or part-time day jobs that make it impossible for them to attend school during ordinary school hours. And some are kids whose history of truancy and failure led them to drop out of other schools. By accepting students who range in age from 17 to 21, by offering intensive ESL and remedial classes, by keeping its doors open from 11:00 a.m. to 11:00 p.m. six days a week, year round, and by keeping in contact with at-risk students and making every effort to persuade them not to give up, the school has achieved a truly astonishing graduation rate—made more impressive by the fact that more than half of its graduates go on to two- or four-year colleges.

Founded more than 15 years ago by educator Howard Friedman, the school occupies a 100-year-old facility originally built as the Hebrew Industrial School for Girls. The building is historically significant: although not officially landmarked by New York City, it falls under the aegis of the New York State Historic Preservation Office, which must approve any architectural changes to the structure. Despite its being in relatively good shape, the building was inadequate to Night and Day's comprehensive program. For example, it had no science labs (science classes were held in regular classrooms), art and music curriculums were severely limited by a lack of appropriate facilities, and the school was also short on office and conferencing space. To correct these deficiencies, a rooftop addition was planned for the building, and the New York City School Construction Authority retained a Manhattan-based firm, Kostow Greenwood Architects, to provide design services for the project.

The challenges encountered while designing and constructing the Night and Day School's rooftop addition, which was completed in 2002, illustrate the range of issues that might arise during the renovation of any vintage, multistory urban school. According to Jane Greenwood, the principal in charge of the design project, concerns ranged from zoning constraints, to unknown site conditions, to the difficulty of accommodating an ambitious program in a very limited space (the one-story addition totals about 5,600 square feet). Of particular importance were accessibility issues: not only did the architects have to find a way to make the new sixth floor accessible to disabled students, but code requirements dictated that the entire building be made accessible at the same time that work on the addition was performed.

Because of the building's historical significance, zoning requirements mandated that the addition be set back so that it is invisible from the street. Although the setback restricted space available for programmatic uses, it did carry a benefit: a portion of the roof—with magnificent views of the surrounding city—can be used for outdoor teaching in fair weather as well as for receptions and other events.

The ambitious program necessitated a flexible design approach. The addition's two general-purpose science labs share a prep room, and a small suite of offices does double duty: one office can also serve as a music classroom, and an office/conference space is outfitted with a folding wall, allowing it to accommodate larger-group meetings when necessary. The addition also houses accessible toilet rooms and a photographic darkroom—a real enhancement to the school's visual arts program.

Accessibility was improved throughout the building by several means. Because the building's first floor is a few steps above grade, a wheelchair ramp was added outside the school's main entrance. Access to the interior stairway was improved on each floor, and designers had to ensure that this stair could accommodate the entire school population in the event of an emergency. (Adding a second interior stair was an architectural impossibility, which meant that a variance had to be obtained.) A small elevator was added to make the basement wheelchair accessible from the first floor, and the school's main elevator had to be completely retrofitted: the new cab has doors that open on either side. Waiting areas on each floor were expanded to permit wheelchair traffic. (Beyond these challenges, designers also had to find a way to create a new shaft running from the basement to the new sixth floor to accommodate the additional ductwork.)

The design vocabulary for the new addition is subdued and, according to principal-in-charge Greenwood, more "adult" in character than at other high schools. So as not to compete with the rich historical fabric of the existing building, the addition is a simple, metal-clad structure. (The metal panels used in its construction also minimize weight.) Clerestory windows permit natural light to suffuse the addition's lobby, where a sense of arrival is created by the curved metal wall enclosing the staircase and by another wall, directly opposite, covered with pale yellow tiles.

Throughout the addition's interior, including the bathrooms, finishes are light colored or white—an unusual choice for a school but one that's justified here by the great respect and care that Night and Day's students have for their environment.

NOTES

1. Admission to the Montessori Magnet Elementary is determined by a somewhat complex formula: 50 percent of its students must reside in Hartford itself, and of that group 50 percent must live in the Frog Hollow neighborhood in which the Learning Corridor is located; within each group—the city kids, the neighborhood kids, and kids who come from suburban districts—students are selected by a strictly monitored, blind lottery to ensure that all applicants have an equal chance of admission. This is all in compliance with state regulations for ensuring racial, ethnic, and economic diversity among magnet school students.

2. The Greater Hartford Academies' programs are half-day rather than full-day for two related reasons. First, the part-time schedule furthers the schools' goal of achieving diversity by enticing students from suburban high schools—students who might not be willing to entirely forgo the often excellent comprehensive programs that their home-district schools offer. Second, limiting the programs to half a day fosters buy-in from the participating districts, since these districts might well be reluctant to lose their "best and brightest" to a full-time magnet. As Howard Thiery, director of the Academy of Math and Science, explains: "We aren't a full-fledged high school; what we are is a *special program* of the 20 or so schools that send students here."

3. This decision reflects one position within an ongoing debate over the comparative advantages and disadvantages of small versus large schools; for good reasons, the small-school movement has many champions, but as others have pointed out, the economies of scale that can be achieved by larger schools enable them to offer students a much greater range of activities than a small school can provide. On the high school level, these activities include varsity athletics, band, and student clubs.

II

CREATING MAGNET, CHARTER, AND OTHER SPECIALIZED SCHOOLS

Planning, Creating, and Funding New Magnet Schools

Charles R. Cassidy

Any magnet school is, first and foremost, a *community* school, and for a new magnet school to be successful, the community must be integrally involved in its formation. Successful planning is a serious undertaking that involves countless hours of effort. Because of the large investment in time and energy that planning a new magnet will entail, it's essential that planners, first of all, carefully examine whether there is in fact a need for such a school. Having established that such a need does exist, it is necessary to survey the community to determine the potential attractiveness of the theme or themes being considered. Rushing headlong into planning for a theme that never has a chance with the public can be disastrous, not only for this particular project but for any future planning of magnet schools within the district.

GAUGING THE PUBLIC'S INTEREST

To learn what kind of theme is most attractive to the parents of potential enrollees, the community's opinions can be surveyed through written questionnaires, telephone polls, and public meetings. The things that a planning committee does early on will color the tenor of all its future activities, and making an up-front effort to gauge the public's interest is not just a way of obtaining information but also helps to build the trust that's so crucial to a project's success. Planners should be prepared to present several different possibilities to the community and to include specifics on school location and goals.

The composition of the planning committee is very important. It should include teachers, administrators, parents, business and community leaders, members of the board of education, and local political representatives. Magnet schools draw students from throughout a district, so residents from all district neighborhoods should be part of the planning process. The district superintendent must be a key member of any planning team, and garnering his or her support from the start can facilitate the navigation of complex conceptual and financial issues down the road.

FUNDING A MAGNET SCHOOL

The central question for any magnet school project is, "How much will this school cost?" Lack of funding has been an insurmountable obstacle for many a magnet school project. Magnets typically have smaller classes than other public schools and therefore require more teachers than would a traditional public school with the same number of students. Because teachers' salaries make up the bulk of any school budget, magnet schools are more expensive than traditional public schools—an average per capita expenditure of between $10,000 and $12,000 is not uncommon. So the question any planning team must first answer is, "Will our district provide the additional dollars needed to make this work?" Some reports indicate, however, that added costs are more frequently found at the high school level and that magnet elementary schools can actually be run less expensively than their traditional counterparts.

Certain themes and grade levels tend to be more costly than others. Science-oriented schools require the ongoing purchase of up-to-date equipment and materials. Special classes in voice, dance, or instrumental music at performing arts schools raise the overall cost of instruction. Transportation is an additional cost for interdistrict magnet schools.

Preparing the school's facility—whether through renovation of an existing building or through new construction—is, of course, the largest initial cost planners must face. The use of an existing, underutilized facility will likely engender renovation costs, but these will probably be lower than those associated with purchasing a site and constructing a new building. Ever-burgeoning enrollments at public schools in cities and suburbs, however, make it increasingly difficult to use extant buildings to accommodate new magnet schools. (Other issues involving the renovation of existing buildings for use as magnet schools are covered in detail in Chapter 7, "Design Considerations for Specialized Schools.")

If no suitable buildings are available, planners have no choice but to build new—either by adding to an existing facility or constructing an entirely new school building. New construction, however, might add a *time* dimension to the project that may be as problematic as its cost: An addition might take two or more years to complete. Depending on the availability of suitable sites, a new facility might take three years—or even longer—to plan, design, and build. If a district must relieve overcrowding or implement a desegregation plan, long delays may be impracticable.

There *is* help available, though planners must often make a concerted effort to find it and exploit all the funding opportunities open to them. Some states, like New York and Connecticut, make sizable grants for magnet schools. Under a court order to reduce racial isolation in its schools, Connecticut invested nearly $1 billion in facilities that were fully funded by the state. The federal government gives school districts assistance of up to $4 million per year (for up to three years) for the startup and expansion of magnet schools. These funds, though, are limited to the operation of the school itself. Other grants are also available to schools in their initial stage of development. The federal government's Voluntary Public School Choice Initiative provides funds under the No Child Left Behind Act as an incentive to establish new school choice programs and expand existing options at the district level.

Magnet schools have historically had a difficult time funding their programs, which have more than once been abandoned when funding streams ran dry. There is never a guarantee that state or federal funds can be obtained, or that they won't be cut back after grants have been made. Planners should explore local and alternative funding sources to ensure the continuing operation of their schools should other options be exhausted. While independence from a school district may be desirable to meet particular educational goals, the consequent lack of a steady funding source can wreak havoc on a school's financial stability.

THE ACADEMIC PROGRAM

Magnet schools are expected to meet the same academic requirements as other district schools, but the curriculum design and delivery for standard subjects like math, science, English, history, and foreign languages should be unique to the school and support its academic charter. The parents of students who attend magnet schools—and the students themselves—often perceive magnets as more academically sound than other public schools. Of course, many magnet school students *do* thrive academically, but students' differing academic abilities and differing levels of preparation mean that magnets must be ready to address the abilities of all students to ensure that they can take advantage of the opportunities presented. Because of their recognition of the varying needs of students, many of these schools have successfully met the challenge of reducing the academic gap between minority and nonminority youth. And beyond academic success, attraction to a magnet school is built around the successful integration of its theme into the very culture of the school; magnet schools are *different*, and this difference should be in evidence throughout the school, especially in its academic program.

The strength of a magnet school lies in its ability to depart from the district's usual offerings through an educational design that reinforces its theme in considerable depth. This theme cannot be merely an addition to existing programs or an offering available only to a small segment of the school's population: it must be of sufficient scope to make the school identifiably different and fully committed to its mission. While a theme provides the overall direction for a school, it does not specify how a curriculum should be implemented. Curriculum specialists should begin by laying out the core academic program: language arts (reading, writing, grammar, speaking, and listening), social studies (citizenship, government, history, geography, and economics), mathematics, science, physical education, and the arts (music, visual arts, theater, and dance). They should then address foreign language instruction and any applied education, or school-to-career, opportunities.

Once these basics are in place, planners should decide how to incorporate the school's special theme into each of these arenas. Most themes can be readily accommodated through at least one curricular area. A language arts curriculum, for example, might easily be adapted to a theater specialization. Social studies courses provide fertile venues for a school built around a political, governmental, international, or multicultural theme. But planners must also decide to what extent their school's theme will be carried out in more specialized programs, and how far the magnet curriculum will diverge from the standard. Specialized courses not available elsewhere in the district will fulfill the school's mission and collectively serve to provide a separate identity from other district schools.

Montessori schools and others whose curriculums are preset have a head start on this, being known commodities after years of operation in the private sphere. Such schools require professionals trained in their method of instruction, and they may also have to meet special accreditation requirements. The costs associated with that training and accreditation process should be considered when developing an operating budget for such schools.

The world outside of school is a heterogeneous one. Magnet schools should take advantage of this diversity by seeking to replicate it in their enrollment and curriculums. A diverse environment and a curriculum that incorporates the learning and traditions of different cultures enhance students' civic values, broaden the academic environment, and better prepare students for both college and the workforce.

Magnet schools are public schools and must be inclusive: once the doors of these schools open, they are open to all. Students will come from a variety of backgrounds. Some will bring strong academic backgrounds and educational experiences. Others students will bring special needs. The variation in students' academic capabilities is a challenge to all schools, and magnet schools must be prepared to teach children of all abilities. It may be necessary to provide remedial programs or accommodate students with special needs or whose first language is not English.

There was a time when instruction was confined to the school building. But today's urban school districts offer a wealth of resources that supplement school-based instruction, and planners should build such community-based resources into their curriculums. Many districts have gone so far as to locate schools at zoos, museums, theaters, and colleges and universities, drawing upon the staffs and special resources of those institutions to enrich their offerings.

Planners should be cautious about duplicating successful magnet schools within a single district, particularly if a goal is to reduce racial isolation. When given a choice, parents will send their children to schools in more affluent neighborhoods, especially if two similarly focused schools are competing for students. This can lead to underenrollment in less affluent sections of the district, especially in smaller school systems. Some large school districts, such as Buffalo, New York, control enrollment at certain magnet schools through an admissions lottery that ensures that the population of each section of the district is represented equally among each magnet school's attendees.

THE SCHOOL-WITHIN-A-SCHOOL OPTION

While many magnet schools are freestanding educational institutions, some have been located in the same facility as a district's traditional programs. This arrangement can lead to its own set of problems. Such an environment makes it more difficult for a magnet school to distinguish itself from the surrounding, more traditionally structured educational model. The larger school can inhibit the flexibility of the magnet program to arrange class schedules that depart from the norm. To save money, such schools often share teachers or core classes required by both programs, and the integration of the magnet school's theme can suffer as a result. Because magnet schools are heavily reliant on staff participation, magnets that share faculty with a larger school face many obstacles with which dedicated magnet schools do not have to contend.

These schools within a school also face fiercer competition for common resources, which must be allocated based on the needs of the entire school building. The specialists that magnet schools use to provide in-service teacher training and program coordination are often the first to go during any budget cuts, threatening the uniqueness of the magnet program. Because these schools tend to have smaller enrollments than the schools with which they share resources, the opinion of the magnet program's administrator may carry less weight in decisions about the day-to-day operation of the school. While magnet schools can and do successfully share buildings with traditionally structured programs, planners should address the potential pitfalls specific to such an arrangement up front. And, for long-term success, it's of the utmost importance that the school within a school have a fair degree of independence and decision-making autonomy.

STUDENT RECRUITMENT AND ENROLLMENT

Unlike other public schools, magnet schools must recruit their students. Planners must determine whether students will be automatically accepted if their brothers or sisters have previously gained admission. A school's sibling policy can impact its ability to maintain racial balance and narrow its potential enrollment pool significantly, so the decision should be taken carefully, *and* should be carefully explained to parents of potential enrollees during all recruiting efforts. Planners should widely disseminate recruiting materials aimed at district students and their parents, and a serious effort should be made to make these materials available in all the languages spoken in the district. Advertisements in local media and open houses for the community are especially effective tools.

A variety of strategies may be employed to ensure that the racial makeup of a magnet school's student body closely approximates that of the city or town in which it is located. The school may decide to recruit students from outside the district. It may create attendance districts drawn largely along racial lines to control diversity in recruiting. Once a sufficient number of applications from each attendance district is received, a lottery can be used to maintain impartiality in the admissions process. The application process must, of course, be open to all students regardless of race, ability, or disability.

As with the development of its academic program and funding base, a magnet school's student base must be a product of a dialog with the community the school is to serve. The most successful schools are those whose programs and enrollment policies have been created with the input of the surrounding community and are well understood by the schools' constituents.

GRANT WRITING: 13 HOT TIPS
By Charles R. Cassidy

Administrators of magnets and other specialized schools are faced with a number of challenges in keeping their schools "magnetic." Schools can lose their appeal over time if they do not keep pace with developments in the theme fields or pedagogical methods. And their magnetism can suffer if the learning technologies that they offer students grow outmoded. Programs can fray—and enrollments drop—if there's not enough money for ongoing operations. Faced with a continual drain on their resources, school systems and individual magnets have turned to grant writing to secure additional funds for a whole list of purposes, including enabling staff development, hiring resource persons, and purchasing needed equipment and materials.

The Internet—and the sheer amount of information on grants that's available online—have made grant writing a lot easier and more user-friendly than it used to be, especially for districts without grant writers on staff. That doesn't mean it's a cinch, however. To help school personnel hone their grant-writing skills, here are 13 tried-and-true tips for successful grant proposals:

1. *Seek clarity.* Look at the proposal as if it were an essay exam. Treat each section as if you were answering an essay question. Ask, "What is this section asking me to do?" For each section, list the information being requested as part of a topical outline. Under every topic, list the pertinent information. Complete this outline before writing the response to the question. This makes the task much less ominous than trying to swallow it all in one gulp.

2. *Be direct.* Many proposals written for state and federal agencies wrongly delay telling the reader what the program is about until ten pages into the proposal. To those reviewing and evaluating proposals, this can be immensely frustrating. If you are doing an abstract or executive summary, you need to spell out the who, what, when, where, why, and how right up front. Hit them at the outset with the basics. When I start reading a grant proposal, I want to know the following:

- Who (what district or districts) will be involved?
- What will this grant attempt to do in terms of activities and outcomes?
- When will this occur? (If the proposal is for a phase-in of different schools, a timeline is mandatory.)
- Why is the money being requested? What need is being met if you are funded?
- How much money is being requested for how many students?

You get the idea. Now do a little role-playing: put yourself in the reader's place. How would you as a reader respond to what you have written? Better than that, get other people in your district to read a draft of your proposal. It is important to include readers from the district's minority groups, since they are likely to be the most directly affected.

3. *Follow directions.* Every grant sets limits. If the grant is limited to $150,000, do not ask for $300,000. (One group I'm aware of did this—and then claimed that the granting agency cut their grant in half!)

4. *Answer all questions fully.* Vague or general responses leave the answers to the reader, who may or may not see the answer in the same light as you. Did you ever have someone start a story and leave out the ending? Frustrating, isn't it?

5. *Be accurate.* Check your math. A good 30 percent of the proposals that I've looked at over the course of time have had to be returned or are delayed because the writer failed to compute the program costs correctly. Check for the agreement between statements made in the proposal and the budget. There is nothing worse than a proposal that creates questions in the reader's mind about the accuracy of your statements. If you say you are going to involve 2,000 students in the program, this number should be consistent throughout. Proposal readers are looking for inconsistencies that will lower the score of your proposal—not things that will increase it. Make sure the information presented throughout the proposal is accurate and consistent.

6. *Be professional.* Proposals should be professional in nature. They should look like serious efforts to obtain a grant. Misspelled words, incomplete sentences, and fragments of thoughts create the impression that the proposal is not a serious effort. Copies should be clear and easy to read. Attachments should be of high quality. I cannot begin to tell you how many proposals I have seen that were poorly copied and illegible. Looking at such a proposal, readers will ask themselves whether the program administrators have sufficient expertise to carry out the proposal in this "information age" of computers and Internet access. Maybe Lincoln could get away with writing on the back of an envelope. Grant writers can't.

7. *Use graphics (graphs, tables, pictures, etc.).* Let graphics help explain your points. Readers tend to be visual and are impressed by things they can see. Of course, there should be balance in the presentation. Provide pictures and graphs, but also in-

clude statements by parents, students, teachers, and administrators that buttress your points. You would be surprised how grants can come alive when you do this. Even presidential addresses try to personalize the material by including statements from constituents. It works for presidents. Why not you?

8. *Provide evidence.* You need to back up your statements with hard evidence and not assume your statements will be accepted at face value. Just because you say it doesn't make it true.

9. *Use consultants.* It is not enough to simply proofread a proposal. You need to run your proposal before someone who can give you feedback on the concept and execution. In years past, the federal government made it a practice to have community groups (as well as the state education department) sign off on magnet school proposals. This isn't a bad idea. Run your grant by minority as well as nonminority readers. If it is an interdistrict or intradistrict proposal, develop a grant review committee composed of parents, teachers, administrators, and (where applicable) local businesspeople and students from participating school districts. This approach results in some of the strongest programs (and proposals) I have seen.

10. *Choose language wisely.* Simple words often get the job done more effectively than more complex terms. Avoid "alphabet soup" and fancy pedagogical terms familiar to only a handful of people. Ask yourself whether including a glossary might be helpful to your audience. Your goal is communication—not obfuscation. I have used acronyms like LEA (local education agency) and SDE (state department of education), expecting people to know what I was talking about. They didn't.

11. *Consider your audience.* This goes hand in glove with tip #10. Remember how your English teacher used to talk about writing *for* a particular audience? The same principle applies to grant writing. Consider who will read the proposal. Will the reviewers be experts in the field, or will they have no particular expertise on the subject? Underestimating your reader will not penalize your proposal. Overestimating your reader will.

12. *Be repetitive.* While eating too much candy can be bad for you, repetition in a grant is not sinful. Do not expect people to remember on page 35 what you said on page 3. If an idea or concept is important, reiterate it frequently.

13. *Be a salesperson.* You can build a better mousetrap, but you still have to market it. You need to sell your proposal to the reader. In the competitive grant process, not all grants will be funded. Will yours? Your proposal is your only opportunity to get your foot in the door and keep it open. If you capture the readers' attention and imagination at the outset, you stand an excellent chance of being funded. Be aggressive in demonstrating why the granting agency should fund your program in particular.

Preparing Students for the Future World of Work

Christine M. Casey, Ed.D.

Specialized schools *are* schools of the future. The very nature of schooling will change dramatically over the next 25 years, as curriculums are reshaped by the demands of the 21st-century workplace and by ongoing research into how the learning process actually works. But already, specialized schools all across the United States—schools that target all grade levels and that focus on many different themes—are beginning to provide the educational choices and opportunities needed to meet the future's demands.

Specialized schools, and the themes they focus on, emerge in different ways. Some districts choose to develop theme-based magnet schools to assist in voluntary racial desegregation or to entice students to attend school in what's perceived as an "undesirable" area. A specialized school's theme may grow out of a grant opportunity, or it may be developed in response to the need for a specialized workforce or the proximity of a particular industry (the presence of an airport in a community, for example, might inspire the creation of an aviation-themed school). But no matter what their origin, such schools capitalize on students' interests and afford them the chance to explore potential careers, and they often provide innovative modes of instruction for those who need a different way to learn.

As the demand for school choice grows, and as specialized schools continue to proliferate, we must remember that the school buildings we design and construct today must accommodate the new approach to education. Teaching children how to think independently and apply knowledge to novel situations requires a setting that in some ways is fundamentally different from those that now exist in most American schools, which still tend to be geared toward the rote memorization of facts.

RELEVANCE *IS* MOTIVATION

In their book *Becoming Adult* (2000), psychologist Mihalyi Csikszentmihalyi and his coauthor Barbara Schneider remind us that until relatively recently, most children had little choice about what they would be when they grew up. As class structures became less rigid and educational opportunities more egalitarian, adolescents' occupational choices were no longer so tightly circumscribed by the lives their parents led. Today, the ever-escalating pace of change heightens that freedom from the past: given the rapidity of technological advance, it even becomes difficult to know what future jobs might *be*.

Moreover, the scope of knowledge is now so vast that previous ways of teaching through content memorization are ineffective. Learning how to learn has become much more important than learning a discrete set of facts. To make this difference clear, think of a dictionary: if we were to ask students to memorize the words in a dictionary, the school year would end before we'd gotten halfway through the letter A. But if we teach students *how to use* a dictionary and have them practice looking up words, they'll be able to integrate this tool into all their schoolwork.

Speaking of the need to prepare students for a future world of work whose demands, in important respects, cannot be predicted, Csikszentmihalyi and Schneider write,

> Now more than ever, young people must learn the skills and values necessary to build successful careers. We have delegated to our schools the responsibility for preparing youth for the future, yet few would claim that schools are well-equipped to prepare youth for realistic careers even in the present, yet alone in the years to come. Somehow we must find better ways to inform youth about the kinds of opportunities that will be available to them when they grow up, as well as the habits, skills, and values they should acquire in preparation for those opportunities. (p. 5)

Csikszentmihalyi's research has uncovered a powerful relationship between students' childhood educational experiences and their ultimate career options. The hands-on nature of specialized programs that allow students to immerse themselves in potential areas of interest and that emulate real-world workplaces can often motivate them in a way that more traditional programs do not. Stressing the importance of the connection between schoolwork and students' future career options, Csikszentmihalyi and Schneider write, "It is particularly important to make sure that children do not fall into the habit of feeling that what they do is meaningless" (p. 235). Making the connection between effort in school and success in life transparent provides motivation, a key component for perseverance.

New American High Schools, a reform initiative sponsored by the U.S. Department of Education during the 1990s, recommended a number of different curricular models incorporating the latest research on successful secondary education. Each model included instruction in computer skills, the opportunity for students to learn about college and careers from real-life experiences, and the formation of "active alliances with parents, employers, community members and policy makers," as well as with colleges and universities. According to a research document supporting this initiative,

> All over the country, states and communities are taking up the challenge of reforming schools and building school-to-work systems for the demands of the global, knowledge-based economy of the twenty-first century. To be effective citizens, parents, and workers in this new economy, all young people will need a higher level of academic, technical, communications and information processing skills. (Visher, Teitelbaum, and Emanuel 1999)

SOFT SKILLS ARE KEY

Although sometimes dismissed as unimportant, "soft" interpersonal skills are absolutely foundational to success at work—even in a highly computerized workplace. Collaborative work environments are critical to contemporary project management, and when employees lose their jobs for performance-related reasons, it's often their soft skills, not their technical prowess, that are at issue. The know-how needed to coordinate work teams from a distance using the telephone, the Internet, and videoconferencing technology is quite different from the skills that employees relied on in the past. In *The Distance Manager* (2000), Kimball and Mareen Fisher describe the successful distance worker as having "highly developed competencies in the areas of leadership, getting results, facilitation, barrier busting, business analysis, coaching and setting an example" (p. 15).

Beyond possessing core competencies in providing customer service and communicating effectively, 21st-century workers must also be able to organize and deliver presentations, manage projects, conduct research online, and word process various kinds of documents. Because information technologies change so rapidly, many skill sets will be self-taught; the development of new hardware and ongoing releases of new versions of standard software demand that workers be life-long learners and highly capable of self-study. They will need to make independent decisions based on data and information. These application-based skills must be practiced in different scenarios in order to be integrated in a knowledge set.

ASSESSING ACHIEVEMENT

The recent standards-based movement in education has not produced the results its champions had hoped for. In an attempt to quantify progress, legislators demanded standardized testing and declared that it would ensure that "no child is left behind." But rather than engendering true academic accomplishment, such testing often produces a regressive ripple effect. Teachers scrutinize the tests and attempt to prepare students for them by focusing their classes on test questions and test-taking techniques. Many districts have even changed their curriculums to better reflect the material in the standardized exams.

Trends in education are cyclical, and the federal government's No Child Left Behind initiative will itself inevitably be left behind. Current standardized tests cannot adequately gauge high-level thinking or assess self-constructed knowledge. The sophisticated assessment tools needed to determine student progress in higher-order thinking must flow from curriculums derived from real work situations, including multimedia presentations, virtual portfolios, and community service—not from the arbitrary measures of standardized testing. It is the application of knowledge that is the new intelligence, and measuring this requires sophisticated and time-consuming methods.

Successful assessment uses a variety of evaluation strategies to compare what students have learned with institutional standards and expectations. In theme-based high schools, alternative evaluations can be linked closely to work-related scenarios to confirm that students have mastered a specialized curriculum. Their measurement is embedded in their course work and comes as a natural result of their specialized studies. The equivalent of a successful evaluation at an aviation high school might be the attainment of a pilot's license, for example. Many vocational schools and some career-oriented magnets (e.g., Las Vegas's ATech; see pages 51–57) already provide access to specific industry certifications, a practice that will likely proliferate. Industry increasingly embraces certifications to ensure life-long learning because they must be periodically renewed. More relevant than required tests imposed by states or districts, these firsthand experiences of the working world enhance students' resumes and even afford them the opportunity to earn money part-time during high school and college.

FOR EVERY UNIQUE STUDENT, A UNIQUE CURRICULUM

Although the means for individualized instruction are available to any teacher who can master simple, computer-based tools, many of this generation's teachers have never taken advantage of them. The open classrooms of the 1970s disappeared, in part, because of the difficulty of maintaining extensive, detailed records on the progress of each individual student. Today, computers can manage that kind of performance-related data. Early computer-aided instruction was more or less limited to replacing workbooks with computer monitors. The newest generation of computer-aided educational programs can adjust to a student's level of mastery of a particular subject by matching the degree of difficulty of a particular lesson to that student's capabilities. The formats include games and other innovative ways to practice skills.

And the technology continues to evolve. To remediate certain learning disabilities, the use of word-prediction software is beginning to take hold. Technology that slows down human speech is revolutionizing the learning of sound/symbol recognition. Computers also facilitate the kind of repetition required by some learning disabilities without wearying an educator or causing a student to feel embarrassed by the number of trials they require to master a particular concept. Assistive technologies that speak for the mute, read aloud for the blind, and write for the physically disabled are smoothing the integration of those with disabilities into mainstream programs. Buildings with wireless local area network access make it possible for such students to work easily from laptop computers.

One of the most important potential benefits of e-learning comes from the seat time it potentially saves. As software and collaborative and multimedia functions become more sophisticated, students will increasingly enjoy the self-pacing this form of instruction allows. It facilitates more flexibility in direct teacher time and attention, in the time a student has to pursue specific tasks, and in the ways students can manipulate information presented and reinforced through visual or auditory means.

CREATIVITY IN THE WORKPLACE—TECHNOLOGY IN THE CLASSROOM

In his book *The Rise of the Creative Class* (2002), author Richard Florida posits that one-third of the working world now makes its living through on-the-job invention, creation, and innovation—a sharp departure from the assembly-line economies of the past. Although today's computers can also analyze information, make decisions, and predict results from models, the human brain makes connections and solves problems in ways computers cannot. That's why human creativity is becoming ever more important in the evolving world of work. As Florida writes,

> The creative class consists of people who add economic value through their creativity. . . . The Super-Creative Core of this new class includes scientists and engineers, university professors,

poets and novelists, artists, entertainers, actors, designers and architects as well as the thought leadership of modern society: non-fiction writers, editors, cultural figures, think-tank researchers, analysts and other opinion makers. (pp. 68–9)

It's inevitable that the rise of this creative class—the people who create new ideas, new uses for things, new ways to do things, and new combinations—will profoundly affect the education we provide our children. But this kind of transformation is, at least on a national scale, all too slow in coming. When I spoke with an electrical engineer about her work, she stated, "I am challenged every day to find a way to solve a problem. I think independently and make decisions." For the most part, however, the current public school system simply does not prepare students to solve problems, think independently, *or* make decisions. No wonder there is a shortage of engineers!

Fortunately, a roadmap to a new kind of educational practice is available. The Education Development Center, Inc., in partnership with the Information Technology Association of America and the National Alliance of Business, has developed a model for training the future workforce. The EDC's document, *IT Pathway Pipeline Model* (Malyn-Smith et al., n.d.), provides guidance for leading all students through technology skills development, with opportunities for pathways into specializations. The document's authors recommend beginning to create awareness of information technology issues as early as first grade, with hands-on exploration in the seventh and eighth grades, and career preparation—including "shadowships," internships, and apprenticeships—in grades 9–12. This document can be used to structure the curriculums for technology-based theme schools.

The Academy for Information Technology and Engineering (AITE) in Stamford, Connecticut, is one such program. A high-tech high school that teaches about technology and uses technology to teach, AITE infuses every aspect of its program with the foundational skills its students will need after graduation. The AITE program was developed in collaboration with local businesses, the chamber of commerce, industry associations, and institutions of higher education. Its students have access to state-of-the-art technology—hard-wired labs, wireless laptops, a Citrix server, Internet access in all classes, ceiling- and wall-mounted monitors, ceiling-mounted projection devices, and a very wide variety of up-to-date hardware and software—and they can earn college credits and industry certifications through their course work. An active industry advisory board assists in program design and curriculum oversight, ensuring relevance to current industry demands. Paid internships, guest speakers, mentoring opportunities, and invitations to professional events round out the students' experience. The effort has been stunningly successful.

Partnering with local professionals is a smart idea for theme-based high schools of many different sorts. The Thomas Jefferson High School for Science and Technology in Alexandria, Virginia, has partnered with local biotechnology companies, as has the Biotechnology Alliance for Science Education in San Francisco, which assigns professors from local universities as advisers to the school's teachers. As with information technology, biotechnology requires a specialized environment, and students benefit from visits to labs and industry sites and from mentoring by working scientists.

HIGH SCHOOL PROGRAMS ON COLLEGE CAMPUSES

Educational alliances in some parts of the country have created "2 + 2 + 2" programs—formalized pathways that begin with a specialized program in the final two years of high school, continue with two years at a community college, and are completed with two years at a four-year college or university. The shortage of skilled technical and professional workers, especially in engineering, science, and computer technology, can provide the necessary economic justification for such programs.

The use of a shared, specialized facility is a practical way to foster these relationships, and proper facilities planning can make this programmatic movement from one educational institution to another even more powerful and cost-effective. A building shared by college and high school students can be utilized at different times for course work at different levels, maximizing an investment while providing high school students a peek at college life. Expensive lab equipment can even become an incubator for private industry, and professionals conducting research in labs used by high school and college students can create opportunities for on-site internships. There is a growing movement, supported by the Bill and Melinda Gates Foundation and other philanthropies, to place public high schools on college campuses, giving students an early familiarity with the college environment, as well as access to high-quality sports facilities, libraries, and of course technology. (For an example of a specialized public high school located on a community college campus, see Chapter 2, "Specialized Schools: Twelve Exemplary Projects," Project #11, pages 65–70.)

CAREER-BASED PROGRAMS

The federal government's five-year School-to-Work Initiative ended in the 2001–2002 academic year. It prepared students for careers and further academic study by matching them with work-world experiences, and it created many outstanding opportunities. Unfortunately, the reforms and revitalization inspired by the School-to-Work Initiative have not yet been institutionalized. While many schools offer apprenticeships, internships, and cooperative programs, less than 6 percent of high school students nationally have actually participated in them (Visher et al. 1998). This is especially troubling in light of research that confirms the benefits of supported, structured work environments for young people.

In 1997, researchers documented gains in reading, math, and science by students who spent 15–20 hours per week in a quality, work-based learning environment (Bottoms, Creech, and Johnson 1997). Findings regarding at-risk youth indicate that those in work-based learning programs have more positive attitudes toward school and are more successful in the job market after graduation (Stone 1995). Such programs provide a context for recognizing the importance of learning and further study, as well as occasions for practicing communications skills and developing relationships with people in the workworld. The extra hours necessitated by such programs also provide students with productive ways to stay occupied after school.

The public has sometimes viewed career-oriented schools simply as vocational programs leading directly to work. Fearing this stereotype, some school districts have sometimes eschewed school-to-work initiatives, wrongly believing that they adversely impact students' preparation for college. In actuality, many students' college plans grow more concrete as a result of school-to-work activities, which underline the necessity of college to their future success. Especially in high-tech industries, school-to-work programs create workforce readiness through hands-on learning experiences in the workworld and interaction with on-the-job professionals. As the *IT Pathway*

Pipeline Model puts it, "It is critical that students have direct contact with the IT industry and related groups within the community in order to see how their developing skills can be applied, to be encouraged and inspired by role models, to network and prepare for careers in IT, and to explore their own careers, interests, and values" (Malyn-Smith et al., n.d., p. 9).

INTERNSHIPS AND SERVICE-ORIENTED LEARNING

The fields of science, technology, and engineering all provide ample prospects for well-structured mentorships, internships, and apprenticeships. One notable program is run by Connecticut Career Choices (CCC), an initiative of the state's Office for Workplace Competitiveness. To "stimulate students' interest and prepare them for careers in technology," CCC operates pilot programs in selected school districts that connect students with professional mentors and that find meaningful, real-world work experiences (including internships) for high school students. The CCC program is designed to help students and prospective employers (and thus to make the state of Connecticut a more attractive venue for high-tech businesses). (For full information on the program, visit www .ctcareerchoices.org.)

Some schools make service-oriented learning a requirement for graduation. At Plainville High School in Plainville, Connecticut, students must provide ten hours of community service learning during their freshman or sophomore years. Although most states do not make such demands on their seniors, high schools around the country have discovered that senior year is wasted for many students and have begun to structure activities especially for the second half of senior year. At Lyman Memorial High School in Lebanon, Connecticut, students work with mentors from the community on their senior projects. In addition to 40 hours of community service, Branford, Connecticut's public schools require seniors to design, develop, and present a major research project that demonstrates the essential skills and characteristics of an autonomous learner.

To accommodate such requirements, new buildings should include space for meetings between students and mentors or advisers, conference space for small-group meetings, and presentation space capable of supporting computer-based multimedia presentations. (Buildings with enough space to accommodate several simultaneous meetings are ideal.) Eventually, all students will employ technology to collect and analyze information and even to synthesize new ideas. Although presentations are currently limited to a two-dimensional computer screen, the use of computer-based robotics will increase as students begin to create three-dimensional presentations. The nature of the labs and equipment to support such projects will necessarily differ from the lab configurations in schools today.

CLOSING THE GAP FOR POOR AND SPECIAL-NEEDS STUDENTS

There really is a "digital divide," and one of the greatest challenges facing American educators is to help special populations—poor students, urban students, disabled students—bridge that gap. Lack of opportunities for children from low-income families is especially pronounced in technology careers, but studies have demonstrated that it is possible to overcome the inequities of this economic divide. A report for the state of Connecticut by the Battelle Memorial Institute, a nonprofit technology consulting firm, recommends involving economically disadvantaged youth in IT-related activities and creating more magnet programs for IT skills development at all grade levels, beginning as early as kindergarten.

At Hundred High School in Wetzel County, West Virginia, students were given laptop computers (with Web access) through a program funded by the U.S. Department of Education. Students used their computers consistently, even during lunch hour, and test scores increased dramatically. The federal study that funded the Hundred High School program found that Internet access and computer technology could be used to motivate and assist poor students in improving their overall academic performance, as well as building specific technology skills. The experiences of educators at Stamford, Connecticut's AITE mirror this research. Students understand the power of the opportunities technology can offer and respond with the hard work needed to master new and often difficult concepts. And school-to-work programs provide role models for low-income children by putting them in direct contact with adults in well-paying jobs.

High-tech, career-focused magnet school programs should include facilities for students with special needs. According to a federal Web commission report, "No group is more likely to benefit from web-based education than people with disabilities." At present, only one-third of the adult disabled population is employed, but computers can level the playing field for the disabled. Not only does such technology foster personal independence, but enabling people with disabilities to work contributes to the health of the overall economy.

Internships and apprenticeships, critical for all students, are especially important for low-income students, minority students, the disabled (including the learning disabled), and girls interested in professions that have traditionally excluded women. Students who work in internships gain an understanding of the different roles and functions within a company and develop an appreciation for the way their school studies can be applied in the workworld. By interacting with coworkers and supervisors, they learn about work-appropriate behavior, and internships help them develop decision-making, goal-setting, and time-management skills.

CLASSROOMS WITHOUT WALLS

As theme-based schools begin to pop up everywhere, schools are beginning to merge with the world outside the classroom. There are now schools in malls, schools in airports, and high schools on college campuses. Learning is occurring both within the school building and in the field. And the community at large is sharing the school building with students—a trend that will gather steam in the future, as parents attend classes to take advantage of the technology available in technology-themed schools and community groups stage performances in the theaters of performing arts schools. It's a two-way street: as high school students move out into the world, those who've graduated come back to the school building to continue their own life-long learning.

This two-way movement—the interpenetration of the worlds of school and work—is, of course, enhanced by technology. Technology increasingly brings the world to students' desks, giving them unlimited access to knowledge and placing life experiences within their reach. The challenge today is to motivate these students to explore the potential that exists for them in that knowledge and those experiences. The analysis and application of this new understanding are key to constructing an education that can properly prepare students for the technology-saturated workplace of the 21st century.

Finding a Home: The Facilities Side of the Charter School Debate

Edwin T. Merritt, Ed.D., and James A. Beaudin, AIA

"**W**ithout a doubt, facilities issues are the number-one problem facing most charter schools," says Ernest Villany, treasurer of the board of trustees of the six-year-old Teaneck Community Charter School in Teaneck, New Jersey. His view is corroborated by Michael Duggan, executive director of the Domus Foundation, a social-service agency that operates Trailblazers Academy, a four-year-old charter middle school in Stamford, Connecticut. "I'd put facilities issues right up there with the need to pay teachers a competitive wage," Duggan says.

It's not hard to find other charter school leaders who agree. When asked about the facilities-related challenges charters face, Charles Knoph, business manager for the Unity Charter School in Morristown, New Jersey, rattles off a litany of problems very similar to those listed by Villany: because their programs must be periodically reviewed and their charters reapproved, charter schools often find it difficult to secure long-term leases; because they can't raise money for capital investments through bond issues, charters are forced to spend a much higher percentage of their yearly operating budgets on facilities- and maintenance-related costs than do regular public schools; and because they sometimes face resistance from local school districts who see them as competing for resources, charters may find that space in existing school buildings—even when such space is underutilized or sitting empty—is unavailable to them.

Given these realities, it's astonishing that amid all the debate that's surrounded the charter school movement in the decade since it began making its mark on American public education, so little attention has focused on charter schools' facilities—by which we mean both the kinds of learning spaces and the technological resources that charter schools offer their students.

There are indications that this situation is changing. Writer/educator Jonathan Schorr's immensely readable book on a parent-led charter school initiative in Oakland, California, *Hard Lessons* (2002), is forthright about the difficulties of *physically* establishing a new charter school. "Building a school from scratch is no small thing," Schorr writes. "The complexities begin with renovations, contractors, codes, and cost overruns." Perhaps it's only now, when many charter school advocates have had a few years' hard experience with actually running the schools they so enthusiastically founded, that we can begin to talk about the importance of good facilities to the success of a charter school.

UP TO PAR?

Are charter school facilities anywhere near being up to par with conventional public schools? With about 3,000 charters now in operation around the United States, the question doesn't admit an easy answer. Some certainly are, and in fact a few possess buildings and technological resources that may be envied by the regular public schools in their districts. That's the case, for example, at San Diego's High Tech High School. Now in its fifth year of operation, High Tech High occupies renovated spaces in the former Naval Training Building, and the school features a "commons" room, individual workstations for all students, project rooms, multipurpose seminar rooms, and a variety of specialty labs. With plentiful support from San Diego's high-tech business community, the school excels in its ability to train students in the use of state-of-the-art high-tech equipment.

But High Tech High is the exception; the great majority of charter schools are, from a facilities standpoint, much humbler operations. Beyond the difficulty of finding appropriate spaces to lease or buy, charters typically wrestle with facilities-related challenges that include everything from problems with indoor air quality and other components of healthy learning environments; to small, inflexible classrooms and inadequate support spaces; to insufficient or outmoded computers.

The kinds of facilities issues charter schools encounter are likely to differ according to whether a charter is in the suburbs or the inner city. Dr. Rex Shaw, principal/director of the Teaneck Community Charter School, says that a charter located in an affluent suburban town can find its facilities choices constrained by a kind of catch-22: real estate prices in the community may be so high that most available, appropriate properties are financially out of reach, but the school's charter may limit it to working within a specific demographic area, meaning it can't venture outside its community in search of a less-expensive facility.

The list of facilities problems that charters may face seems almost endless. Many charters function without their own gyms, playgrounds, cafeterias, or auditoriums. We're aware of a charter whose program is almost entirely dictated by its building's minuscule classrooms. We've even heard of one charter that's housed in an almost windowless building, where no classroom has any natural light (a bad idea, since the absence of daylight has been found to affect learning). Charter schools' ability to find solutions to these kinds of challenges is critically important for several interlocking reasons. Inadequate or inappropriate facilities affect the quality of the educational experience a charter can provide; a not-so-good facility may hurt a charter's enrollment by discouraging parents who might otherwise be willing to let their children give the school a try. And substandard facilities may affect a school's ability to get started and retain its charter over the long run.

LEARNING FROM CHARTERS

No matter what one's feelings about the charter movement as a whole—and to be frank, our own are mixed—it's clear that American public education is moving toward expanding the variety of choices available to parents and students, and that charters will remain an important strand in the fabric of public education for years to come. That's not said grudgingly; in fact, we're consistently impressed by the creativity, innovation, and degree of parent involvement evidenced by many charters—and by the sheer amount of effort that so many charter advocates are willing to expend to make their experiments succeed.

We even think that leaders of regular public schools—and designers of public school facilities—have some things to learn from charter schools' experience. For example, though architects and building committees pay a great deal of lip service to flexibility in learning-space design, some of the flexibility that's built into today's educational environments doubtless goes unused. By contrast, many charter schools don't let inadequate facilities hobble their programs; instead, they apply every available ounce of creativity to transforming constrained spaces into environments that are as flexible as they can be. (Similarly, some charters don't let tight operating budgets stand in their way when it comes to investing in technology; for instance, the Teaneck Community Charter School took advantage of the fact that many of its students' parents work in high-tech fields by forming a Technology Committee that advises the school on implementing technology and holds regular events to raise money for equipment purchases.)

Making-do can be the mother of inventiveness in other ways as well. Contemporary educational theorists are always talking about the need to dissolve the barriers between the classroom and the wider world beyond. Some charters have taken the lead in doing just this, by making field trips an essential adjunct to their in-class curriculum. "We're *always* taking trips," says Teaneck Community Charter's Shaw, who emphasizes that field trips are integrally related to his school's modular curriculum. "For a module on World War II, we went to the *Intrepid* [the sea-air-space museum housed in a 1940s aircraft carrier docked on Manhattan's West Side]. For a module on medieval history, we traveled to the Cathedral of St. John the Divine in New York, so that the kids could see how the Gothic cathedrals were built."

Philadelphia's Charter High for Architecture + Design has used local resources in an especially intriguing way—one that goes far beyond the typical field trip. During construction of Philadelphia's new Kimmel Regional Performing Arts Center (completed in late 2002), CHAD organized an independent study project for a small group of students that focused on the center's design and construction. The students paid regular visits to the construction site (just seven blocks away from the school), met with construction-industry professionals involved in this massive building project, and traveled to New York City to visit the studio of the performing arts center's architect, Rafael Viñoly. The study project, which continued for more than two years, served as a model for the development of other, similar projects at CHAD—and might well be worth imitating by other charters and career-oriented magnets. (For more on CHAD, see pages 57–62.)

IMPROVING CHARTER FACILITIES

Curricular creativity can take charters only so far in working around their facilities' limitations. As Trailblazers Academy's Duggan puts it, "It all comes down to the dollar," and a great many charters are perpetually short of cash. For his part, Duggan advises charters against taking out large loans for long-term leaseholds or to pay for extensive renovations. Charter school legislation, of course, differs widely from state to state, and some states (e.g., New Jersey) forbid their charters from taking such loans. But Duggan says he's heard of New England charters burdened by debts of $1 million or more—loans whose repayment can eat up a significant chunk of the operating budget. While Duggan is all in favor of constantly pressing state and local governments to make more money available for charters, he rues the fact that many charters are forced to spend so much precious time looking for ways to enhance their facilities budgets, fund renovations, and so on.

PRO BONO ARCHITECTURAL WORK

What can charters do to improve their facilities—or to escape their facilities' limitations—without busting their budgets or spending huge amounts of time on fund-raising? One tactic is to search for an architect who will provide pro bono assistance. Many architecture firms, large and small, do a certain amount of pro bono work, and some are willing to lend a hand in helping a charter evaluate potential sites, assess a property's long-term value, bring a facility up to code, or design a renovation and help oversee construction.

As with so much else that charters do, success in finding a willing architect may well depend on person-to-person connections. That's what happened at Stamford's Trailblazers Academy: a Trailblazers board member had an architect-friend who donated his services in readying the school's classrooms for occupancy.

USE OF COMMUNITY FACILITIES

Often, charter schools can make up for some of what they lack, facilities-wise, by working out arrangements with other community institutions. Of course, some charters are actually *housed* in other community institutions. Unlike many—especially suburban—charters, the inner-city Trailblazers Academy has a good working relationship with the state DOE and the local school district, which made it possible for the school to lease space in an underutilized public school building, the J. M. Wright Technical School. The Unity School, mentioned above, operates out of the social hall (reconfigured as six classrooms and a common area) in the Columbian Club of Morristown, and Jonathan Schorr's book describes a number of charters that began their existences in the schoolrooms of Oakland churches.

But suppose a charter school has no gym. That's more or less the case at Trailblazers Academy, whose access to the gymnasium in the building it now shares with Wright Technical is extremely limited. According to Trailblazers' Duggan, the school has compensated by working out a deal with a nearby YMCA, which allows the school to use its facilities for physical education classes on weekday afternoons, when utilization by the Y's members is very light. Charters that don't have auditoriums or large-group meeting spaces might work out similar arrangements with local theaters.

COOPERATIVE OWNERSHIP

Probably every charter school that doesn't have a building of its own longs for a permanent home. But that dream can be indefinitely deferred because of budget limitations and state-imposed restrictions on a charter's ability to borrow money. One possible way out of the impasse may be to enter into a cooperative arrangement with a local private or parochial school. At the time this chapter was written, Teaneck Community Charter School was trying to do just that. For several years prior, it had leased space in a building (a former office facility) owned by a girls' yeshiva, but in 2002 the Teaneck charter was in negotiations with the yeshiva to co-op the building and share ownership.

Whatever approach a charter takes to solving its facilities problems, one thing has become very clear through all our discussions with charter school leaders: it takes a lot of time and an enormous amount of effort to find an acceptable facility and to do the work necessary to get that facility ready for school. Schorr's *Hard Lessons* details the logistical nightmare of trying to prepare an Oakland building for its new role in only 151 days. Doing all the things that need to be done in that short amount of time may not make for an auspicious beginning. As Teaneck Community Charter's Villany puts it, "I recommend that facility planning begin at least a year—at a minimum—before the first day of school."

We couldn't agree more. In their enthusiasm for curricular innovation, parent involvement, and close student-teacher interaction, charter school founders should not downplay the fact that effective education requires an acceptable learning environment.

6

Special Ed That's Even More Special: Designing Schools for Autistic Students

Patricia A. Myler, AIA, Thomas A. Fantacone, AIA, and Edwin T. Merritt, Ed.D.

No one really knows why it's happening, but the incidence of autism is skyrocketing. Back in the 1970s, it was estimated that autism affected only about 1 in 10,000 children in the United States; today, 4 to 6 out of every 1,000 children in this country are being diagnosed with autism or one of a spectrum of related disorders, such as Asperger's syndrome or pervasive developmental disorder (PDD). That means that currently about 1.5 million Americans—most of them children— are autistic or similarly disabled. Some observers expect the number to top 4 million within the next decade.

For educators, these statistics are sobering. The alarming jump in the number of children with autism spectrum disorders presents American public education with a set of unprecedented and bewildering challenges. It's not an exaggeration to say that the "autism explosion" is one of the greatest problems facing American public education today. Why? Because it's so difficult to treat these disorders, and so expensive to educate those afflicted by them.

The symptoms associated with autism and related syndromes can vary remarkably from child to child, meaning that educational and treatment programs must be highly individualized. Also, because "social deficits"—the inability to communicate or interact successfully with other human beings—are among the most pronounced and intractable of autism's symptoms, most autistic students, unlike other students with disabilities, cannot easily be mainstreamed into ordinary public schools, or not until comparatively late in their school careers. (In this regard, the education of autistic children often runs counter to the prevailing trend in special education, which emphasizes the integration of disabled children into mainstream schools.)

The social deficits associated with autism also mean that the education of autistic children relies, especially in the early stages, on intensive, one-on-one work aimed at establishing a close, trusting bond between student and teacher. Depending on the educational technique employed, a teacher may spend upwards of 30–40 hours a week working with a single autistic pupil. The staffing requirements of schools for autistic children are therefore exorbitant. Thomas Parvenski, who directs the River Street School in Windsor, Connecticut—an autism education/treatment center operated by that state's Capitol Region Education Council—compared his school's staffing demands to those of an ordinary elementary school: Whereas a typical K–5 school might have 45

99

or 50 staff for a student population of 800 or so, the River Street School, whose program serves 135 autistic individuals ranging in age from toddlers to young adults, has about 180 staffpeople.

Moreover, for autistic individuals, education and treatment are two sides of the same coin—meaning that schools for autistic children must incorporate diagnostic, medical/therapeutic, and social support services that are much more extensive than those possessed by ordinary public schools. Add in the fact that children with autism respond best to education that's consistent and continuous—necessitating programs that are year-round, or nearly so—and you're just beginning to grasp the enormous expenditures of money and resources needed to address this problem.

School systems—on the state, regional, and district levels—are developing a variety of strategies to deal with these financial and logistical challenges, which are almost always too great for a single school district to bear. In some places, as in Connecticut, regional education centers serve autistic students from a number of school districts. Elsewhere, public school systems enter into arrangements with private institutions specializing in educating and treating autistic individuals. No matter what the strategy, however, it is very clear that the need for specialized educational facilities for autistic children is being sharply felt around the country, and that this need will only intensify in the years to come.

The specifics of design for a given autism education/treatment facility will differ somewhat according to the particular approach to educating autistic individuals employed by the school. (There are currently a half-dozen or so widely accepted approaches.) The basic guidelines outlined below are, for the most part, generally applicable, though we note a few issues on which autism educators diverge.

A NONSTIMULATING, NONTHREATENING ENVIRONMENT

Effective design for autism education contradicts some of the received architectural wisdom. For example, it's a truism of education-facility design that learning spaces should *stimulate* the children who occupy them. Designing schools for autistic kids turns this basic principle on its head. Because autism and the spectrum of related disorders are marked, in most cases, by extreme, debilitating sensitivity to sensory stimulation—sound, light, color, and pattern—it becomes of primary importance that schools for autistic children tightly control the amount and kind of visual and aural stimulation that students receive from their environment.

This need to strictly delimit sensory stimulation affects design decisions regarding everything from wall finishes, to flooring materials, to mechanical systems, to the use of natural light. For example, many of today's mainstream elementary schools employ a bright, diverse palette of wall colors, and VCT flooring—especially in a school's corridors and public spaces—may be a lively patchwork of geometric shapes and patterns. In a school for autistic kids, design decisions like these would introduce a level of complexity into the visual environment that many autistic children would have difficulty processing. Color was one of the first aspects of school design mentioned by the two directors of educational/treatment programs for autistic individuals interviewed for this chapter—the River Street School's Tom Parvenski, and David Holmes, who heads Princeton, New Jersey's Eden Institute. Though Holmes pointed out that there are no hard data on color-related distractibility, both educators concurred that a muted, subdued palette—pastels, neutral beiges and browns—and plain, unpatterned finishes are the sensible choices for schools for autistic kids.

Controlling sensory stimulation goes hand in hand with the need to provide a comfortable and nonthreatening environment. Temple Grandin, whose books on her own experience with autism have been national bestsellers, has written that fear—including a terror induced by the spatial disorientation autistics experience in overlarge, busy, and unfamiliar environments—can overwhelm autistic individuals to a degree that those without autism have trouble even imagining (see Grandin 1995). As parents and teachers of autistic kids know all too well, fear can cause an autistic child to completely shut down—effectively blocking out the outside world. An appropriately scaled facility can help guard against this happening. Among other things, this means keeping ceiling heights low, spatial volumes small, and learning spaces intimately proportioned, especially in the early years, when most teacher-student interaction is one-on-one. (And it certainly means avoiding the soaring lobby spaces and atriums so beloved by architects!)

For autistic toddlers and elementary school children, the transition between home and school can be significantly eased if the educational environment is residentially scaled. In fact, according to Holmes, the Eden Institute has often preferred to adapt actual residences—ordinary suburban homes of 1960s or 1970s vintage—for use in its infant/toddler programs. The bedrooms of such houses become the learning centers where one-on-one instruction takes place. Bedroom closets are rebuilt as observation rooms whose doors open into adjacent corridors. Living rooms become the locus for small-group activities. Observation rooms, by the way, are an essential component of autism education facilities, since students' problems and progress must be closely monitored to ensure that educational strategies are working, and because parents are often invited in to watch what goes on so that they can replicate the techniques and methods used in the classroom in their own interactions with their children at home.

Holmes was also insistent that educational facilities for autistic individuals—of whatever age group—be *noninstitutional* in character. Beyond increasing students' comfort, settings that don't seem institutional carry another benefit, according to Holmes. "We want to stay away from creating an 'institution,'" said Holmes, "because institutions tend to create a set of values that are different from prevailing societal values. If they're too separated off from the outside world, staff might accept behavior—screaming, for example—that won't be accepted elsewhere." In other words, noninstitutional-type settings advance the ultimate goal of autism education and treatment, which is to enable autistic individuals to function to the best of their ability in the society at large.

Nondistracting, nonthreatening, and noninstitutional environments—these are just a few of the basic principles underlying the design of schools for autistic children. There are other overarching concerns: for example, regional education/treatment centers (like the River Street School) often serve students who range in age from toddlers to people in late adolescence or even their early 20s. Moreover, a school's population—even within a given age range—is likely to be highly diverse developmentally and in terms of level of functioning. In such a facility, it becomes highly important to segregate students of different ages and developmental stages, both for reasons of safety and of psychological/emotional comfort. At the same time, though, architectural design must provide a strong sense of continuity and predictability throughout the facility, to ease the transitions as students progress from simpler, more contained learning environments to those that are larger and more complex. As River Street's Parvenski said, autistic students must be introduced to "the chaos of the outside world" in an extremely gradual way.

Now, let's turn to some issues in facility design to see how these general principles are applied to specific building systems and components.

INDOOR AIR QUALITY

Autism spectrum disorders are extremely complex, symptomatically. Parvenski pointed out, for example, that the extraordinary sensitivity to light or sound suffered by many autistic children is often accompanied by heightened sensitivity to other components of the environment, especially airborne contaminants such as dust, mold, and pollen. According to Parvenski, a majority of River Street School's students have chronic upper respiratory problems of greater or lesser severity—and poor indoor air quality can definitely interfere with their education.

River Street's long experience with students' respiratory problems—which had always grown more pronounced during the spring and fall pollen seasons—led Parvenski to insist that River Street's new facility be equipped with an air filtration and ventilation system that, he said, "is almost up to hospital standards," achieving seven complete air changes each hour. "We could probably have done with less—maybe three or four air changes," admitted Parvenski, but he also noted that respiratory distress has become a much less significant problem in the decade or so since River Street's new facility opened.

ACOUSTICS

Mechanical systems for schools for autistic children must also be designed to be as acoustically unobtrusive as possible. According to Parvenski, those who study autism speculate that autistic individuals have trouble processing sound—as evidenced by some autistic kids' tendency to cover their ears even in environments that nonautistic people find acoustically comfortable. The problem isn't just noise: an autistic child who can't "foreground" and "background" various sounds—distinguishing sounds that are important from those that aren't, and recognizing meaningful patterns of sound—can all too easily become distracted from a learning task if he or she locks onto a sound coming from a nearby fan or duct.

Controlling the acoustical environment isn't just a matter of attenuating sound generated by the air system, however. Learning spaces—especially those that accommodate both one-on-one instruction and small-group activities—must be configured in ways that control sound transmission. Adjacencies between classrooms and noisy spaces (such as cafeterias and loading docks) have to be meticulously worked out, and acoustical treatments introduced where necessary. Though the proximity of school buildings to sources of noise—heavily trafficked roads, for example—is always considered when siting new educational facilities, such considerations become even more critical when deciding where to locate an autism education/treatment center.

INJURY PREVENTION

Since VCT and other hard-surfaced flooring reflects sound and can create or amplify a din, carpet is often used more liberally in schools for autistic children than in mainstream schools. But carpet can serve purposes other than just controlling sound. Children with autism spectrum disorders are often prone to seizures and may also, in some cases, engage in behaviors—self-injury, tantrums—that can cause physical harm to themselves or others. Soft surfaces like carpet can reduce the potential for injury. Eden Institute's Holmes said that in facilities operated by his organization, carpet is sometimes installed on walls as well as floors in areas designated for children with extreme auditory distractability or whose potential for self-injury is especially great.

But carpeting carries some drawbacks. It's more difficult to clean and maintain than hard-surface flooring, for example. Carpet that's wet or dirty can provide a medium for the growth of mold and other air contaminants. And most new carpeting gives off volatile organic compounds (VOCs) that can also negatively affect indoor air quality. Discussing these drawbacks, River Street's Parvenski recommended that carpet be used judiciously (a music room at the River Street School is partly carpeted, partly tiled) and that designers do careful research before specifying carpets—choosing those, for example, that have proved acceptable in hospitals and other settings where maintaining good indoor air quality is of equally critical importance.

The potential for physical injury can be reduced in other ways, as well. Parvenski cautioned that designers of schools for autistic children have to become aware of dangers that can lurk in the details of architecture or furnishings—details that might seem inconsequential in other, more typical educational environments. (The corners of whiteboard marker trays or of windowsills, for example, can present unintended hazards.) The overall softness of the environment can be increased through the use of other materials besides carpet. For instance, rubberized flooring might be appropriate in some areas, and Parvenski mentioned that, in a school for autistic kids, drywall might be preferable to masonry construction for certain walls: what one loses in durability one gains in protection against injury, since drywall—unlike concrete block—gives, at least slightly, on impact.

LIGHTING DESIGN

Lighting also presents quandaries for designers of autism education/treatment centers. Granted, today's fluorescent lamps are much more visually comfortable than fluorescents used to be, but even so, all fluorescent lighting flickers. That flickering may not be discernible to most people, but it can be distracting—even harmful—to individuals with autism. Parvenski spoke of cases in which autistic children, seemingly intentionally, lock their gaze onto a fluorescent fixture, whose subtle flicker can set off a seizure. (Apparently, some autistic children deliberately induce seizures in themselves because of the pleasurable rush of endorphins that accompanies the neurological event.) Obviously, it would be better to light an autism education facility with full-spectrum lighting, but there's a rub: nonfluorescent lighting uses considerably more energy, and it's unlikely that the operations budget will allow for this long-term expense. A solution, according to Parvenski, is to use only *indirect* fluorescent lighting so that the lamps are never visible to students. At the River Street School, pendant indirect fixtures are augmented by hidden downlights at the ceiling perimeter, which softly wash the walls with light.

Designers must also be extremely cautious in their use of natural light to illuminate the interiors of autism education/treatment centers. In most school design today, natural daylighting is usually considered an unqualified good, enhancing students' sense of well-being and—according to some studies—improving academic performance. But windows with exterior views may have the opposite effect on autistic students, offering undesirable distractions. Clerestory windows and sky-lights—other common strategies for introducing natural light into interiors—may likewise be counterproductive, since shifting patterns of daylight can complicate the visual environment. These caveats don't mean that natural daylighting can't ever be used—it is, after all, a very good way of introducing full-spectrum light into an interior—but rather that the locations of windows and skylights must be carefully considered. At a new facility for the Eden Institute in Princeton (which is awaiting construction until local roadway issues are resolved), skylights are used—but very sparingly, and only in some corridors.

STORAGE SPACE

Storage space is always at a premium in school buildings, and this is yet another area in which the ante is upped in facilities for autistic children. Since a great deal of the education of autistic youth (particularly in the early developmental stages) involves work with objects of various sorts, and since it's so important that the learning environment remain uncluttered and visually undistracting, the learning centers and classrooms of schools for autistic children have extraordinary storage requirements. Parvenski estimated, for example, that a classroom space of 400–500 square feet might require as much as 100 additional square feet of storage space.

Storage strategies differ according to the particular educational approach employed at a given school, so this is one area where interior design must be responsive to differences in educational philosophy. Staff at the River Street School, for example, prefer closed storage, in which objects are put securely away when not in use. (Parvenski said that large plastic boxes serve this purpose well.) By contrast, the Eden Institute generally opts for open-shelf storage. "We tend not to child-proof the environment," said Director Holmes. "Those who don't use open shelving are trying to protect the equipment, but at Eden we try to teach students to respect the environment."

ART AND MUSIC EDUCATION

Educators of autistic children place differing emphases on the place of art and music in the educa-tion of autistic kids. Parvenski admitted that a decade ago he would have discounted the impor-tance of music in his school's curriculum, but that his experience since then has changed his mind. What began to turn him around, he said, was the case of one autistic boy at the River Street School—a child with a severe speech handicap—who first began to communicate through singing. "You see that enough, and your eyes have to be opened," Parvenski said, though he was quick to point out that arts and music education are introduced to River Street students in a gradual and very systematic way so that their potential to help individuals can be carefully gauged.

In her writings on autism, bestselling author Temple Grandin—herself an engineer and a world-renowned designer of livestock-handling facilities—often highlights the picture-making skills of some high-functioning autistics like herself, recommending, for example, that courses in drafting and computer-assisted design be offered to autistic students who demonstrate visual arts talent. But heavy emphasis on visual and musical arts may not fit every education or treatment philosophy or match a given student population's needs, so here, too, architectural design—

including the types, sizing, and number of spaces for arts instruction—must be responsive to the particular school and the educators who run it.

TECHNOLOGY AND OTHER ISSUES

The list of design-related issues goes on and on. Among other important items on this list is the need to accommodate a wide variety of computer technologies, in terms of space and infrastructure. Computers and other electronic devices—including handheld augmentative communication devices, which enable those with severe speech disabilities to "talk" with their teachers—typically play an extremely important role in autism education. Autism education has, in fact, become a proving ground for a wide variety of computerized learning tools that may be useful in other kinds of special education and mainstream educational settings. But an autism education center's computer requirements also include the need for information systems of greater capacity and sophistication than those used in most mainstream schools because of the vast amount of recordkeeping involved in tracking students' progress and because all the many professionals engaged in educating and treating students—and in providing them and their families with an array of support services—must remain in constant communication with one another.

We've barely begun to touch the full range of issues that comes into play in the design of autism education/treatment centers. Occupational therapy and physical education spaces may, for example, require additional structural reinforcement because of the specialized, ceiling-hung equipment (including swings) used in what's termed "adaptive physical education." Toilet rooms in toddler and early childhood areas may have to be oversized so that other learning activities can be pursued during time-consuming toilet-training sessions. Special attention must be paid to the finishes and furniture used in time-out rooms so that children do not injure themselves. Meeting rooms for parent conferences should be especially comfortable, since the issues discussed in such conferences can be so emotionally trying.

Architects tend to view issues like those outlined in this chapter as absolutely critical. But let us reiterate something we said near the beginning of this essay. Despite all the good that a well-designed facility can do, it's what goes on *inside* the facility—especially the interaction between teachers and students—that's of paramount importance. As a society, we certainly need to focus on the need for specialized facilities for educating and treating autistic children, but we need to focus even more directly on the crying need for teachers trained to work with this very special group of students, whose numbers are burgeoning day by day. Effective buildings can help. According to Holmes, they foster "a harmonious interaction of spatial configuration and the training of individuals." And for Parvenski, "The building can eliminate a lot of problems and allow staff to get to the skill acquisition that will make the kids more successful in life." As design-industry professionals, we can't help but be humbled by the dedication, perseverance, and spirit of the educators who commit themselves to helping America's autistic people lead productive and rewarding lives.

Design Considerations for Specialized Schools

Trying to outline basic design considerations for specialized schools puts one in an immediate quandary. How can designers develop rules of thumb for a set of schools that are so different from one another? From a design point of view, what would a magnet elementary school employing the Montessori approach share with a magnet high school for the performing arts? What would either of these share with an underfunded K–8 charter that—for lack of a better place to go—takes up residence in a strip mall or warehouse? Or with a regional school for autistic children that serves a population of disabled youth ages 5–21?

The very differences among these kinds of schools give us, we think, a place to start. Designers are always talking about designing "to the program"—making sure that architectural design is intimately geared to what will happen inside and around a building, and is as responsive as possible to the needs of that facility's users. If anything, that architectural rule of thumb is even more true when it comes to designing a specialized school. The school's unique mission, particular curriculum, and specialized instructional modes—as well as the specific needs of its student population and other users (faculty, administrators, and the community)—all have to be closely considered before making any design decision.

As a starting point, this guideline—we might call it the "anti–cookie cutter" principle—may seem pretty vague. It does, however, provide us with a useful caution. Below, we'll outline some other, better defined principles that we believe should guide specialized school design. But we've always got to keep in mind that almost any of these principles might have to be rethought in a particular case. When it comes to the design of a specialized school, nothing trumps the specificity of that school's mission, program, and population. Nothing.

ARCHITECTURE VERSUS "ANTI-ARCHITECTURE"

Let's turn to another dilemma that designers of specialized schools have to puzzle over. Most school architects (and most educators) would agree that successful school design provides schoolchildren with a strong (and strongly positive) sense of place—a sense of home, identity, belonging, and well-being. Because children spend so much time in school, it's inevitable that their identities

---

The text of this chapter is largely based on two roundtable discussions held at Fletcher-Thompson, Inc.'s Shelton, Connecticut, offices. Participants in those discussions included James A. Beaudin, Timothy P. Cohen, Daniel Davis, L. Gerald Dunn, Thomas A. Fantacone, Julie A. Kim, Edwin T. Merritt, Patricia A. Myler, and James Waller.

will, in some deep way, be connected to the physical environments they inhabit for so many hours of the day, so many months of the year, so many years of their lives. If you think back on your own educational experiences, you'll immediately see how true this is: if you feel pleasantly nostalgic about your schooldays, it's likely that that good feeling is at least partly tied to the physical character of the schools you attended; if recalling your schooldays makes you a bit queasy, the discomfort you feel probably has partly to do with something that was wrong with your school's physical environment.

Good school architecture, then, is architecture that strongly defines an environment—and that makes the school building a distinctive, safe, comforting, and altogether special place. The trouble is, there's a competing principle—one that might undermine the specialness that's an earmark of successful school design. And this competing principle is extremely important; in fact, it is now a watchword of good design. It goes by the name of *flexibility.*

There's no doubt that maximizing flexibility is essential to contemporary, future-oriented school design. But there's also no doubt that flexibility and what we think of as "architecture" can be in direct conflict with one another. The most flexible space imaginable would an "anti-architectural" space in the sense that it would be utterly nondistinctive—anonymous, really. Think of a plain box capable of being divided up or otherwise manipulated at will—utterly flexible and, from an aesthetic point of view, utterly humdrum. A building filled with ultraflexible spaces might be a pretty homogenized, characterless place—not much of a *place* at all. (Somewhat ironically, a totally flexible environment would also be extremely costly to build.)

This conflict between sense of place and easy adaptability to multiple purposes must be addressed, and compromises found, in the design of most specialized schools, because both sides of the conflict—"architecture" and flexibility—may be equally critical to fulfilling a specialized school's mission. Providing students with a strong, strongly defined identity—which can be enhanced by the facility itself—is, after all, a central aspect of the mission of many specialized schools. On the other hand, specialized schools—especially those forward-thinking schools that experiment with numerous, highly variable approaches to learning—require a very high degree of flexibility to easily accommodate those diverse instructional modes. Making sure that a school building is flexible enough to accommodate present-day and future styles of learning while not skimping on architectural excellence can be a tall order. (But it can be done—as is witnessed by many contemporary museums, which achieve the enormous flexibility required by shifting exhibitions while, at the same, being beautifully designed.)

The contest between architectural design and flexibility is dramatically illustrated by the MicroSociety Magnet Elementary School in Yonkers, New York.[1] The interior of this school, which opened in 1992, remains a visually stunning example of clever, sophisticated, and innovative educational design. (The building's designers, the Rye, New York, firm of Anderson LaRocca Anderson Haynes, won several well-deserved architectural awards for the facility during the year after its opening.)

The MicroSociety Magnet's classroom wings open onto a large central area, dubbed "Freedom Square," which is designed to look like a small-town commons. In keeping with the MicroSociety theme, which emphasizes student participation in the many different kinds of institutions—retail, financial, political, and so on—that constitute a real, functioning society, the central square is surrounded by a series of specialized learning spaces that emulate the businesses and offices one might find in an actual city. There are market, government, media/publishing, and manufacturing

Figures 7.1 and 7.2.   Freedom Square, the central gathering space at the MicroSociety Magnet Elementary School, is surrounded by shopfronts, with a specialized learning space behind each. *Photographs by Charles R. Cassidy.*

spaces, as well as two "banks"; each space has been given a real-looking, though somewhat stylized, shopfront, complete with appropriate signage. The effect is charming—even exhilarating: walking into this commons, one is immediately persuaded that this school is far from ordinary.

But, as you might have guessed, there's a problem. As planned—and as originally used—the various spaces surrounding the square were designated for specific kinds of educational experiences. Over the course of any week, class groups would travel to one or another of the spaces for hands-on learning (conducting transactions at the bank, for example). Over time, however, the MicroSociety concept implemented at the school has suffered—and the overall MicroSociety program there has deteriorated—because of the Yonkers school district's budgetary woes. (Staff cutbacks, for example, spelled the loss of the school's magnet program director some time ago.) Although MicroSociety principles still guide some of the learning that goes on in the school's classrooms, the specialized spaces surrounding Freedom Square are now rarely if ever used for their intended purposes.

That doesn't mean these spaces go unused. Some, for example, are used for weekend adult-education classes and for group meetings of various sorts. Unfortunately, however, these highly specific spaces are rather inflexible and serve their new purposes somewhat uncomfortably. When you know all this, your impression of the architectural design subtly and unavoidably changes: though Freedom Square is still visually impressive, there's something sad about it. For better or worse, the school is "stuck with" an architectural expression that no longer suits it. Freedom Square has the aspect of a small-town center whose commercial buildings stand empty because suburban "big box" stores have robbed them of their business.

The lesson here is that, to remain successful over the long term, specialized-school facility design *must* anticipate change—not just technological change and change in educational philosophy and practice but also the much more banal, everyday changes that might occur in a school because of a weakening economy, for example, or cuts in funding. And anticipating change equals being flexible. This doesn't mean magnet schools can't or shouldn't be aesthetically pleasing, but it may well put certain limits on the expressiveness of a school's architecture, especially when it comes to the design and configuration of interior spaces.

SPECIALIZED SCHOOLS—OTHER SIMILARITIES

We talk, above, about *difference* as the one thing that all specialized schools "share." That's inarguable, but, as we explain in this book's first chapter, there are a few other characteristics that many (not all) specialized schools have in common and that may have a significant impact on design. To reiterate those similarities:

1. *Urban location.* Many specialized schools (magnets, charters, and alternative schools) are urban schools. From a facility planning and design perspective, this is important for several reasons, especially those involving a school's site and the school's relation to the surrounding community. (Because of the scarcity of appropriate, affordable land for new construction in many cities, urban location relates directly to characteristic #2, below.)

2. *Preexisting buildings.* Many specialized schools—either by choice or through lack of alternatives—occupy already existing buildings, either older school buildings or buildings originally designed and used for noneducational purposes (warehouses, office buildings, or retail buildings).

Issues having to do with adaptive reuse—and prior questions about which sorts of existing facilities make the best candidates for conversion into schools—therefore come more strongly to the fore when planning and designing specialized schools.

3. *Small size.* Most specialized schools are significantly smaller—in terms of student population and thus facilities—than their conventional public school counterparts. (Even the largest magnet high schools, such as Las Vegas's Advanced Technologies Academy [see pages 51–57], are much smaller than comprehensive highs.) Small size in some ways restricts design—for example, smaller schools may often incorporate fewer amenities. But small size, coupled with unique programmatic requirements, may also free the designer's hand.

4. *Uncertain long-term funding.* Even in cases where capital costs associated with design and construction are taken care of—for example, where the state picks up the bill (or almost all of it) for building a new magnet—coming up with adequate funds to sustain ongoing operations can be a real problem for many specialized schools. The design impact of this reality is easy to understand: a school's long-term financial viability is supported by high-performance building systems and easily maintainable components and materials.

5. *Self-selecting populations.* The student bodies of many specialized schools are largely self-selecting, that is, parents must intentionally decide to send their children to these schools (or students must decide that they want to go to them). This characteristic relates to design in that a well-designed facility might well be a selling point for a magnet or charter—something that will attract parents and students, helping the school meet and retain enrollment targets.

Let's take a closer look at some of these shared characteristics and their relation to planning and design considerations.

Location, Location, Location. As they say, location is everything. That's true—or *almost* true—for many magnet and other specialized schools. In some cases, the site-related issues are obvious: It's a no-brainer that a marine-science magnet high school should be located on or very near the water, that a zoo-themed magnet should be adjacent to (yes) a zoo, and that a museum-themed magnet would do well to have a museum within shouting distance. The reverse of this kind of proposition, however, may not be quite as obvious: that a school district's natural resources, business strengths, and major cultural institutions should play a determining role in deciding the particular focuses of the district's magnet schools. Would it make sense to found an aviation-themed magnet high school in a county without an airport or any aviation-related industry? Or, to take a less clear-cut example: what benefit would a performing arts–themed magnet confer in an area where theaters, dance companies, and symphony orchestras are few and far between? (The issues in this case wouldn't have to do only with an absence of local career opportunities for the school's graduates—after all, they might well go on to college or move to New York City!—but also with the difficulty of finding good, professional-caliber faculty to teach at the school.)

But siting issues get a lot more subtle than this, especially with regard to urban specialized schools. Chapter 10, "Site Design and Landscape Architecture for Urban Magnet Schools," covers many of these issues—creating safe environments, accommodating vehicular traffic, ensuring adequate outdoor recreational space, and improving urban ecologies—in detail. But there are other considerations as well. These include:

- The need to take steps to ensure that a neighborhood will welcome, not resist, the presence of a new specialized school in its midst.

• The desirability of locating new magnet schools in places where the presence of the school may foster or assist neighborhood revitalization.

An urban community's residents may understandably fear the quality-of-life impact of a new specialized school. These fears would likely be greatest in the case of a school designed to serve a certain special-needs population—say, a specialized high school for emotionally/behaviorally troubled young people. But fear and opposition may also be generated if local residents believe that a new specialized school will cause traffic disruption on nearby streets, or put undue burden on local resources, or if the school's construction will require the condemnation of nearby houses and the displacement of people who live in them. (For an example of how neighborhood fears delayed the design and construction process for one urban magnet, see the case study of New London, Connecticut's Regional Multi-Cultural Magnet, pages 20–25.) Whatever the potential reason for community opposition may be, care must be taken to understand the community and to address residents' concerns early on in the project's life.

Far from harming a community, however, it is possible that a new magnet might give a boost to neighborhood revitalization efforts, and that appropriate siting of a new school might foster a synergy between educational improvement and the enhancement of quality of life in the surrounding community. That this can indeed happen is clearly illustrated, for example, in the case of Hartford, Connecticut's Learning Corridor (see pages 31–33), a four-school campus whose purpose, in part, was to improve the character (and reputation) of the city's Frog Hollow neighborhood. In Waterbury, Connecticut, the presence of a new performing-arts magnet has inspired the renovation of that city's Palace Theater. An even more intentional synergy between school construction and neighborhood revitalization occurred in New Haven, Connecticut, where the full-scale renovation of the K–8 Wexler-Grant Community School was simultaneously accompanied by the building of an adjacent HOPE VI housing development. Though not a magnet per se, Wexler-Grant is magnet-like in that its student population is drawn from all over New Haven.[2] And there's anecdotal evidence of school-neighborhood synergy elsewhere in the country. Miami, Florida's well-regarded Design and Architecture Senior High (DASH), a charter school that occupies a former warehouse, is located in a neighborhood filled with new art- and design-related businesses. Which came first—the school or the galleries and designers' offices? That chicken-or-egg question is hard to answer; what's clear is that school and neighborhood go hand in hand.

The New (Old) Schoolhouse. As just noted, Miami's DASH charter high school lives in a former warehouse. So does East Hartford, Connecticut's Polaris Center, a residential and day school for emotionally troubled youth. These specialized schools are hardly alone in occupying buildings originally meant for some other, noneducation-related purpose. As Chapter 6 relates, autism treatment/education centers are sometimes located in revamped suburban houses. Hartford, Connecticut's new Coltsville autism education center occupies a renovated factory building. Philadelphia's Charter High for Architecture + Design (CHAD) began its life in an office building. The Greater Hartford Academy of the Performing Arts once lived in a refashioned funeral home. The facility used by San Diego's renowned High Tech High is a former naval training center.

Besides all the specialized schools housed in what were originally nonschool buildings, countless others occupy older school buildings—some of which have been moved into "as is," and others of which have been slightly or significantly renovated for their new purpose. (Four of the schools represented in Chapter 2, "Specialized Schools: Twelve Exemplary Projects," occupy preexisting school buildings.) So far as we know, there are no national statistics on the number of magnets and other specialized schools housed in older school facilities, but our guess is that there are plenty. It's interesting to note, for example, that none of the magnet schools in New York City's extensive magnet program occupies its own, purpose-built facility; all are housed in school buildings that already existed when the magnets were founded.

Why do so many magnet, charter, alternative, and other specialized public schools use existing buildings? This question has several answers:

- Many specialized schools start small—very small—and are somewhat experimental in nature, in the sense that it may be unclear, even to the schools' staunchest proponents, whether they will succeed and grow, or fail. Very small schools like these rarely have the need or the capital for their own, purpose-built facilities. (A good number of them, at least at the beginning, may take over space within a larger school from which the specialized school operates independently or semi-independently and some of whose resources and facilities the specialized school shares.)
- Charters, especially, often operate on shoestring budgets that don't allow them to build (or even purchase) their own facilities. (For more on charters' facilities-related issues, see Chapter 5, "Finding a Home.")
- In densely built urban areas, there may simply be no place to build a new school—or such open land as does exist may be prohibitively expensive.

But these are "negative" reasons for deciding to move into an existing building rather than building new. There may well be positive reasons, too. For instance, in the case of the Wexler-Grant Community School mentioned earlier in this chapter, the New Haven Board of Education decided to renovate an existing elementary school rather than demolish it and build anew because there was a real facilities-related advantage to doing so: the old building contained a sizable auditorium that today would *not* be included in the program for a new K–8 school. And then there's the fact that, despite their sometimes-dire state of disrepair, many of the old school buildings that dot inner-city neighborhoods across the United States are remarkable buildings, architecturally—well worth preserving, renewing, and reusing. Architect Robert A. M. Stern (2000) has forcefully argued for the renovation and reuse, for educational purposes, of New York City's many late-19th- and early-20th-century public school buildings, which he considers treasures of American civic architecture. Beyond their inherent architectural value, many such buildings—in New York and other cities—are beloved by their communities. Saving and renewing them builds community "ownership" and pride.

But the educational reuse of older buildings—whether schools or nonschool structures—can raise some real architectural challenges. Here are just a few of the problems that designers might encounter when renovating an older school building or designing an "adaptive reuse" project in which a commercial (or other nonschool) building is transformed into an educational facility:

- *Environmental remediation.* Older buildings (and their sites) may require significant environmental remediation before they can be renovated for educational use. Remediation efforts, such as abating asbestos or other hazardous materials within the structure itself, can add astronomically to a project's expense—so much so that it may turn out to be much cheaper to build anew elsewhere.

- *Code compliance.* In some cases, it may be extremely difficult to bring an older building into compliance with present-day building codes. These codes—which cover everything from fire protection and life safety to accessibility by physically disabled students—tend to be especially stringent for educational facilities; moreover, changing a building's use— say, from a factory to a school—often triggers code-related upgrade requirements. (It may therefore sometimes be easier, from a building-codes standpoint, to reuse an existing school building rather than adaptively reuse a commercial structure for educational purposes.)
- *Structural issues.* Like human beings, buildings grow "creaky" with age. Older buildings may have developed structural problems over their lifetimes that render them unfit for reuse as schools or that may require "rehabilitative" measures that are too costly to perform. What's more, structural problems besetting an older building often remain hidden until interior demolition begins, and measures to stabilize the structure may add hefty, unanticipated costs and scheduling delays to the project. And these aren't the only structure-related issues: for example, older buildings were designed under less stringent codes that did not incorporate requirements for seismic (i.e., earthquake-resistant) design; it may be impossible to bring such structures up to current seismic code.
- *Building systems.* Mechanical (heating, ventilating, and air conditioning) systems, electrical power systems, and telecommunications systems all require pathways through a building, both vertically and horizontally. It may be difficult or even impossible to introduce new HVAC, power, or telecom pathways into an existing structure.
- *Landmarking or historic preservation regulations.* Sometimes, the extent and type of architectural interventions that can be performed on a historically significant older building are fettered by local or state landmarking or historic preservation rules. If such regulations will interfere with the proposed program, it might be wise for a school to look for a home elsewhere. Concerns about preserving historical "fabric" can sometimes extend beyond the existing building: for example, a new addition to a historically significant structure may require building materials that are "in keeping" with the older building's grandeur—and that may be much more expensive than the kinds of materials usually used in school construction today.

To this list must be added the fact that existing buildings—whether schools or commercial structures—may just be plain unsuitable for contemporary educational standards and practices. In older school buildings, classroom spaces—which because of structural considerations may be impossible to alter or expand—may be much smaller than today's standards. And there's sometimes the danger that an unusual or "quirky" configuration of interior space might dictate the program rather than the other way around. When an interior configuration can't be altered (for structural reasons, say), the programmatic changes necessitated may affect learning and damage a school's ability to fulfill its special mission.

But let us end this section on a more upbeat note. In many, many cases, the reuse of an existing building makes a great deal of sense, architecturally and otherwise. Although it's not often seen as such, renovation or adaptive reuse can be an immensely valuable contribution to environmental sustainability. By reusing older buildings and putting them to new uses, we're not only paying homage to our architectural legacy. We're also maximizing resources—"recycling," so to speak. We're refusing to squander much of the energy and natural resources that went into the creation of the original building—its brick, its terrazzo floors, its stone. We're not "drawing down" yet more of our shrinking heritage of undeveloped land. For these reasons alone, renovation and adaptive reuse are well worth pursuing, wherever and whenever it makes sense to do so.

Smaller = Better? A consensus is emerging among educators and those who study academic achievement that smaller schools are better schools. Limiting the size of a school's student body helps ensure, for example, that no student "falls between the cracks." Large schools can be fairly forbidding, anonymous, and even uncaring places for a sizable fraction of the student body. Small schools are better at fostering socialization, encouraging peer relationships, and promoting focused interaction between teachers and students. But do smaller schools permit a greater degree of architectural freedom, and are the designs of new, smaller schools likely to be better—more nurturing of alternative approaches to education—than those of larger schools? We'll hazard that the answer to this question might well be "yes."

Why? A few reasons come to mind. First, design of all new buildings is to some extent driven by code requirements, and those requirements, especially as they concern fire protection and safety, are likely to be more stringent for larger buildings than for smaller ones. (A comparatively large building will require a comparatively larger number of exits, placed at fairly regular intervals, that can be readily accessed in an emergency. These requirements, in turn, tend to impose a certain regularity on the overall design.) Designers of small schools aren't free of code-mandated strictures—hardly!—but they may have a somewhat freer hand in this regard than designers of large schools.

Large schools must, of necessity, also be much more "regular"—*repetitive* might be the better word—in the provision of spaces than smaller schools. A large comprehensive high school, for example, will require dozens of classrooms that are essentially the same in dimensions, in the ways they're equipped and outfitted, and so on. This necessary repetition might well constrain a designer's creativity when it comes to organizing space. The ability to "play with" different kinds of organizational schemes, different kinds of adjacencies, will probably be quite limited for a large school. A smaller school's comparatively few spaces permit greater flexibility in how those spaces will be arranged, that is, in how they (and the groups that use them) interact with one another.

In addition, it may well be the case that a small school can spur design creativity for the simple reason that the designer has greater leisure (comparatively speaking, of course) to focus on each component in greater detail—to spend more time making every design element as good as it can be.

Long-Term Viability. Because of relentless pressures to keep a tight lid on first costs, most school facilities built today are not very durable. While concrete masonry unit walls and terrazzo floors are common in older school buildings, the materials used in newer construction—gypsum board for interior walls and vinyl tile for flooring—are cheap, and, to put it bluntly, you get what you pay for. Less expensive, less durable materials equal higher maintenance costs, and significant maintenance/repair/replacement needs are likely to occur much earlier in a building's life cycle than they would had more expensive, more durable materials been used instead.

Moreover, public schools today generally aren't built as well as they could be from a performance standpoint—top-of-the-line energy-saving ("high-performance" or "green") components are passed over for cheaper alternatives. The motive, once again, is that of controlling first costs—and once again, life-cycle costs are the victim of the myopic, first-cost-centered approach. It seems clear to us that the penny-wise approach is pound foolish no matter what kind of school you're building, since cheap materials and relatively low-performance mechanical systems will add massively to school systems' operations and maintenance expenses over the course of time. The approach seems particularly unwise when it comes to building new magnet schools, whose long-term O&M budgets are in many cases very insecure. (This does vary from state to state, depending on how magnet education is funded.)

There is some good news here. First, there are ways of improving a new school building's long-term energy performance without enormously increasing initial construction costs. Some of those are detailed in the description of the proposed Academy of Information Technology and Engineering building in Chapter 2 (Project #1, pages 9–15). Second, in cases where districts receive full (or nearly full) reimbursement from the state for magnet school construction, it may be possible to specify costlier, more durable materials than a district could otherwise afford. And, as is mentioned elsewhere in this chapter, the rock-solid construction of many older school buildings is one of the qualities that makes them attractive as venues for some magnet and other specialized schools.

"Magnetic" Buildings. The committee of "visionaries" who planned Las Vegas's Advanced Technologies Academy (see pages 51–57) knew they might be facing an uphill battle in enticing parents from all over the Greater Las Vegas area to enroll their children at "ATech," which would be located in an older, somewhat run-down section of the city, just northwest of downtown. So they made what in retrospect seems a very smart decision: to make the building a showpiece designed to "wow" prospective students and their families.

Now, more than a dozen years after ATech's founding, the school has no difficulty attracting students: its well-regarded, highly successful program (a 2003 Blue Ribbon School award winner) does that job handily. But during those first, critical years, the building's attractiveness—and its designers' decision to situate some of the school's showier high-tech learning and support spaces front and center—were crucial to ATech's ability to meet enrollment targets.

The principle embodied in the ATech example is a simple one: a magnet school's "magnetism" can derive, in part, from the school building itself. To succeed, magnet schools must do a good job of selling themselves to their potential market, and the strategy employed at ATech is as old as retailing itself: "show the merchandise." By locating the school's main server in a glass-walled space near the front entrance and placing its then state-of-the-art distance-learning lab in the media center, also adjacent to the entry lobby, designers emphasized the magnet's theme and, in doing so, all but guaranteed that parents visiting the school would drive away *very* impressed.

Strategies like ATech's "front and center" approach can be used by any specialized school, new or old. For example, at the Museum Magnet Middle School in Yonkers, New York—all of whose schools are magnets, meaning that they're all in competition with one another for the same "market" of parents and students—we were very impressed by the dramatic, skylit main lobby, as well as the roomy gallery space, displaying students' work, adjacent to the reception desk. The same approach is in evidence at Philadelphia's Charter High for Architecture + Design (see pages 57–62), where anyone entering the school is immediately greeted by a vibrantly colored Sol Lewitt mural, where the wall facing the reception desk showcases artwork by CHAD students, where the corridor leading to the classrooms is outfitted as a museum-caliber gallery, and where prospective students and their parents are interviewed in an office that's a model of contemporary workplace design.

Of course, a facility's magnetism extends well beyond the front-and-center spaces that greet visitors upon arrival. We're sure, for example, that the overall attractiveness of the Advanced Technologies Academy building also helped woo ATech attendees' families. We're equally certain that the design excellence epitomized throughout the Montessori Magnet Elementary School in Hartford, Connecticut's Learning Corridor (see pages 33–41) is a deciding factor for at least some of the parents who consider sending their children there. But the lesson is the same: a specialized school's facility can create a powerful impression, and what might be called the "WYSIWYG factor"—What You See Is What You (and Your Children) Get—shouldn't be underestimated by anyone planning a new specialized school. In fact, specialized schools' need to attract students and their families may be reason enough to eschew the dull conservatism that characterizes too much contemporary school design; when the building itself functions as a public relations tool, there's something to be said for dramatic, innovative, unusual, and truly future-oriented design.

The benefits of good design, of course, are hardly limited to the early phase of a specialized school's life. A well-designed facility might also help underwrite a school's long-term success by boosting achievement outcomes—outcomes that will, in turn, attract more parents and children to the school. Granted, one usually can't draw a direct connection between the quality of a school building and how well that school's students perform on standardized tests or other assessment measures. But it does seem clear that run-down, dilapidated school buildings are one factor behind poor academic achievement. Depressing environments yield disappointing results. One of the ways we can do better by America's inner-city schoolchildren is to give them school buildings that—at the very least—don't hinder learning. And we believe that magnet schools, especially, can take the lead in accomplishing this transformation.

POWERS OF TEN

There are two ways of looking at what specialized schools, especially theme- or career-based magnets, do. The first—more common but also more limited—way of viewing these schools is to see them as providers of specific kinds of knowledge and technical know-how. In this view, the primary purpose of, say, a marine magnet high school would be to develop students' knowledge and expertise in marine biology, aquaculture, oceanography, and related fields.

But there's another, and we believe better, way of viewing such schools—which is to see them as places where students learn how to learn. Looked at this way, the career focuses of theme-based magnets and specialized schools serve a primarily motivational purpose. Yes, the school's particular theme attracts students by appealing to their personal interests and strengths. And yes, the educational experiences offered by the school do provide solid background and preparation for future careers in a certain field or fields that a student *might* chose to pursue. The school's more important function, however, is to help students develop problem-solving skills, learning habits, and attitudes toward learning that can be applied throughout life, no matter what career the student ultimately chooses. It's this dimension of the educational experience offered by magnets and some other specialized public schools that really distinguishes their philosophy from the older, vocational-technical model, in which students were definitely slotted into certain narrowly defined career tracks.

It's also very significant that this newer, theme-based educational model is meant to raise academic achievement across the board. To take just one example: at Philadelphia's Charter High for Architecture + Design (CHAD), the stated focus is on preparing students for careers in the design professions, but the school strives to help students learn to apply similar problem-solving methods to *every* area of study—English, social studies, science, math, and so on. CHAD's advocates believe that these problem-solving skills are widely transferable across disciplines and that, applied appropriately, these skills—though "borrowed" from architects and other designers—can be just as useful in helping students improve in reading as in enabling them, say, to build an architectural model.

Understanding this more important goal of magnet and other specialized education has aided us in developing a set of design considerations that can be applied to any specialized school. Of course, many of the specifics regarding the precise kinds of spaces and equipment required by specialized schools will differ from case to case: a performing arts high school might well need a near-professional-caliber theater, complete with a full-scale stagehouse and sophisticated lighting and sound systems; a science and math magnet will most likely require a range of sophisticated technical equipment that goes well beyond what one would ever find in an ordinary comprehensive high. But by putting those highly specific considerations aside and concentrating, instead, on what architecture can do to foster learning how to learn, we can discover many potential design-related commonalities among all specialized schools. One of the most important commonalities, to our minds, is that each such school will need a comfortable and appropriate mix of small, medium, and large spaces, because different kinds of learning require different—and differently sized—spaces.

There's a short film, produced in 1977, that's a favorite of many architects. It's called *Powers of Ten*, and it was made by a famous husband-and-wife design team: Charles and Ray Eames. (The Eameses are especially noted for their furniture designs; many of their pieces—including the "potato chip" chair and the Eames recliner—are icons of mid-20th-century design.) The film, all of nine minutes long, is an architect's favorite not because the Eameses were themselves design professionals (who moonlighted as filmmakers) but because of the movie's thought-provoking structure—which stresses the *continuity* and *connectivity* of all things, throughout the whole universe.

The film begins with a shot of a man and woman picnicking in a Chicago park; the man is lying on a blanket that's been spread out on the grass. This first shot, which lasts ten seconds, is taken from above, at a distance of one meter. Throughout the first section of the film, the viewer's distance from this picnic scene increases by a power of ten every ten seconds: the second shot shows the scene from ten meters away, the third from a height of 100 meters (i.e., 10^2), and so on. As the distance increases, one gains an ever-widening perspective: the whole park comes into view, then the city of Chicago, then the Great Lakes region of the United States, then planet Earth, then the solar system, the Milky Way galaxy—until, eventually, the entire visible universe is within the viewer's "frame." At this point, having achieved the widest possible "camera angle," the film reverses direction. Now—speeded up so that the shot changes every two seconds—the distance from the original Chicago park scene *decreases* by a power of ten. Within very little time, we've descended from intergalactic space back down to where we started: the picnicking couple. But the film doesn't stop when it reaches this point. From one meter above, the shot zooms to the man's hand, and the film then goes on to explore "inner space," showing us increasingly microscopic views of tissues, then cells, then molecules, then a single atom, and, finally, a single proton in the atom's nucleus.

The film's effects were fairly inventive for 1977, but as must be obvious, that's not why we mention it here. Our reason for bringing this superb little film to your attention has to do with its marvelous ability to underline the importance of relationships of scale. The parts of the universe as depicted in *Powers of Ten*—from the farthest-flung reaches of space to the tiniest constituents of the atom—may appear very different from one another, but they represent a continuum, and each part is essential to the whole.

That's why we think the film is germane to a discussion of designing facilities for magnet and other specialized schools. For no matter what a school's specific mission is, a successful design of its facility must foster a continuum of learning and must integrate a variety of spaces of differing scales that serve differing (but always related) learning purposes.

Let's employ our own Powers of Ten approach to the future magnet/specialized school, looking first at individual learning spaces, then at spaces for one-on-one interaction, then small-group spaces, then classrooms and labs, then large-group spaces, and, finally, the architectural strategies that link the school to the wider world beyond. This pattern is, we believe, a fertile way of approaching school-facility design, since it replicates in spatial terms the multidimensional structure and purpose of education itself: that of bolstering and nurturing the individual student's ego and of integrating him or her into social groups of various kinds and sizes as well as into the greater society and culture. On the route toward that integration of self and world, architecture should both facilitate and, yes, inspire.

Individual Learning Spaces. Contemporary educational theory and, to a large extent, pedagogical practice have been transformed by the discovery that different people learn differently. This insight, epitomized in the "multiple intelligences" theory propounded by Harvard University's Dr. Howard Gardner, has spawned numerous pedagogical innovations, including, for example, the "reading styles" work of Dr. Marie Carbo.[3] We single out Carbo for mention here because she, in her writings, has been so adamant about the educational folly of requiring diverse students— with diverse learning styles—to adapt themselves to a single, rigidly structured way of doing things in school. Education, she believes, should adapt itself to students, helping them to learn in the ways they learn best.

That pedagogical attitude provides a good starting place for discussing how a specialized school's facility should accommodate the individual learning styles of individual students. Following Carbo's lead, we believe that a well-designed facility would, first of all, offer a diversity of spaces where students can pursue learning alone, on their own—both inside and outside the classroom. Think about how you yourself like to read. Sitting upright at a desk? Or lounging in a comfortable chair? Do you like to read in an environment—like that of a library reading room— where you're surrounded by other people, each absorbed in his or her own book? Or do you prefer to be alone and undistracted by others' presence? Do you find it easier and more enjoyable to read in a brightly lit room, or in a room with a low level of ambient light but bright, focused task lighting? Obviously, different adults will answer these questions differently; Carbo's point is that young people are just the same: they prefer to learn in different ways—and those differences have to do with physical environment, among other factors.

Understanding this, it's possible to imagine a school incorporating a wealth of different kinds of spaces and places where students can pursue individual study and work on individual projects:

cubbies and workstations inside and outside of classrooms; tables and carrels in a school's media center; upholstered chairs and benches where students can stretch out, slouch, or curl up while reading; and individual practice rooms or studio spaces for students engaged in arts projects. Certainly, cost will play an important role in determining how many and what kinds of individual learning spaces/places a school building can incorporate, but—before deciding what's affordable—it may be wise to put together a wish list of the kinds of individual learning spaces that would best suit a school's program and the learning styles of its students. It's this kind of "visioning" approach that led, for example, to the innovative interior design at the Greater Hartford Academy of Math and Science (see pages 47–50), where academic-wing corridors are lined with workstations at which students can plug in their laptops and work on individual projects whenever the opportunity presents itself.

Beyond accommodating diverse learning styles, the planners and designers of specialized schools—of all schools, in fact—need to think about students' need to have a place to call their own. Traditionally, schools partly accommodated this "territorial urge" by assigning desks (each of which had a storage compartment) to elementary school students and by giving lockers to junior and senior high students. But, on the elementary-school level, those individual desks of yore have in most cases long since been replaced by simpler tables and chairs that, in many cases, can be easily rearranged to accommodate groups of various sizes and different kinds of activities. That flexibility is a good thing, but it does diminish the chance that an individual student will feel "ownership" toward a particular place. And more and more communities have decided to eliminate lockers from new or renovated middle and high schools because of concerns about security and safety. This, too, may be a reasonable move, but once again, it deprives students of a place of their own. One can easily imagine a day when, at most public schools in the United States, a student's private, personal space will be limited to the backpack that he or she lugs around—perhaps supplemented, virtually, by the student's own website or blog.

Elsewhere in this book (see especially Chapter 4), we recommend that at least some specialized schools be designed along the lines of the contemporary workplace. So let's take a lesson, right now, from workplace design. In the early to mid-1990s, office designers experimented with a number of new ways of organizing interior space, including radically "open" offices in which, for example, private offices were completely eliminated, as were most physical barriers between workstations. Some of this experimentation worked well, at least in certain applications: often, breaking down the physical barriers between employees enhanced communication and creativity, raising productivity levels. Some of the experiments did *not* work so well, however. For example, the concept known as "hoteling"—in which no employee had a designated place of his or her own but rather "floated" from one desk to another and from workstation to conference room and back again as business needs dictated—proved disastrous and has largely been abandoned. Why? Because to function effectively, human beings need their own personal spaces—some sort of "home" to return to. Companies that instituted the more radical forms of the hoteling concept suffered from extremely high turnover rates—employees simply didn't like working for them and soon looked for jobs elsewhere. This experience should serve as a lesson to school planners and designers.

How can a school accommodate this need for a place of one's own? San Diego's High Tech High—one of the nation's most innovative and successful charter schools—includes suites of individual workstations, and each student is assigned his or her own. The suites resemble contemporary offices in which partitions between workstations are low enough to allow for visibility and easy communication but high enough to provide a modicum of privacy. This is obviously an expensive proposition and requires a lot of floorspace—roughly 20 percent of the school's net square footage is given over to the workstation suites—but it works. Of course, High Tech High has a very small student population (and, as charter schools go, is well funded), so the solution may be inapplicable to schools with larger student bodies or that are strapped for space or cash. But even so, giving each student a "home base" (of some sort) should be seriously considered by any school. (It's one of the key ideas influencing the design for the proposed AITE facility in Stamford, Connecticut, discussed on pages 9–15.)

Beyond providing students with their very own workstations, High Tech High's facility epitomizes what we were saying above about connectivity and continuity between spaces of various sizes and purposes. It's notable, for example, that each of the four workstation suites at High Tech High is adjoined by a "project room" to which students can go to participate in small-group projects and conferences—another way in which High Tech High's floorplan emulates that of many contemporary offices, in which groups of workstations are adjacent to smaller conference rooms that are immediately accessible by employees in need of a space to engage in discussion without disturbing others.

One-on-One Spaces. From the individual learning space—the place, that is, where a student pursues his or her own work, alone—it's a small step to the "one-on-one" space, where a student works with another student or discusses work with a teacher or other facilitator. Obviously, "individual" spaces and "one-on-one" spaces will often be the same: two students working on the same project may want to sit together in front of the same computer screen, and teachers may sometimes need to look over the shoulder of a student engaged in an individual task to discuss the project while he or she works on it.

Acoustical considerations come to the fore when one-on-one spaces are located within classrooms or other common areas. How can such spaces be designed or situated so that one-on-one conversations won't disrupt—or be disrupted by—activities or other conversations going on nearby? How can design help ensure that one-on-one discussions can be reasonably private? These questions interest us because we're fans of what, in architecture schools, is called the "desk crit"—in which the instructor and student together examine the student's work and in which the instructor gives the student a frank assessment of where he or she is doing well, where the work falls short, and where progress needs to be made. Since these open and honest interchanges aren't usually the kind of thing that a student (or teacher, for that matter) would want others to horn in on, a certain level of privacy is desirable. By the same token, it often makes sense to conduct this kind of critique "at the desk," that is, in the actual environment in which the student is performing the work. The challenge of seeking a balance between privacy (and the benefit of sharing ideas via "over the shoulder" conversations) and openness is similar to the challenge that architects face in designing open office environments, where one must weigh the pros and cons of ensuring good communications versus creating a disturbance.

Of course, some kinds of one-on-one conversations demand greater privacy than could be achieved in any shared setting. Tutorials and counseling sessions, as well as specific kinds of therapy required by students with physical or learning disabilities, call for small, private (sometimes soundproofed) spaces. The number and nature of these spaces must, of course, be determined on a school-by-school basis, keeping in mind the school's specific mission and program and the special needs of its student population. As Chapter 6 relates, for example, spaces for one-on-one teacher-child interaction are critical to autism education/treatment centers, especially during the early years of an autistic child's education. (Those spaces have their own special requirements—including adjacent observation rooms.)

Small-Group Spaces. Small-group learning spaces come next, as we travel up our Powers of Ten ladder of spatial connectivity and continuity. We've already mentioned one such space—the project room adjacent to each workstation suite at San Diego's High Tech High—but there are numerous other possibilities. In fact, High Tech High possesses other special-purpose, small-group spaces: a series of "seminar rooms" in which several students might gather with a teacher for group tutorial instruction that supplements the learning that occurs in the school's labs and studios. (High Tech High is notable in that it has no traditional "classrooms" per se, but rather a combination of specialized labs and studios, seminar rooms, and the workstation suites and project rooms discussed above.)

Other design strategies for facilitating small-group interaction include the "breakout spaces" that lie just outside the doors to the laboratories at the Greater Hartford Academy of Math and Science—very similar in essence to the breakout spaces that one might find in many a contemporary research and development facility, where such spaces spur informal collegial interaction. And specialized schools of whatever level might emulate contemporary elementary and middle schools, which often place kiva or agora spaces outside or between classrooms. (The word *kiva* comes from the name of the communal gathering place in the Native American pueblos of the Southwest; *agora* is the ancient Greek word for "marketplace," the public space in which philosophers like Socrates engaged the townspeople.) Sometimes, the kiva (or agora) will sit at the center of a cluster of classrooms; this type of multipurpose space can accommodate individual study, small-group study among students from a given class, or group learning among students from different classes or even different grades.

Yet another strategy for organizing space to facilitate small-group learning is embodied in the design for the Middlesex County Academy for Science, Mathematics, and Engineering Technologies (see pages 65–70), where small, wedge-shaped computer labs are set between paired classrooms. One noteworthy feature of these spaces—which can accommodate individual as well as small-group work—is that they are visually linked to the surrounding classrooms by interior windows, which permit supervision even when a teacher is not in the computer lab and which, just as important, make visible the continuity of learning from the classroom, to the small group, and to the individual student.

Our list of possible small-group learning spaces ought also to include outdoor spaces, whether these are styled as "outdoor classrooms" or just as places—equipped with benches, tables, amphitheater seating, or other components—where students can gather informally during fair weather.

Classrooms, Labs, and Studios. Let's start our discussion of the specialized-school classroom by asking a deliberatively provocative question. Especially in the context of theme-based specialized secondary schools, are traditional classrooms even necessary? Although in most cases the answer is probably "yes"—at least for certain subjects—we believe the question must be asked. It's clear to us that, for magnet or other theme-based education to realize its fully potential, we must move away from the educational model that sees the classroom as the necessary center, or core, of in-school learning.

As we mentioned earlier, San Diego's High Tech High has done away with the traditional classroom entirely. High Tech High is obviously a rare case, but one can see similar kinds of movement away from traditional classrooms at a number of the schools featured in Chapter 2's "Exemplary Projects." To take a few examples:

- Traditional classrooms are few at the Greater Hartford Academies building (pages 41–51); instead, most classes in both the Arts and Math and Science wings of that building are conducted in specialized laboratories and studios. (The Math and Science Academy does have some fairly typical classrooms for mathematics classes, but even the language-arts classes in the Arts Academy are held in specialized rooms, such as a living-room setting for the creative writing seminars.) Of course, it's true that the Greater Hartford Academies don't really need much in the way of traditional classroom space, since both operate half-day programs, and Academy students take many of the classes required for graduation at their home schools. But even so, the relative absence of traditional classrooms in this building is noteworthy.
- Even where a school's architectural design is largely based on a traditional classroom model—as at Las Vegas's Advanced Technologies Academy (pages 51–57)—classrooms may be so altered in actual use that they hardly resemble "classrooms" at all. At ATech, that's true of the classroom that houses the network-technology lab: over the course of time, that room's interior has been "rebuilt" by the lab's teacher and students so that it looks like the hands-on workshop that it is.
- On the pre-K, primary, and elementary level, the idea of the traditional classroom is challenged by, for example, Hartford, Connecticut's Montessori Magnet Elementary (pages 33–41). As befits the Montessori method, the classrooms in that school have a residential quality—with kitchens, eating areas, napping areas, and comfortably outfitted work-spaces—that distinguishes them from classrooms in most other pre-K–5 schools.

By raising the possibility of the traditional classroom's obsolescence, we're not at all suggesting that there's no need for learning experiences that bring together medium-size groups of students. Just the opposite, in fact. Many kinds of learning experiences work best with groups of 10–25 students—and groups of this "medium" size can play an important role in schools' nonacademic purposes: assisting in children's socialization, for example, or providing the right environment for learning the basics of democratic process. What we're saying is that the classroom itself—as traditionally conceived and designed—may be outmoded. On one hand, traditional classrooms can—and perhaps should—be replaced by a variety of specialized learning spaces that, depending on a school's mission, might include physics labs, dance studios, automotive-technology shops, "living rooms" for English seminars, and so on. On the other hand—especially on the pre-K–5 level—the traditional classroom concept can be expanded to facilitate a much wider range of internal configurations, and, hence, to accommodate a much greater variety of learning activities. At the very least, it's something to think about.

It should also be noted that the traditional classroom concept can perform very poorly when applied to certain kinds of medium-size group learning. When two of the compilers of this book visited the Museum Magnet Middle School in Yonkers, New York, we found ourselves pulled aside—*cornered* would be more like it!—by two computer-lab instructors eager to find a listening ear for their complaints about the design of the room in which their classes are held. What was so instructive about our discussion was that their computer lab was so very typical—the sort of computer lab that one might find in schools across the United States. It was modeled, of course, on the traditional stand-and-deliver classroom: a teacher's station at the front, and rows of stationary tables, each holding five or six PCs, spanning the rest of the room. Space was tight, so there was no easy way for instructors to move through the room and behind students' chairs, to supervise work and offer help, or even to make sure the students were doing what they were supposed to. Lighting in the room was abominable, that is, for the room's purpose. The overhead direct-lighting fixtures created glare, so the lights had to be dimmed for students to be able to see what was going on onscreen. (A window wall facing the corridor provided some ambient illumination within the room.)

Hearing these instructors' reasons for their consternation—which included the fact that their suggestions for configuring and outfitting the lab had been ignored by the facility's designers—we were reminded of the following thought, from Charles H. Stallard and Julie S. Cocker's groundbreaking 2001 book, *The Promise of Technology in Schools: The Next 20 Years*. Stallard and Cocker write: "The persistence of traditional school architecture may be the best example of the lack of awareness and understanding . . . of how IT has impacted the rest of society and how society is changing." To which we would add: the persistence of the traditional classroom model may be the best example of the lack of awareness on the part of school designers and planners of how information technologies work and how their use can best be taught.

For its purpose, that Yonkers magnet middle school computer lab was a disaster—crowded, poorly lit, and difficult to navigate. More worrisome, however, is that this ill-considered way of designing IT spaces remains so common, even years into the IT revolution. It's to be hoped that the coming wireless revolution—especially the ability for students to wirelessly access in-school networks and the Internet from anywhere within the school building—will also revolutionize the design of technology-education environments. But that transformation may well entail abandoning the traditional classroom model and looking elsewhere for inspiration.

Let's assume, however, that the classroom—in more or less its traditional form—will remain useful for at least certain kinds of purposes in at least some kinds of specialized schools. What kinds of changes in classroom design might be advisable? We can think of several possibilities. First, there's a need, in many specialized school contexts, for classrooms to incorporate much more storage space—of different kinds—than is typical in most standard classroom design. The reason is simple: specialized schools of many different types encourage hands-on, exploratory learning in which students make, build, and create things. Not only is there need for room to safely store all that stuff once it's been created, but there's an equally great need for a place to store the materials from which it's made. At almost all the schools—newer as well as older—that we visited in compiling this book, storage and related issues were critical: At Las Vegas's ATech, the separate storage room adjacent to an engineering classroom was barely large enough to hold the components of a shed that first-year engineering students were building. At the Greater Hartford Academy of the Arts, the director pointed out that backstage set-building and storage areas were too small (this was the one fault he found with the facility). At another magnet academy, a librarian complained that—barely two years after the school had opened—the media center had just about run out of vital storage space. And these are all thoughtfully designed facilities!

Having crusaded for more storage space, however, we're now going to say something that might sound contradictory: we believe that, in many cases, schools might benefit if classrooms were smaller than the current standard. Here, we're talking about programmatic space—the space within the classroom that's actually used for learning purposes. We've already made reference to the difficulty, within a shared environment like a classroom, of establishing adequate acoustical separation between, say, a one-on-one conference in one part of the space and a group activity nearby. The question naturally arises: how many different, acoustically competing activities should a classroom be required simultaneously to house? To aid in that acoustical separation, why not shave some square footage off the classroom and add it to other learning spaces in the facility—kivas, breakout rooms, and so on?

On our travels to various specialized-school facilities, we happened upon another rationale for making classrooms a bit smaller. At one magnet middle school, we were informed that classrooms were deliberately sized to hold no more than 25 students. Why? So that the school could not physically accommodate larger class groups in the event that it was pressured to increase class sizes. A brilliant (and somewhat "subversive") design maneuver, we thought.

There's much more that could be said about classroom design, but let's limit ourselves, here, to just a few more ideas:

- Though a great deal of lip service is paid to the virtues of interdisciplinary learning—especially in the specialized-school context—not nearly enough has been done, from a design point of view, to facilitate cross-disciplinary instruction. One tried-and-true way of enhancing opportunities for interdisciplinary education (and team teaching) is to make the walls between classrooms movable. Granted, placing demountable walls between classrooms is a relatively expensive option, but that expense may be worth it if it creates opportunities for teachers (and classes) to work together in ways that cross disciplinary boundaries.[4]
- Students benefit from "nonprecious" learning environments—spaces where they can engage in hands-on learning without having to worry that they'll do damage to the architectural fabric of the room.[5] This is the attitude that many artists take toward their studios, and art-studio spaces in schools are often designed in a nonprecious manner so that it doesn't much matter if paint gets splattered, and so on. But what we're recommending is the more widespread application of the concept to at least certain classroom-type environments, to give students greater freedom to build things—make stuff—when building and making serve an educational purpose. This suggestion directly connects with what we, in the beginning pages of this chapter, call "anti-architecture": the nonprecious space is designed, of course, but it's designed to be as free as possible of the architectural elements that connote "design" to most people.

Large-Group Spaces. From the medium-size environment (classroom, studio, and lab), we now move to the large-group learning space. We've already talked about the desirability, in certain contexts, of installing movable walls between classrooms in order to foster team teaching and interdisciplinary learning. But that strategy can only bring together two—or perhaps a few—class groups. On occasion—and we believe such occasions should be rather frequent—the entire school needs to come together as a community. Different schools accommodate large-group assemblies in different ways:

- *Atriums/lobbies.* Some schools have large atrium or lobby spaces capable of holding all, or many, of a school's students at the same time. That's the case, for example, at the Yonkers MicroSociety Magnet mentioned earlier in this chapter; there, the central atrium space—called Freedom Square—is large and open enough to accommodate a variety of large-group activities. The day we visited the school, Freedom Square was playing host to a series of Thanksgiving banquets, each of which brought together several class groups (as well as parents who'd assisted in the preparation of the food). Obviously, however, such spaces don't generally work well for performances, "town meetings," and other, similar large-group events.

- *Cafetoriums.* Because full-scale auditoriums (to which we'll return in a moment) are so expensive to build, many schools are forced to compromise—making cafeteria spaces do double-duty, when necessary, as assembly spaces. These "cafetoriums" are often outfitted with permanent or portable stages, sound and lighting equipment, and other features that facilitate their transformation from lunchrooms to auditoriums. Well, sort of. The trouble is, cafeterias are never easily adapted to other purposes, for a couple of reasons. First, there's no way to rake the floor, so sight lines from the seating to the stage or platform are always somewhat impaired. Second, and more important, cafeterias are almost never acoustically appropriate for assembly-type purposes as they have to be kept clean, which means they're full of hard, smooth surfaces that can easily be wiped down or mopped. Acousticians call these surfaces "reflective": they *reflect* sound waves, bouncing sound around inside the room (which is why school lunchrooms are often so noisy). Yes, there are acoustical treatments of various sorts that can be applied to diminish the din, but the result is seldom entirely satisfactory. The cafetorium option is better than nothing, certainly, but—having designed a number of such spaces ourselves—that's about the most we can say for it. (Using gymnasiums for assemblies has, by the way, similar drawbacks.)

- *Large multipurpose rooms.* A better option—especially for smaller schools—is the large multipurpose room, outfitted with a flexible furniture system that enables the room to be quickly reconfigured as changing purposes dictate. (Such a room will probably require storage space where the furniture can be put away when it's not needed.) This is the option chosen by the designers of Hartford, Connecticut's Montessori Magnet Elementary, whose multipurpose room can support learning experiences that bring together several class groups, as well as other kinds of meetings (receptions for parents, etc.).

The Hartford Montessori Magnet has an advantage that many specialized schools do not: it shares a campus, and therefore resources, with three other magnet schools. The Learning Corridor campus, of which the Montessori school is part, has a Commons Building—where a shared media center and food-preparation service are located—as well as a theater (see pages 50–51) that is available for use by each of the campus's schools. On those comparatively rare occasions when the Montessori school requires a full-scale auditorium, it can book the theater.

That sort of solution—grouping specialized schools together to take advantage of economies of scale—is, we believe, a viable one, especially in urban areas. Since, as we say above, so many specialized schools have relatively small populations, it may only be by joining forces with other such schools that they can afford the full complement of amenities that other, larger schools might enjoy all by themselves.

Another word needs to be said about auditoriums: at many schools, full-scale, purpose-built auditoriums might well be considered a needless expense because such spaces are used relatively infrequently. But there are ways of increasing an auditorium's utilization—and thus of making it a more essential space from a programmatic point of view. One approach might be to equip the auditorium for use as a lecture hall. Another—which we've seen implemented at a number of schools—is to design the auditorium so that portions of the "house" can be easily be partitioned off to serve as separate learning spaces, allowing the overall space to be used simultaneously for several different purposes involving different-sized groups. In a variation on this theme, in one of the magnet schools we visited, a classroom-type space—equipped with whiteboard and movable desks—was situated in the theater directly behind the stage. This interesting solution permits theater classes to move directly from classroom-type instruction to hands-on stagecraft whenever such a transition makes educational sense.

Of course, these days, an entire school community can be "brought together" virtually as well as physically. Intensifying the sense of community, of shared purpose, and of continuity and connectivity across grade-levels is certainly a major purpose of the television-broadcast program so extensively employed at the Gilbert Magnet Elementary School in Las Vegas, Nevada. (See the sidebar.)

TV TECHNOLOGY FOR THE YOUNGER SET

At the Gilbert Magnet Elementary in Las Vegas, Nevada, every school day begins with a TV broadcast—viewed in every classroom—of student-produced programming. To a visitor, the programs are amazing: the news and features that make up these daily broadcasts—produced by elementary school writers, editors, camera people, and on-air "talent"—are of nearly professional quality, right down to the special graphic effects that enhance some of the segments. About the only thing that distinguishes this programming from the local nightly news (aside from content, of course) is that the nine- and ten-year-old anchors are often better, more natural performers—and in some cases better readers of the teleprompter—than their adult equivalents.

Architecturally, the school is no great shakes: the main building dates from the mid-1960s, and though it has some admirable features—including a large central room where a number of class groups can gather for performances and other events connected with the school's multiculturally oriented curriculum—the facility is otherwise unremarkable. The school began life as an ordinary elementary, then for a brief period became a "sixth-grade center" when the Clark County school district experimented with grouping lower-grades students together by grade (that experiment was soon abandoned). About ten years ago, the school was reorganized as a magnet, and since then it has flourished. Not only has it achieved and maintained target enrollments, but about 90 percent of its students matriculate from first all the way through fifth grade. It's a very lively, vibrant place. The school's arts focus is everywhere in evidence—classrooms and common areas are chock-a-block with brightly colored, student artwork.

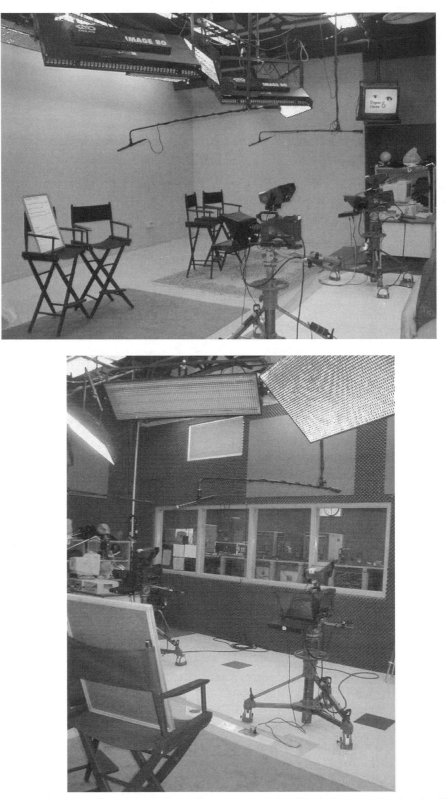

Figures 7.3 and 7.4.   The TV studio at Las Vegas's Gilbert Magnet School is of almost professional caliber—but it's been designed with elementary school children in mind. *Photographs by Charles R. Cassidy.*

It was about five years ago that Gilbert added a performing-arts building to its campus. The new building—which houses a large theater as well as a broadcast television studio and control room—stands on a lot next to the one occupied by the older elementary school building. The theater is well equipped and well used, but it's the TV studio that's the real heart of Gilbert's arts curriculum.

Gilbert kids begin using the studio as early as the second half of their first-grade year: six-year-olds attend taping sessions in the studio, where they sit on risers and "learn appropriate audience behavior," according to Gilbert's magnet program director, Tim Dearman. By second grade, some students are already appearing on camera (reading the day's lunch menu from the teleprompter, for example). Hands-on training in the use of the studio's equipment begins in third grade, and by fourth and fifth grade, the kids are doing more or less everything all by themselves—with the gentle guidance, of course, of an in-house broadcast media specialist. They even work "on location"— taking portable videocams into the school's hallways and classrooms to tape stories "as they are happening" and engaging fellow students in "person on the street" interviews.

Designing the technical aspects of a TV studio that would be used by half-pint journalists and producers was a challenging task. According to Ken Baird, the system engineer who designed Gilbert's setup, it was critically important that equipment be chosen to ensure that it could be operated rather simply, that it would be durable, and that it would not become too quickly obsolete. (Commercial broadcast operations can replace expensive equipment frequently, but the components employed in Gilbert's system would have to last an average of five to seven years.) According to Baird—whose Las Vegas–based consulting firm, Visual Communications Systems, has designed broadcast systems as elaborate as that for the Command and Control Center at the 2002 Winter Olympics in Salt Lake City, Utah—the primary components of Gilbert's system are software-based, "so that when you upgrade the software, the system is upgraded." Baird warns schools against choosing hardware-based components that may be initially cheaper but rapidly become obsolete.

The Gilbert system is a sensible mix of industrial- and consumer-grade equipment. For example, the three Sony cameras used in the studio are professional caliber, as are the pedestals they sit on—to ensure that this expensive equipment could weather a fair amount of inadvertent abuse. The videocams that kids use "in the field" are consumer-grade digital video recorders; in this application, cheaper consumer-grade products make more sense, since the risk of breakage is higher. (The DV format was chosen because the consumer orientation of such products means that prices are likely to continue to fall over time.) But the three VCRs in the studio's control are, once again, industrial grade to ensure their long-term durability. The software-based system that ties all the components together allows for the easy integration of "disposable," consumer-grade products and industrial-grade components. Baird says that the system has undergone five software upgrades in as many years, allowing it to keep pace with developments in the field and "to do everything done in a major studio today."

That capacity and flexibility are a great spur to children's creativity, and Baird applauds the extent to which Gilbert has integrated the TV broadcast program into the school's curriculum and into its life. "You *can't* stop students once you've got them excited," he says—and Gilbert does everything to inspire the kids' enthusiasm and give them the freest possible creative rein. Baird stresses, too, that learning how to produce TV programming provides children with valuable life lessons: creating a daily news program makes students aware of what it means to be "on deadline," and using an hour-long class to develop a 30- or 60-second spot teaches the value of perfectionism.

What's more, the system will soon play a role in involving parents more deeply in the life of the school. A districtwide gigabit backbone is now in the works. Once it's set up, Gilbert parents will be able to electronically access the programming their children have created—not just "today's news," but also past programs stored in the network's archive.

Connections to the Wider World. In recent years, schools have become much more "permeable" than they used to be. Many schools—including some specialized schools—open their doors to community users, both after school hours and, in some cases, while school is in session. School planners and designers have recognized that the presence of a new school building within a neighborhood has a real impact on that neighborhood—and in many places, they have strived to ensure that the school will benefit the surrounding area's residents, businesses, and institutions. Moreover, the telecommunications revolution of the past decade has "opened the school's doors" in a virtual, electronic way: students in many of the nation's schools have immediate access, via speedy broadband connections, to the resources of the Internet; remote learning communities are increasingly being brought together by distance learning; and parents and others enjoy electronic access to what's happening "inside" a school through e-mail, school websites, and Intranet-type networks of various sorts.

Designing a school to enhance its connectivity and continuity with the "outside world" has, therefore, several aspects:

1. The organization of space—especially the relation of academic areas to shared, common areas that might also be used by community members—within the building.
2. The siting and landscaping of the school—and related issues involving, for example, lessening the impact of school-related traffic on the surrounding neighborhood and appropriate planning for the school's use of neighborhood resources.
3. The design of specialized spaces and the implementation of other strategies to enhance a school's electronic connectivity to the wider world beyond its doors.

The second and third of these aspects are discussed in great detail elsewhere in this book. (See especially Chapter 5, "Finding a Home: The Facilities Side of the Charter School Debate"; Chapter 9, "School Technology: A Sensible, Future-Oriented Approach"; and Chapter 10, "Site Design and Landscape Architecture for Urban Magnet Schools.") But we do need, here, to take a closer look at the first aspect in the list above: organizing space to foster community use.

Permitting individuals and groups from the surrounding community to avail themselves of some of a school's resources and facilities can be a great help in fostering community acceptance of the school and integrating the school into the life of the community. The list of possible "outside" users—and of the core, support, and other school-facility spaces they might use—is potentially quite a long one. Local theater groups might book a school's auditorium for rehearsals and performances. Municipal government agencies might hold town meetings or public hearings in an auditorium or cafeteria. Voluntary associations of various sorts might use in-school auditoriums and conference rooms for meetings. Nearby community colleges and other educational institutions might relish the chance to use a school's classrooms or other facilities for continuing-education programs. Parents and other community members might like the opportunity to work out, mornings or evenings, in a school's weight-training room. And so on.

In designing for such uses, two major issues must be considered:

- *Safety and security.* Protecting the school building and its contents from vandalism and theft—and, more important, protecting schoolchildren and other members of the school community from harm—are obviously the most crucial requirements. Often, adequate protection can be ensured by grouping together the core spaces that will be accessed by community users, situating all of them near a main entry or lobby space, and "zoning" off the rest of the building (including academic areas and storerooms)—making sure, of course, that areas to which outsiders are denied access can be locked down. (Such a strategy was employed, for example, at the Rotella Magnet Elementary School in Waterbury, Connecticut; see pages 15–19.) The issue becomes more complicated, however, in cases where community groups will be permitted to use classrooms as well as when outsiders are allowed to use certain school facilities—the media center, say—during school hours. Does such a situation require the posting of security personnel throughout the facility during periods of after-hours use? Maybe, but there are electronic solutions on the horizon: for instance, all visitors might be issued electronic badges at the front desk—badges that would allow their movement through the facility to be continuously tracked from a central location. Of course, each school will have to decide the particular combination of physical, electronic, and human security measures appropriate for its mix of uses.
- *Accommodating community users.* This can actually be a trickier matter, since accommodating the needs of community users may involve determining ahead of time who those users might be—or which potential users the school might want to attract. Cases in point: a local theatrical company might be much more likely to book a school's auditorium if that auditorium is outfitted with professional-caliber lighting and sound equipment (as well as adequate backstage set-building areas, dressing rooms, etc.) and if the auditorium has a box office and a roomy, comfortable lobby for pretheater and intermission gatherings, and so on. Local sports teams will undoubtedly require full-size basketball courts, regulation-size athletics fields, and the like. Local visual artists and arts groups will be enticed by extensive, well-lit gallery spaces. These are obviously commonsense determinations, but they need to be carefully worked out during the planning stage. We might also mention that designers of an elementary school that intends to invite community users into its facility need to take pains to ensure that at least some of the furniture and facilities (e.g., toilet rooms) in the common areas are sized for adult users.

WHERE GREAT ARCHITECTURE HAPPENS

A brilliant school designer once said, "Great architecture happens between the net and the gross square footage." In other words, the real opportunities for architectural inventiveness and creativity often occur in the spaces that are not designated for programmatic uses per se—for example, hallways, lobbies, stairwells, courtyards, and so on. As we see in some of the exemplary projects featured in Chapter 2, these are indeed the spaces where specialized school design can really shine: Think, for example, of the multipurpose "nodes" placed outside each classroom's corridor door in the Montessori Magnet Elementary in Hartford, Connecticut, or of that school's wondrously designed courtyard (pages 40–41). Or think of the workstations that line the hallways outside the labs at the Greater Hartford Academy of Math and Science, or the continuous benches that skirt the window wall facing the Greater Hartford Academies building courtyard (see below). Or of the gallery spaces—some displaying student work, others housing changing exhibits from the National Design Museum—that greet the visitor entering Philadelphia's Charter High for Architecture + Design (pages 57–58). Creative responses, all, to spaces that are too often neglected as mere connectors between one programmatically "valuable" place and another.

"Nonprogrammatic" spaces—if well designed—can actually be a great boon to a school's mission and program. Corridor breakout spaces and workstations provide venues for individual and small-group study. Hallway benches allow students to interact informally—and, at the Greater Hartford Academies building, allow students in the arts curriculum to get acquainted, and share ideas, with their colleagues from math and science. The Montessori Elementary's specially built nodes and the garden planters in its courtyard encourage playful, hands-on learning. And the gallery spaces at CHAD and other schools discussed in this book—for example, the Museum Magnet Middle School in Yonkers, New York—offer opportunities for the school community to celebrate itself and focus attention on students' creative achievement.

Figure 7.5. At the Greater Hartford Academies building, a continuous bench along the window wall facing the courtyard provides a place for students from the Math and Science Academy and Arts Academy to study alone or to meet for informal conversation. *Photograph © 2001 by Robert Benson; used by permission.*

Designers of magnet schools—especially magnets that are fully or almost completely funded by a state's department of education—may enjoy greater-than-usual freedom in paying real design attention to these spaces, because designs for such projects may not be as efficiency-driven as those for conventional schools. (Budgets may contain a little more elbow room, that is.) But no school design ought to ignore these spaces, which—as the examples show—can heighten the connectivity and continuity that we've been emphasizing throughout so much of this chapter.

ADDITIONAL DESIGN CONSIDERATIONS

Other architectural issues may sometimes come to the fore in specialized-school design:

- *Support/administrative spaces.* Certain kinds of specialized schools—we're thinking especially of education/treatment centers for autistic children (see Chapter 6)—require a much greater than usual number of support and administrative spaces. Offices, conference rooms, observation rooms, therapy rooms—the list can grow quite long, especially when a school must accommodate a range of professionals (therapists, specialists of various types), and when the school does some of its own fund-raising. (Autism education/treatment centers, even where they receive public dollars, must often supplement their operations budgets through their own development work.)
- *Special-needs populations.* In fact, the "special needs" that identify special-needs populations can often have as great an impact on overall facility design as does curriculum. Autism education/treatment centers are an obvious case in point, because their students' exceptional needs can dictate everything from the sizing of learning spaces, to lighting, to the color palette used in furniture and finishes, to the quality of the center's mechanical system (see Chapter 6). And schools for other kinds of special-needs students will carry their own specialized design requirements. For instance, at East Hartford, Connecticut's Polaris Center—a recently fully renovated residential and day school for emotionally and behaviorally troubled adolescents—durability of building materials was of greater-than-usual concern, as were security and safety measures (to make sure students remain on site, as well as to lessen the chances for self-harm). The Polaris center's designers were also more than ordinarily concerned about the affect of design on students' emotional well-being.
- *Magnet academies.* Sometimes, high school magnet programs are organized as "academies" that are housed in or attached to conventional comprehensive high schools. That's the case, for example, at the Brien McMahon High School in Norwalk, Connecticut, which houses the Center for Global Studies magnet program (pages 62–65). The concept here is much like the "house" or "school within a school" concept that's widely employed to create smaller, more manageable and caring learning communities within especially large schools. The academy arrangement can offer some real advantages to a magnet program, whose students can use the comprehensive high school's gym, media center, and other resources that its small program could not afford were it housed in its own, stand-alone facility. (Magnet program students often take some of their classes within the comprehensive high school as well.) There are, however, some potential drawbacks. Some of these disadvantages can't really be offset architecturally—for example, the magnet-academy stu-

dents often have more, and better, technological resources at their disposal than do students in the conventional high school program, which can lead to envy on the part of students in the regular program (and also the teachers who teach them). Such intramural rivalry must be dealt with carefully by administrators to prevent resentment from growing. There's also the danger that the magnet academy might lose its unique self—be swallowed up by the larger school in which it makes its home. Architectural design *can*, to a certain extent, guard against this happening—for example, by giving the magnet-academy portion of the school a distinctive design vocabulary and by making sure that the magnet program's academic facilities are somehow physically separated from the school at large.

- *Spaces for parents.* Parental enthusiasm and involvement are often critical to the success of a magnet or other specialized school. Schools have therefore sometimes taken the step of "inviting the parents in" by creating special spaces just for them. Parent rooms should be comfortably outfitted and furnished with conference tables and plenty of chairs for group meetings, as well as with computer stations so that parents can easily access the school's network on site.

- *Spaces for teachers.* Sadly, teachers are often *the* most neglected constituency when it comes to planning and designing a new school building—and on the whole, specialized schools are not much better than conventional schools at accommodating teachers' needs for space in which to study and prepare lessons, relax, interact with colleagues, and confer with students and parents outside the classroom. There are a variety of ways to address these needs through architectural design, including the provision of separate offices, shared departmental offices (allowing for faculty interaction as well as individual work), and adequately sized and comfortably furnished faculty lounges and lunchrooms. To ensure that this important aspect of good school-facility design doesn't fall through the cracks, however, it's critically important that teachers be invited to participate in the planning and design process, and that the desires of individual faculty be balanced with the needs of departments to achieve the right (and affordable) solution.

Talking about how to address teachers' needs brings us neatly to the point with which we'd like to end this chapter: the critical importance of involving the educators who will use a building in the planning and design of the whole facility. That, in turn, may involve encouraging teachers to think about school design in a truly futuristic way. We should let educators be our visionaries, for it is they who really know about the nuts and bolts of educational process—and it is they who, more than anyone else, will guide our children into tomorrow.

NOTES

1. For more on the MicroSociety approach to education, visit the MicroSociety website at www.micro society.org.

2. For more on the Wexler-Grant Community School, see an earlier book in this series, Edwin T. Merritt et al., *The Middle School of the Future: A Focus on Exploration* (ScarecrowEducation, 2004), pp. 13–14.

3. For more on Dr. Marie Carbo and her work, visit the National Reading Styles Institute website at www.nrsi.com/nrsi.htm.

4. Very creative use is made of demountable walls between classrooms at the Ocoee Middle School, Ocoee, Florida, which is featured in one of this series' previous volumes. See Merritt et al., *The Middle School of the Future*, pp. 17–20.

5. See Merritt et al., *The Middle School of the Future*, where we make a case for the inclusion of "nonprecious" learning environments in most schools.

A Draft Magnet School Operations Plan

Each of the previous volumes in the Schools of the Future series has featured a "Draft Educational Specification" (for an elementary, a middle, and a high school, respectively). "Ed specs," as they are called, serve as the foundational documents for most conventional schools, laying out—sometimes in great detail—a proposed school's mission and programmatic requirements. Magnet schools, by contrast, typically rely on a somewhat different kind of foundational document: an operations plan. Magnet school operations plans differ markedly from case to case, depending on the proposed magnet's mission, its theme or career focus, the community or communities it is intended to serve, the funding mechanisms that will pay for its construction and support ongoing operations, and so on. The operations plan that follows, developed by LEARN, southeastern/coastal Connecticut's Regional Education Service Center (and reprinted here with permission), is presented not as a "typical" operations plan—there could be no such thing—but rather as an exemplary document of its type. (Note that the Marine Science Magnet project described here is still under development.) After the operations plan has been produced, the architects engaged to design a magnet school will produce a programmatic specification for the facility.

OPERATIONS PLAN: MARINE SCIENCE HIGH SCHOOL OF SOUTHEASTERN CONNECTICUT, MAY 2001

School Vision and Design

The mission of the Marine Science High School of Southeastern Connecticut, a model regional collaborative among the towns and related agencies of southeastern Connecticut, is to prepare students for marine-related employment and/or higher education by addressing a wide range of marine-related topics and disciplines with a challenging, experiential curriculum responsive to the diverse interests of a broad spectrum of students.

Guiding Statements

- Students will acquire and apply both practical skills and theoretical knowledge.
- The school will be founded and operated upon an ongoing partnership among educators, industry, and other community resources.
- The core curriculum and related activities of the Marine Science High School of Southeast-

137

Figure 8.1. An early computer rendering of the proposed Marine Science Magnet shows the facility at a possible harborfront location in southeastern Connecticut. *Image: Fletcher-Thompson, Inc.*

ern Connecticut will focus on marine subjects and current and future marine-related opportunities.
- Direct access to experts in marine science, aquaculture, and related technologies will be crucial to student success.
- The school will serve as a resource to the region by:
    - providing professional development for teachers
    - sharing innovative marine technologies
    - providing continued training for adult learners
- The school will be committed to innovation, flexibility, and continuous improvement.
- The school will foster:
    - critical thinking
    - problem solving
    - transferable employment skills
- The school will be committed to environmental stewardship.

Approximately 250 students will make up the school enrollment. It is anticipated that no more than 30 percent of the student population will reside in any one town. The basis for the responsive curriculum will be studies of the ocean and related sciences and technologies. These related sciences and technologies include, but are not limited to, aquaculture, environmental studies of the ocean, and the marine trades.

The Marine Science High School of Southeastern Connecticut curriculum will focus upon career and higher education opportunities in marine science including chemistry, pathology, anatomy, physiology, bacteriology, nutrition, and genetics. The curriculum will also include fin-fish and shellfish farming, nautical science, and marine technologies.

The school will provide a college preparatory and marine career preparatory program with a marine education focus. Students will engage in theoretical and applied courses whose basis will be oceanography, marine biology, aquaculture, chemistry, and marine technology. Out-of-school-time activities will include internships, service learning, commercial and recreational fishing trips, and community activities related to the ocean and its environment.

Community involvement will occur via combined community and business support. The following institutions had varying levels of involvement in the regional planning as requested by the Commissioner of Education:

- Ledyard Agri-Science program, Ledyard Public Schools
- Waterford Public Schools
- Stonington Public Schools
- Connecticut Maritime Coalition
- OceanTechnology Foundation
- The Connecticut Marine Trades Association Connecticut Marine Industry Cluster
- UCONN (University of Connecticut) at Avery Point
- Mystic Seaport
- Project Oceanology
- Mystic Aquarium

It is anticipated that these and other organizations will be involved in the continued development and support of the school.

Learning Objectives

- Students enrolled in the Marine Science High School of Southeastern Connecticut, in cooperation with their teaching staff and families, will:
  - demonstrate a sense of self as a learner
  - demonstrate a sense of responsibility to self and others
  - demonstrate effective functioning, individually, and as a member of a group
  - demonstrate the ability to think critically, solve problems, reason, and question
  - use language to communicate, convey, and interpret meaning
- The Marine Science High School will encourage the learning of environmental ocean sciences, including wise natural resource management and an appreciation of coastal waters for commerce, recreation, and food production.
- The Marine Science High School will provide supervised occupational experiences to build a basis for a growing experienced future marine workforce.

- The school will provide continuous educational opportunities for families to participate in the education of their children.
- The school's program will engage the families and students in regular multicultural activities to promote awareness, acceptance, and appreciation of diversity.

Education Program

The Marine Science High School of Southeastern Connecticut . . . will offer full-day sessions. The curriculum will be offered in a series of three 12-week modules per year. Students will access the rich community resources in southeastern Connecticut. As requested by the Commissioner of Education, LEARN researched the impact of operating this school on such programs as Ledyard Agri-Science, Project Oceanology, Mystic Aquarium, and Mystic Seaport. The planning consortium and other dedicated community and business members have committed to designing a unique, creative offering that complements and enhances the already marine-rich environment of the shoreline. The school will promote social, emotional, physical, cognitive, and creative growth of high school students. The school will collaborate with the home district of each student for ease of transition, achievement of graduation requirements, and so forth. The ever-evolving curriculum will be based upon marine science, aquaculture, and marine technologies. Technology skills will be a continuous thread throughout the curriculum. All students will develop proficient English language skills. The school will comply with all federal and state requirements regarding Limited English Proficient (LEP) students and students identified with special needs and work closely with the home school district. . . .

Instruction will integrate reading, writing, speaking, listening, computing, calculating, hypothesizing, creating, assessing, and practicing. Instruction will recognize the developmental aspects of students' learning. Assessment of student learning will be directly related to the curriculum and the concepts assessed on the CAPT (Connecticut Academic Performance Test) exams. Critical thinking, problem solving, life skills, employability, and real experience will be the essence of instruction, professional development, and administrative reflection. The planning committee members recognize that the most effective way to increase learning is to integrate concepts and disciplines.

Curriculum

The Marine Science High School of Southeastern Connecticut curriculum will focus upon career and higher education opportunities in marine science, including chemistry, pathology, anatomy, physiology, bacteriology, nutrition, and genetics. The curriculum will also include fin-fish and shellfish farming, nautical science, and marine technologies.

The school will provide a college preparatory and marine career preparatory program with a marine education focus. Students will engage in theoretical and applied courses whose basis will be marine technology, oceanography, marine biology, aquaculture, and marine chemistry. Out-of-school-time activities will include internships, commercial and recreational fishing, and community activities related to the ocean and its environment. . . .

All students will participate in community service, internships, and on-the-job training. Furthermore, all students will be required to pass a swimming test, a CPR and first-aid test, and a safe boating test.

Each class will incorporate projects that improve students' communication skills, reading skills, writing skills, technical writing skills, and technical presentation skills. Teachers will utilize interdisciplinary approaches for classes. Internships, on-the-job training, field experiences, and field trips will be incorporated into each course as appropriate.

Student Assessment

Student assessment will be closely tied to the school's curriculum. Connecticut's Common Core of Learning and subject-specific Curriculum Frameworks as delineated for 9–12 students will serve as the basis for continued curriculum development and enhancement. Given the nature of the school and the curriculum, assessment will need to be a collaborative endeavor among all the staff and community partners.

Assessment will be formative and summative, with an emphasis on performance-based and portfolio development including collection of student work samples; student, teacher, and parent reflections; and teacher observations to supplement criteria-referenced testing modeled on the CAPT. The linkages to Connecticut State Department of Education assessments will include standard requirements for high school graduation.

Specifically addressing performance-based assessments, each graduating student will be required to produce a final project or product as a result of his or her work with the marine industry. Each student will be required to create and maintain a cumulative portfolio that will be reviewed by the teaching staff. Time for reflection will be an important part of the students' portfolios. There will be exit criteria performance-based assessments in each of the applied marine science areas.

The students will also have traditional assessments in the way of academic tests, quizzes, and homework. Students will have opportunities for skill exhibition both in the classroom and as a part of their required internships. Community partners will collaborate with school staff for assessment of students participating in internships and on-the-job experience.

Individual Education Plans for students with identified special needs will be developed, implemented, and monitored in conjunction with the home school district.

Monthly team reviews and teacher and administrative reflections will serve the dual purposes of monitoring student progress and providing an impetus for programmatic change.

Additional program assessment will take place through family surveys related to how the family views their student's progress and learning and parent satisfaction questionnaires related to the curriculum, staff, administration, and environment of the school.

School Governance

The continued development of the magnet school will look to increase cooperation by continuing and expanding the regional involvement of appropriate community members. It is hoped that by continuing the planning and development during the construction phase of the school, a definitive balance of theoretical, academic, and practical features of the school will be reached. By continuing this planning, the likelihood of achieving the mission of the school increases. The continued planning and development process will allow the region to maintain a mission-based focus by organizing and prioritizing all goals and tasks with maximum participation.

Day-to-day management responsibilities will fall primarily to the director of the school and his or her administrative team and the partners of the school. The principles of consensus decision-making, including total quality processes, will be incorporated into staff meetings, parent meetings, steering committee meetings, and board meetings.

In consultation with the governance committee, LEARN will be the fiscal agent. As such, LEARN is responsible for fiscal management of the school, supervision of the school, supervision of the staff, recruitment and enrollment of families, local and state reporting, and policy implementation. LEARN, in conjunction with the governance committee and partner committee, will develop any new policies that may be required to meet the unique needs of the school.

New employees will be recruited and employed by LEARN. All teachers will have appropriate certification, experience, and expertise specific to the mission of the school. Consultants, including business owners and those in higher education, will be utilized to enhance the instruction, curriculum content, professional development, and practical experiences.

The school calendar will include 180 educational days for students and a maximum of 187 days for teaching staff. . . . Enrichment classes, hands-on experience, internships, and work opportunities with a focus on achieving the mission of the school will be offered. Programs for families will be incorporated in the culture of the school.

The school calendar of Waterford Public Schools will be the calendar used by the program to ensure ease of access and smooth operation of the school.

Evidence of Support

School District Support is evidenced by the attached original "Applications to Establish a Regional Vocational Agriculture Center" and governance agreement. *[Editor's note: Attachments are not included here.]* These were submitted in 1998 to the SDE. Along with these applications, Ledyard Public Schools submitted a proposal to expand their current program. The Commissioner requested that one regional proposal be designed and submitted. A regional committee comprising representatives from education, community resources, business, and the private sector has been meeting since February 1999. The committee has submitted a building construction grant application in June 1999.

Other evidence of support can be found in the results of the regional survey. This survey, developed with the assistance of SDE, was distributed to 3,000 students in (grades 5, 6, and 7). Of the 3,000 distributed, 1,150 surveys were returned, revealing a strong interest in a school with a marine science, aquaculture, and other marine technologies.

A 1997 survey of marine-trade labor indicated the need for employees with skills in all of the marine trades and technology. Marinas, boatyards, and charter boat owners all have expressed the need for qualified employees. The expansion of the Mystic Aquarium, UCONN Avery Point, and Pfizer, Inc., as well as the creation of the Connecticut Maritime Coalition, all highlight southeastern Connecticut as an area rich in opportunities in aquaculture and marine industries, from apprenticeships to highly sophisticated technical, research, and management positions. The Ocean Technology Foundation, as a prime contractor to the Department of Economic and Community Development, explored the opportunities of creating a Marine Cluster. To that end, 11 companies were recruited to form the Connecticut Marine Cluster Advisory Board. Two members of the Ocean Technology Foundation have been involved in this recent planning process. The Marine Cluster is positioning Connecticut as a recognized world-class marine center by enhancing the competitive position of Connecticut marine businesses in the global marketplace. As a result of the Ocean Technology Foundation's work with the Marine Cluster, there is clear support for this school. The executive director of the Connecticut Maritime Coalition has been involved with the Planning Consortium since March 1999. The marine industry hopes that the school will "challenge students and develop critical thinkers, with multi-functional skills across a wide array of disciplines." They are committed to "employment opportunities for graduates as well as participation in curriculum formation, validation, classroom instruction, internships, partnerships, and funding." It is clear that partnerships with business and higher education have been established for the school.

A report on the world's fisheries found that nearly 70 percent of fish stocks are fully exploited, overfished, depleted, or rebuilding from prior overfishing. World production reached 101.13 million metric tons in 1993, not counting 27 million tons of by-catch that is discarded at sea. Population growth will drive up demand by 20 million tons by 2010. Aquaculture, which doubled to 14 million tons between 1984 and 1992, will have to double again by 2010 to meet current consumption rates as ocean catch declines. . . .

School Demographics

Given the current ethnic and economic demographics of the towns of southeastern Connecticut, enrollment from each town will ensure diversity. An estimate of student participation based on the demographics of the LEARN region as evidenced in the 1998–1999 strategic school profiles is 75 percent white and 25 percent minority. The students will be selected from each participating town by lottery, with no more than 30 enrollment from any one town. (Percentages of minority and white students, as well as those participating in free/reduced lunch programs, are given by district and region in Table 8.1.)

All students will develop proficient English-language skills. The school will comply with all federal and state requirements regarding Limited English Proficient (LEP) students. The school will work closely with school home districts to ensure a complete program.

It is anticipated that students with identified special needs will be enrolled in the school as a result of the lottery. Home districts will be responsible for any costs related to implementing the IEP of the student in the Marine Science High School of Southeastern Connecticut.

Student Admissions Policy and Criteria

- Lottery to recruit students the first year with no more than 30 percent from any one town. A lottery will be held in subsequent years to ensure a total population of 250 students.
- Established residence in a participating southeastern Connecticut community.
- If a student enters as a 9th, 10th, 11th, or 12th grader, he or she is guaranteed enrollment until graduation.
- Siblings are not guaranteed admittance.
- Transfers and late entries will come from the lottery list.

Table 8.1. Minority and White Students: Percentages in Participating Districts and Regions

Town	Percentage of minority students	Percentage of white students	Percentage receiving free/reduced lunch
Clinton	8.8	91.2	10.2
Chester	5.7	94.3	5.7
Deep River	4.2	95.8	4.9
East Haddam	2.9	97.1	6.6
East Hampton	3.1	96.9	6.6
East Lyme	7.9	92.1	6.6
Essex	5.8	94.2	6.6
Groton	21.9	78.1	23.3
Guilford	5.6	94.4	3.5
Ledyard	12.4	87.6	1.9
Madison	3.9	96.1	2.1
Montville	11.0	89.0	14.4
New London	73.2	26.8	61.0
North Stonington	5.0	95.0	6.9
Norwich	28.5	71.5	44.2
Old Saybrook	6.4	93.6	8.8
Preston	4.2	95.8	12.6
Salem	3.0	97.0	5.5
Stonington	4.5	95.5	11.0
Waterford	9.3	90.7	6.2
Westbrook	5.2	94.8	9.2
Region 4	4.2	95.8	5.2
Region 17	3.7	96.3	4.0
Region 18	3.2	96.8	4.6

Grade Range and Enrollment

The school will serve students in grades 9, 10, 11, and 12. Students will be able, through lottery, to enter the school at any point in their high school career, based on the availability of space.

Plans for Recruitment of Local and Interdistrict Students

The interdistrict/interagency planning committee has recommended a variety of recruitment methods including, but not limited to:

- Presentations to Board of Education, administrations, councils, and PTO
- Employment of a staff person or securing a loaned executive to do recruitment
- Public service announcements (TV, news, radio)
- Coordinating with the current community agency programs
- Presentations to marine-related businesses
- Utilizing community resource outreach opportunities such as: town/city hall, youth service bureaus, guidance counselors, business leaders, librarians, realtors
- Hosting interdistrict marine-related activities for students in grades 5–8 commencing the year prior to the school's official operation

Plans to Ensure Effective Public Information to Attract a Diverse Student Body

News releases on the operation will occur at regular intervals several months prior to the school's opening. The lottery in each town will be conducted in the spring prior to the September opening of the school. Students will be located from contact with the list above and through public notices posted in the local newspapers. Materials will be printed in language(s) other than English. Recruitment will occur at agencies that focus on specific ethnic populations and that offer marine related programs, as well as at marine-related businesses.

How the Policies Further the Mission of the School in a Nondiscriminatory Manner

As fiscal agent for the Marine Science High School of Southeastern Connecticut, LEARN's policies will be in effect. LEARN has an affirmative action packet and standard assurances on file with the State. LEARN, as a regional education service center, has policies regarding discrimination, sexual harassment, community relations, administration, business and noninstructional operations, employees, and students. Policies that may be necessary to serve the unique needs of this school will be approved by the LEARN Board of Directors upon the recommendation of the executive director after consultation with the partners committee and approval by the governance committee. LEARN is an Equal Opportunity Employer.

Human Resources Policies and Information: Hiring Criteria and Standards

The process for recruiting, selecting, and hiring staff will be in accordance with LEARN's policies, procedures, and practices, under advisement of the governance committee. Members of the Partners Committee will serve on hiring teams. The result will be a diverse, talented, and committed staff with a range of teaching experience and subject knowledge. New employees will be recruited and employed by LEARN. Staff and consultants will have experience and current knowledge with regard to best practices. Teaching staff will have appropriate certification.

Staff Size and Teacher-to-Student Ratio

It is anticipated that the school will follow practices that best fit the mission of the school and the learning needs of high school students. When at full capacity, it is anticipated that there will be one teacher for every 18 to 20 students. Staff will include administration, faculty, noncertified staff, Coast Guard–approved staff for boating, guidance staff, clerical staff, special education staff, consultants, volunteers, and experts from the marine science field.

Professional Development

The planning committee recognizes the unique needs of opening a new school that is regional in nature. Therefore, they are recommending three strands of professional development. All professional development activities will have continuing education units attached to them.

Strand 1: Team Building (Priority 1/Ongoing)

- Developing Common Core Values
- The Stages of Team Development
- Effective Communication Techniques

Strand 2: Curriculum Development (Priority 1/Ongoing)

- Examining Best Practices in the Marine Industry
- Introduction to Marine Technology
- Examining Standards of Marine Science
- Aquaculture and Other Technologies
- Recent Marine Science Research
- Examination of Marine Science Curriculums
- Marine Technologies
- Designing the Marine Science Classroom
- Studying Marine Ecosystems
- Developing Thematic-Based Experiential Learning Rubrics
- Examining and Developing Assessment Tools
- Portfolio Development for Students

Strand 3: Diversity (Priority 2/Ongoing)

- Multicultural Literature
- Anti-Defamation League Diversity Training

School Building

The program requires construction of a new building. The school will be located at Mago Point in Waterford, Connecticut.

Transportation

The students will be transported according to the policies of student transportation in each district, with each district being responsible for its own students. Districts transporting students outside their community boundaries will be responsible for completing all necessary forms for reimbursement as per the relevant legislation to support the costs of providing transportation to an out-of-town approved magnet school. Parents will be responsible for out-of-school-time transportation.

III

ISSUES IN SPECIALIZED-SCHOOL PLANNING, DESIGN, AND CONSTRUCTION

9

School Technology: A Sensible, Future-Oriented Approach

Let's dive right into the issue of school technology by asking some big questions:

- Technologically speaking, where are America's schools today? How well are public schools and school systems dealing with the technological revolution that has restructured virtually every sector of our society and culture?
- For all the talk about educational technology, what is it that we really want technology to do in our schools? That is, how should schools be using technology in the teaching/learning process?
- In this era of breathtakingly swift technological change, what can America's public schools do to help ensure that the systems and components they install now will remain serviceable for as long as possible—while still acquainting students with current technology and its best use?
- Relatedly, how do we manage technology—the technology we have and the technology we're going to get—to make certain that systems remain up, running, and usable to the greatest extent possible? How do we do this in a way that accurately assesses the real life cycles of infrastructure, hardware, and software? And how do we ensure that technological tools aren't misused?
- Where are America's schools ultimately headed, technologically? What kinds of advances in learning technologies and other IT systems are on the near and distant horizons?

As you might guess, the rest of this chapter represents our attempt to provide at least partial answers to this challenging—and very important—set of questions.

WHERE ARE WE NOW?

This question is difficult to answer in a precise, generally applicable way, for American public schools today represent a patchwork—no, make that a crazyquilt—of approaches to the acquisition and use of information technologies and other advanced technological systems. A few of Ameri-

---

Donald Bodnar, Robert Dixon, Jeff Leavenworth, Edwin T. Merritt, Gary Therrien, and James Waller all contributed to this chapter.

149

ca's schools remain in the Stone Age, technologically speaking—with just a limited number of nonnetworked computers and (maybe) some dial-up modems for Internet access. Some are way too advanced for their own good—with lots of up-to-the-minute equipment that isn't used to nearly its full potential.

Most schools, of course, lie somewhere along the broad middle of this spectrum, though we find it very significant that in some American public schools today, the entire learning community—including parents—has become quite used to communicating through electronic bulletin boards and e-mail. More and more schools have their own websites—as do individual teachers and, increasingly, students as well. Ceiling-mounted and portable computer projection screens—on which, for example, students can display PowerPoint presentations they have designed—are becoming common. And distance-learning programs, including ones in which college professors and other experts offer special classes to high school students—are really taking off. (Distance learning has proved especially useful in connecting teachers with students in especially remote areas; Wyoming, for example, uses real-time teleconferencing to link up individual students on far-flung ranches and in tiny rural communities with instructors at schools in larger towns; see Dillon 2003.)

Interestingly, wealth doesn't always equal technological sophistication. A recent technology survey of Connecticut's public schools revealed that you can't always judge how well or sensibly a district or individual school is making technology-related decisions by how rich or poor that district or school is. Some affluent districts lag far behind the technological cutting edge, even as some schools in low-income districts are making savvy use of federal eRate subsidies to develop IT systems that beautifully complement their curricular programs.[1] Rather than wealth, the deciding factor in how well a school uses technology often seems to have to do with enthusiasm and commitment on the part of faculty and staff.

The fact that there is this very wide continuum (from next-to-nothing to much-too-much) stands to reason, since there have been very few reliable, truly future-oriented guidelines to help schools and districts make intelligent technology decisions. Sure, there are lots of technology consultants dispensing lots of advice—but how do you know whether the advice really fits a particular school's needs, and what are the baseline decisions that a school or school system should make today that will increase the chances that the networking infrastructure, hardware, and software selected will be appropriate to a school's mission and program and that the system as a whole will be flexible enough to serve the school for years to come?

WAGGING THE DOG

In all too many cases, schools and school systems purchase and install technology without giving much consideration beforehand to how that technology will serve specific educational purposes. To our minds, that's the IT equivalent of the tail wagging the dog. The first question that should be asked is *not* "What (and how much) should we buy?" The first question is "What do we want or need the technology to *do*?" Or, to put it another way, "How do we envision technology furthering our school's educational goals?" Technology decisions might well differ according to who your school's students are, what they need to learn, and the particular pedagogical approaches your school employs. For example, is your school's primary educational goal among those listed below?

- To prepare students for competitive business careers in the global marketplace.
- To help students become life-long learners capable of intensive individual study.
- To equip students with good, basic reading, writing, and math skills.
- To train students for careers in the performing arts (or any other specialized field of endeavor).
- A combination of any of the above.

And what are your corollary goals? Do they, for example, include any of the following?

- Expanding the curriculum to include areas that in-house resources can't cover. (For example, distance-learning programs might cover subjects that teachers at your school aren't qualified—or certified—to teach.)
- Providing a knowledge base on how information-technology devices work and how they can serve as tools for other learning.
- Equipping teachers with better tools to educate.
- Providing support for teachers in designing a better curriculum.

The point we're making is that one size doesn't necessarily fit all. To take just one, obvious example: equipping a school with loads of hardware and software for the production of graphic-arts materials—everything from high-quality color printers, to AutoCAD programs, to graphic-design software—may make perfect sense if the school is a design-focused magnet or charter but little or no sense in another context.

But it should also be said that there are dangers in being *too* specific about what the technology is intended to accomplish. Even where a learner-centered approach remains constant, specific educational goals and methods may evolve over time. To some extent, these are the prerogatives of individual teachers, department heads, or principals and will therefore change as staff changes, so you need the flexibility to adapt as easily as possible to new teaching methods and curricular content. You also want to avoid getting locked into a system that can't easily—and at reasonable cost—be managed, upgraded, or expanded.

Moreover, beyond the many possible approaches that individual schools might take, there's an important commonality that everyone involved in making school technology–related decisions ought to keep constantly in mind: today, *every* school, of every kind and grade level, should be preparing students for participation in a culture that is ever more saturated with technology. As the developers of one general model for linking educational uses of IT to the postschool world put it, "Everyone in today's complex society must acquire some degree of computer literacy to succeed, even to function, in today's IT-dominated world. . . . Although many educators do not view their function as preparing students to enter the working world, they do want their students to be successful in work and life" (Educational Development Center 2000). For this reason, decisions about the integration of technology and learning are among the most important that educators will ever make.

These two aspects of the technology question—how to make certain that technological systems serve an individual school's learning goals and how to ensure that the school is adequately preparing students for entry into a fully "technologized" culture—aren't really at odds. The authors of a provocative recent book on school technology—who themselves strongly back the learner-centered approach—describe the current situation as follows: "Today, the discussion of IT in education quickly turns to the single issue of how to get more of it into schools or how to best connect schools to the Web rather than *focusing on what we want K–12 schools to become in the face of the kind of restructuring that IT is driving across society*" (Stallard and Cocker 2001, p. xi; emphasis added). In other words, the technology must suit the school—and, simultaneously, the school must prepare students for work and life in the larger, technology-driven culture.

Of course, considerations beyond those that are strictly educational also play—or *should* play—an important role in deciding what a school's IT or other technological systems should do and how they should be designed, and in the selection of their individual components.

Will an individual school—whether a new facility or an existing school undergoing a technology upgrade—function as a stand-alone entity technologically, or will its IT/telecommunications system be part of a larger campus-, district-, or municipality-wide network? Some districts are making the expensive decision—at least in terms of first costs—to build their own wide-area or metropolitan-area networks (WANs or MANs; see Kretchmer 1999 for an early though comprehensive look at self-owned school district MANs). Some municipalities are managing to save on first costs by requiring that, when installing new fiber-optic networks, local cable TV or telephone service providers build in additional capacity, so that all of the municipal government's arms—including the board of education—can piggyback onto those cable pathways. In other, more recent efforts, some school systems have leased or otherwise gained long-term use of other parties' fiber-optic cables to build these networks. (Such an approach is far less costly than building your own end-to-end multischool network.)

Obviously, these kinds of moves depend on budget, on technical feasibility, and sometimes on serendipities of timing. But in any case, the wisdom of such actions all depends on what you want the technology to do. For example, do you want local police officials to be able to make security-related announcements over a school's intercom system from a remote location? Do you want students and staff to be able to easily access resources that aren't available locally—things like lesson-plan banks, scholarship lists, field-trip guides, and policy guidelines, as well as human resources? Do you want to save (enormously!) on the long-term costs of a school system's or municipal government's voice telephony service by replacing a series of stand-alone PBX telephone systems with a single Internet-protocol (IP) voice system?

Even if the school's system will be stand-alone, how integrated should the technology be? Should building management functions be supported by the same infrastructure and protocols that carry the school's voice and data? What about electronic security functions like digital surveillance video and electronic access control? In fact, might it not make sense to integrate *all* of the school's automated functions—everything from voice telephony, to library-book checkout, to financial management—on a common cable-distribution system employing a common protocol? Some schools have already done this: the Ocoee Middle School, in Ocoee, Florida, employs a Schools Interoperability Framework (SIF) network, run on a common cabling system, that integrates these and other functions throughout its campus.[2] More recently, the Town of New Canaan, Connecticut, expanded a "free" fiber-optic network to serve many municipal locations, including schools. Both the town and the school district have implemented integrated voice and video systems over this single-backbone "data" network.

SUCCESSFUL TECHNOLOGY INTEGRATION—SOME GUIDELINES

Charles H. Stallard and Julie S. Cocker's 2001 book, *The Promise of Technology in Schools: The Next 20 Years*, cited above, is a must-read for anyone needing a comprehensive grasp of school technology–related issues. In it, the authors provide a number of basic guidelines for ensuring that the integration of technology into schools is as smooth and successful as possible. The following recommendations are culled from that book's pages, supplemented by our own experience:

- Information technology should be viewed *not* as an add-on that can be cut when budgets are tight, but rather as an integral aspect of every education-related task.
- In general, teachers' attitudes toward the use of information technologies in the curriculum have improved in recent years, but many have yet to accept the imperative of using technology to improve learning. The task of changing many teachers' minds about technology— away from viewing it as a distraction to the "real business of learning" or as merely a replacement for stand-and-deliver, lecture-format instruction and toward an openness toward the manifold ways in which technology can assist the learning process—belongs to every principal, every superintendent and board of education, and especially to teachers colleges and university departments of education around the country.
- In the same vein, it is urgently necessary that teachers colleges and university departments of education provide their students—soon to join the ranks of America's public school teachers—with meaningful preservice training in the use of technology in the classroom. (Training the existing teacher workforce in the effective use of new and emerging technologies must also be improved.)
- On the state and district levels, it is critical to streamline procedures for the procurement and installation of technology. Labyrinthine and slow-moving protocols for buying and installing technology can interpose incredibly long delays between the time equipment is ordered and the time it is set up and ready to be used in a given school.
- On the regional and district levels, school systems desperately need to find workable ways of sharing the staffing and budgetary burdens imposed by schools' increasing use of information technologies. Among other measures, Stallard and Cocker recommend the development of multidistrict, regional "consortia" capable of supplying schools throughout the region with tech-support help—lessening the need for individual schools or districts to spend precious resources on their own separate staffs of IT personnel. Such assistance is needed for two reasons: (1) to help people understand and use what they have effectively, and (2) to help them keep their technology working well and to plan and then implement improvements. As school technology burgeons, it's vitally important to foster measures for avoiding unnecessary and expensive duplication of effort—while ensuring that individual schools' IT systems always remain in as good a working order as possible. Nothing deflates enthusiasm for learning technology as quickly or seriously as a broken computer or malfunctioning software—and the discouragement deepens if there's no one to fix the problem

or no money to pay for necessary upkeep and repair. (We explore critical issues related to operations and maintenance in the sidebar on pages 162–63.)

What this list of extremely sensible recommendations doesn't address, though, are the particular choices regarding infrastructure and equipment that schools and school systems should make *now* to ensure maximum flexibility and adaptability over the years ahead.

Granted, it's difficult to make across-the-board recommendations. Stallard and Cocker believe, as do we, that IT should be chosen to fit specific programs and further specific educational goals, so a rather high degree of customization is inevitable. That doesn't mean, however, that it isn't possible to specify certain baseline recommendations for particular kinds of schools. In fact, work on developing widely applicable school technology guidelines was under way as the present book was being written. The Construction Specifications Institute (CSI), together with several other industry groups—the Institute of Electrical and Electronics Engineers (IEEE), the Telecommunications Industry Association and the Electronics Industry Alliance (TIA/EIA), and the Building Industry Consulting Services International (BICSI)—has just published much better standards for information technology components in various types of new buildings, including schools. (For detailed information on these standards, consult CSI's website, at www.csinet.org/masterformat.) These standards do not, of course, replace the design effort for any particular facility, but they do give guidance on decisions regarding many components to make sure that technology installation is not an afterthought in new building design and construction.

In any event, a school technology planning process must—at the very least—address the following issues:

- How will the wide-area connection to the outside world be established? Through a router and carrier circuit to the Internet service provider? Will there be a router port for each dedicated circuit to content partners?[3]
- How will the central server and data repository spaces be designed? (Issues include the amount of rack space, as well as power-supply and air conditioning requirements.)
- How will print service centers be set up—centralized or distributed in a number of nodes? What kinds of printers will be used: monotone, color, photo/graphic sheet printers, CAD roll printers, or some combination of these?
- How will the network be organized? The physical connections can be grouped by wing, floor, or building and by wired or wireless nodes. The network also needs to be logically organized by user type (e.g., administrators, teachers, students, and parents). Rights and privileges are assigned, and use is controlled, based on both physical area and user type. Should the network be organized through wired backbone connections from a central server room to distribution closets housing switches and patch-panels (one for each floor or wing, major labs, and libraries)? Or through wired connections to wireless hubs in classrooms and gathering places where people want to use electronic tools? Will there be wired outlets where needed to support desktop PCs, laptops, cameras, monitors, and other devices? Will wireless adapters be available for PCs, laptops, and handhelds? What sorts of PCs, laptops, handhelds, and other devices—or combination of devices—will the network accommodate?

Besides finding answers to those questions, school technology planners have to abide by a number of basic rules of thumb, including:

- Building the wired plant to meet current quality standards (currently Level 5E or 6).
- Specifying any "legacy" products (i.e., existing equipment) that must be supported to extend the life of previous school investments.
- Selecting new equipment so that, wherever possible, capacities can be expanded or grown modularly to any rational top-end the budget will allow and technology evolution will likely support. (For example, you might select a router that supports a basic fractional T-1 frame-relay circuit as low as 128 kilobits per second to start, knowing that this equipment can be expanded with just a card swap to support a full 1.5 megabits per second. Or a switch in a closet might have 24 ports, but another module of 24 ports could be stacked atop the original unit and plugged in.)

As we say repeatedly throughout this book, magnet and charter schools exhibit an extremely high degree of variability on virtually every score; by the same token, however, a specialized school of a particular type is likely to share a great deal—including a similar set of technology needs—with other schools of that type. Recognizing this, it's possible to map out different scenarios detailing the basic technology do's and don'ts for any magnet school of a given type. Here are three possible scenarios:

SCENARIO 1: A 300-STUDENT K–8 CHARTER SCHOOL IN A TEMPORARY, LEASED SPACE

Principle: Minimize any investment that isn't portable.

- Do acquire high-quality routers and a few switches designed for modular growth and reconfiguration.
- Do acquire and use one or more wireless hubs so that their use can be learned by staff and students.
- Don't try for ubiquity yet. Fewer dollars should mean fewer devices, so you'll have to find ways of equitably sharing what you can afford to buy.
- Seek a partner (such as a cooperative regional group of schools, or perhaps a private IT service provider) that will help manage what you acquire for minimal cost, and that is in it for the long term.
- Consider working with a content partner, so the on-site server/storage need is minimized, at least for now.
- To control costs, limit printer availability and use.

SCENARIO 2: A 300-STUDENT ARTS-THEMED MAGNET MIDDLE SCHOOL

Principle: Graphic-arts and similar technologies are inherently more complex and specialized, therefore more expensive to acquire and use.

- Do make certain that high-bandwidth capability is designed into both the network and each device.
- Be cautious about expecting wireless solutions to meet users' bandwidth requirements.
- Admit that at this type of school, new technologies are likely to be adopted more quickly and more often than at other kinds of schools. (Sometimes they'll be used on a temporary or experimental basis.)
- Acknowledge that some projects will demand a large number of devices and connections or special configurations, which will create a commensurately larger need for management.
- Determine how to accommodate certain students' or classes' demand for high quantities of graphical printer use and output.

SCENARIO 3: A 500-STUDENT MATH/SCIENCE/TECHNOLOGY MAGNET HIGH SCHOOL

Principle: The demand to use the latest technologies in this type of school will test the limits of any solution, so emphasizing adaptability is more important than buying the "best and most."

- Do make certain that high-bandwidth is available in the connections to the Internet and content providers.
- Expect that some locations will not be in use much of the time, but will be "full-throttle" when put to use.
- To meet the many occasional needs, establish a central manager and a good scheduling tool for device sharing.
- Pay special attention to system security to control nascent hackers who will test the limits.
- Consider specifying "hardened" laptops for science labs to withstand the rigors of chemical spills or electrical surges.

THE TECHNOLOGY PLANNING PROCESS (AND HOW TO SUSTAIN THE PLAN OVER TIME)

How does a school board or building committee plan for technology needs? It turns out that planning for technology isn't so different from other planning tasks.

The Planning Team. First, you need to put together a small planning group or committee—a team that represents, to the fullest extent possible, all those who have a stake in how technology will be used at the school. The planning team must determine what the school and community need, and why. Committee members don't have to have the technical know-how to decide how the plan will be accomplished, although it helps if participants are somewhat technology savvy. To be effective, however, it *is* important that the committee members possess subject-matter expertise in the areas affected and that they be able to think outside the box and in a holistic way, that is, from the Big Picture (everybody's needs) down to the needs of individual departments and teachers. Since not all needs can be met, needs must be prioritized in a way that recognizes budgetary realities and that best serves the school as a whole. It's also crucial that the committee members be able to work well as a team, developing consensus answers whenever possible. Remember, it's this team that will have to champion the plan that evolves.

Who are the stakeholders who should be represented on the planning team? Certainly, teachers need representation, because they are at the forefront of using technology to improve children's education. The school administration should also be represented, to make sure its needs are accommodated and to identify areas where educational and administrative IT needs overlap. Educators responsible for developing curriculum are also important stakeholders, since technology options can have a huge impact on their work. Depending on the size of the building and the desired degree of technology integration, it may be prudent to include someone from the school's operations and maintenance staff to ensure that the infrastructure will accommodate building management requirements, too. Other possible stakeholders include parents, school librarians, and anyone who will be responsible for supporting the technology that gets implemented.

It is important to stress that team members should strive to represent *everyone* who will utilize the technology—not just their own parochial interests. They must take the time to communicate with others to define what is needed and why and to develop a plan for implementing the results. They must be able to develop requirements that everyone can buy into and be able to promote the results with a vision and plan that evolves from the process. In this connection, it may be wise to include one or two "nay sayers" on the team; developing enthusiasm for a technology plan among a school's most conservative, "antitechnology" faculty members—and getting them to buy into the plan—may well require including them in the planning process.

Long-Term Management. Managing and sustaining the plan over the long term are just as important as developing it in the first place. The hard work that goes into developing the technology requirements of a new or renovated school will not be effectively leveraged if no one takes responsibility for maintaining the plan into the future. For instance, some person or group will need to update technology requirements on an ongoing basis—which involves monitoring changes in the school's needs, studying technology trends, and making appropriate recommendations to accommodate them. To ensure that ongoing technology investments remain appropriate, this person or group must be in a position of "ownership," that is, must be responsible and accountable for meeting technology needs and for fighting for funding and support over the long haul. How changes and updates actually get done depends, of course, on how the school is governed and how its budgets and facilities are managed. While a good plan will not change significantly if it is completed shortly before expenditures are made, there can often be a gap of several years between the time requirements are assessed and the actual implementation. Even when a new building is completed and the initial technology is in place, a committee representing the stakeholders should remain in place to keep the technology plan current.

That last point is critically important, and it leads us to mention one crucial fact that school boards too often ignore or find difficult to accept: technology life cycles—whether for infrastructure, hardware, or software—are comparatively brief. Because of this, someone needs to continue the IT planning process over time, and to articulate to the board the school's ongoing needs (and consequent funding options). If well designed and constructed, a new school building may serve its community for decades and decades to come. By its very nature, technology isn't nearly so long-lasting: the cabling that's installed now may serve your school's needs for ten years at most. The PCs and other devices you select may remain "good enough" for five years at the outside. (It's helpful to remember that businesses commonly replace PCs—upgrading to newer, more powerful models—every three to four years.) And software life cycles are even shorter. Because of term licenses and forced upgrades, software is consuming an increasing share of schools' IT budgets. Increasingly, software licenses are restricted to a fixed term (perhaps one year). New versions may be issued annually or even more often, and users are often forced to buy the upgrade, even if it offers no discernible benefit. Sometimes using a "hosted application" (through the Internet to the provider's location) is a better option than buying and installing numerous copies that may not be used fully.

These realities mean that it's incumbent on technology planners to admit that solutions adopted now will inevitably prove inadequate several years down the road. (Likewise, school districts need to face the fact that the need to purchase new technology will never, ever go away.) But these realities also mean that technology *must be used*—and used quickly and widely and well—to justify its cost. If it just sits around growing obsolete, you're wasting your money.

Life-cycle considerations should also play a role in determining whether the costs of purchasing technology fall within a school system's capital budget or its operating budget. Many school systems put such costs in their capital budget on the principle that it may only be possible to undertake large, technology-related expenditures at the time a new facility is being created or a full-scale renovation is being performed. But such an approach may ignore the ongoing need to purchase new technology as systems and devices become outmoded or obsolete.

Setting Standards. Once the committee has defined the educational and infrastructure requirements for a new school, it needs to look at how those requirements will be met. To ensure future adaptability and flexibility, the group needs to define the key technology components in an architectural overview and then get help developing standards for them. For example, the network wiring and electronics that provide connectivity within the school and to the outside world will be designed around certain capacity requirements that will depend on the school's educational and infrastructure needs. But if the technical requirements get defined as actual technology products instead of standards-based connectivity components, proprietary solutions may result that will lock the school into a current technology capability or tie it to a particular vendor. Standards will allow more of a "plug and play" approach—resulting in a system that can be updated more easily and allow a changes in vendors when needed.

Utilizing standards to define requirements is not difficult—and it's usually the case that technical help is available through municipal or state agencies. (And it's always possible to bring in an outside consultant.) Typically, there are only two or three choices for most major components. Do note, however, that while some technology standards (e.g., wire installation standards) are relatively stable, newer technologies (e.g., wireless interfaces) must be monitored more often for change. When standards are utilized to define requirements, infrastructure adaptability is increased immensely and the need for wholesale swaps of equipment is nearly eliminated. To the greatest extent possible, we need to ensure that the IT products and services used in our schools meet published federal or industry standards, because those that do tend to have longer life cycles, and such components are more easily managed because they're easier to integrate and interoperate more smoothly.

WIRELESS NETWORKS

One of the most pressing questions facing school-technology decision-makers today involves just how far to buy into the wireless technologies that promise to revolutionize telecommunications.

This, too, is a difficult question to answer—and once again, the answer depends on what you want your school or school system's technology to do. Obviously, wireless networks can immensely enhance portability within a system, but to take full, truly effective advantage of wireless networking, a school or school system has to be willing to invest in laptops for all its students.[4] But the layout of money isn't limited to the initial purchase of equipment and software and its maintenance, repair, upgrade, and replacement over the course of time. In all probability, that investment must also cover the salary of a full-time IT technician whose job it is to supervise the school's laptop program—including the checkout and return of laptops at the beginning and end of the school day—and to make sure the system and its components remain shipshape. Obviously, this person would need an office and workspace, and there has to be adequate and appropriate storage space for perhaps hundreds of computers—which, despite their small size, take up a lot of room when you put them all together!

Is it worth the investment and trouble? For some schools, it might be worth temporarily resisting the peer pressure to "go wireless" *unless* technology planners are convinced that the immediate implementation of a wireless, laptop-based system can do wonders for the academic program. But more and more schools seem to think such systems can indeed make a sizable difference. And by aggressively pursuing federal educational-technology grants, a school can significantly offset some of a laptop program's costs—including personnel costs.

The fact is that except for special applications requiring large graphic displays or specialized processors (such as UNIX), laptops are growing in capability to meet most user needs and are now suitable for many school-related purposes. The advantage of being able to place more devices where they are needed at a given moment might well outweigh the burden of tracking and securely storing these assets. Moreover, the cost of laptops is dropping precipitously even as this book is being written. Maintenance and software upgrade issues are really no different from those for desktop machines, though laptops are somewhat more fragile and require careful handling by all. An ever-increasing portion of new models are being manufactured with wireless capabilities integrated right into the computers, and it won't be long before all laptops have some form of wireless capability as a standard feature.

Whether or not you jump into the new wireless/laptop world immediately, it's certainly the case that new schools and those undergoing significant renovations or technology upgrades should plan for the ultimate adoption of wireless—and take steps now to ensure that that adoption, when it occurs, is relatively painless. For instance, if a school is being newly constructed or undergoing a gut renovation, it probably makes sense to install a network connection for a future wireless receiver/transmitter in each learning space, which will make the eventual conversion to wireless all that much easier. But despite all the hoopla over wireless, and despite its very real value in certain educational contexts, there are three drawbacks to wireless that make its immediate, widespread adoption somewhat problematic:

- Wireless technologies are still developing, and products have not stabilized, meaning that their lifespan is even more uncertain than that of their wired counterparts.
- Wireless networks' functionality is still hobbled by limited bandwidth, which restricts the speed with which large amounts of information can flow through a network. For Internet connections, wireless simply can't compete, at present, with cable.
- Wireless networks remain much more susceptible to security breaches than wired net-

works. It's much easier to hack into them. Even when designed to work only in a classroom or a small part of a school, such networks can be scanned and intruded upon from nearby locations—even by laptops in a vehicle driving by. Wireless networks must therefore be managed especially closely.

Granted, the standards for wireless connection are evolving rapidly to deliver greater bandwidth capacity and security, and these problems will doubtless be solved in the long run. We just don't know when. What we *do* know is that today's cabled networks can deliver vast amounts of data to the desktop very rapidly, and that they're reasonably secure. We're enthusiastic about wireless's possibilities—who isn't?—but we nevertheless remain just a bit cautious when it comes to the immediate application of wireless networking in educational environments across the board.

WIRELESS NETWORK DESIGN CONSIDERATIONS

A distinction needs to be made between wireless local area networks (LANs) and wireless wide area networks (WANs). A LAN is any communications network constrained within a facility, whereas a WAN is any communications network between facilities or providing connections to public networks such as the Internet. (Other commonly encountered terms include the *campus area network*, which provides communications connections within a campus environment, and the *metropolitan area network*, which links various sites within a metropolitan area, but for simplicity's sake we limit the discussion to LANs versus WANs).

When designing a wireless LAN, a school system first needs to define its goals in providing wireless services to students and staff and perhaps even to the public (say, by parents coming to the school and wirelessly connecting to the school's network). Is the district looking to reduce costs? To provide students with mobile network access throughout a school campus? To allow for mobile computer labs? Or is the driving factor a need for greater flexibility (as might be the case, for example, if a school can afford only a limited number of computers but wants to increase their availability by making them usable in various parts of a facility)? The answers to these questions depend on economics, security, and the limitations of current wireless technologies.

Mobile computer labs are relatively easy to provide. Outfit a computer cart with laptops equipped for wireless operation and the cart becomes a "computer lab" that can be moved from room to room throughout the school. All that's required is a network drop (connection) in any room where the mobile computer lab is to be utilized. (These network drops might be given more capacity than typical end-user outlets—say, 1 gigabit per second versus the current default of 10–100 megabits per second, but this is typically accomplished by a single card in a switch and is not an issue of how or where the drop is wired.)

Creating an environment where students, faculty, and administrators have wireless access to the network throughout the facility poses a greater challenge. One limiting factor involves the physical construction of the facility. Wireless signals cannot pass through certain types of common building materials, so creating a facility-wide wireless network will definitely have an impact on the economics of building construction. Too, bandwidth is effected by how far a wireless computer is from an access point, or "cell." Facility- or campus-wide wireless networks are constructed in very much the same manner as are national cell phone networks: having a greater number of access points in a given area (within engineering specifications) enhances the stability and speed of wireless communications. But the need to install a large number of access points also has obvious economic implications.

Moreover, the wireless network options just described operate on the same frequency (2.4 Gb) used for a variety of other "short haul" wireless purposes, including Bluetooth (used in many computer peripherals, such as printers, scanners, PDAs, and wireless keyboards) as well as the signals transmitted by many utility monitors and alarms. Care must therefore be taken to avoid interference from competing devices.

In the local-area environment, wireless communications connect individual computers or computer-type devices (e.g., PDAs) to a network. By contrast, in the wide-area environment, wireless communications connect networks to networks (buildings to buildings) or networks to the public domain. Mobility is not an issue (buildings do not physically move), but environmental conditions do impose limits on the feasibility of wireless WANs.

WAN wireless communications may be used in circumstances where it is not economically feasible to provide a physical link between two or more facilities but where these facilities are within the line of sight of one another. For a single, short-distance "hop," infrared systems offer relatively high bandwidth for the cost. At the high end, digital microwave systems can be used to transmit over distances as great as 50 miles under certain conditions; however, they are expensive to acquire and require licensed technicians to maintain. Something as simple as bad weather, however, can limit connectivity over a wireless WAN; therefore, care should be taken when deciding what kinds of information are sent over wireless links. (Data transmissibility may not be impacted, while voice or Voice or Internet Protocol [VoIP] communications may fail.)

A MAGIC SLATE FOR TODAY'S CLASSROOMS

Let's put aside the complex issues related to wireless technologies and turn to a kind of educational technology for which we have unreserved enthusiasm. This technology—in use in some schools for more than ten years though only now becoming more widespread—is the *interactive whiteboard*.[5] Interactive whiteboards (in case you've never seen one in use) vastly expand the multimedia resources available to the instructor—and vastly increase the teacher's (and students') ability to immediately and effectively manipulate those resources.

Sound complicated? The technology is certainly sophisticated, but the real virtue of interactive whiteboards is how friendly they are to users. The whiteboard is linked to a computer, and text and images (even video clips) are projected onto the board through either a front- or rear-projection system. But the whiteboard is much more than a projection screen: teachers and students can directly interact with the board—which is actually a plasma or liquid crystal display panel—by touching it or writing on it with an electronic pen. The work that occurs at the board, including notes written on the screen, can easily be saved for retrieval, reference, and reuse. Too, interactive whiteboards have proven their value in distance-learning applications: if each of the linked remote locations is equipped with one of these boards, then all the learners can participate, interactively and *in real time*, in the manipulation of the information appearing on the board. These boards really are magic slates for today's high-tech approaches to learning.

The trouble with interactive whiteboards is that they're expensive—costs might amount to as much as $5,000 per classroom for fixed technology—and the price of equipping every one of a school's classrooms with this technology can be prohibitive. (Though in the case of this technology, too, there are grants available that can help offset costs.) At some schools where interactive whiteboards are in use, costs are controlled by limiting the number (and types) of classrooms in which the boards are installed: only upper-level classrooms, for example, might be equipped with the boards, or they might be installed only in math classrooms or science classroom-labs. We understand the financial exigencies, of course, for limiting interactive whiteboards' use, but here is a technology that—unlike wireless networks—already has amazingly well-developed capabilities, and obvious uses across the curriculum.

OPERATIONAL SUPPORT AND MAINTENANCE CONSIDERATIONS

Operational support and maintenance costs constitute a substantial factor determining the effectiveness and functionality of any network. These costs cover everything from IT staff, to spare-parts pools, to contracts with third-party systems integrators. In school networks, a great deal of effort must be spent to implement and ensure security to protect against unauthorized activities inside the school as well as external intrusions from the Internet. Technical assistance for necessary internal changes and improvements can be provided using internal or contract staff, or through service providers who monitor the network and modify systems primarily from remote centers. Purchasing manufacturer service contracts through third-party vendors is somewhat akin to buying insurance: the more money you are willing to spend, the less risk you'll assume in maintaining the system (and vice versa). Before such decisions can be made, the school's needs must be understood well enough to document assumptions for a contract period. Developing an IT operations plan is the best means to document these needs; it should supplement the information-technology strategic plan used to design and acquire all of the school's technology infrastructure.

The more critical the information that flows over the network (voice or data), the more important it is for the network to be continuously up and for the school to have a quick-response policy should trouble arise. Depending on the particular environment and the applications supported, it may be acceptable for a network to experience some limited periods of downtime. (For example, some downtime may be tolerable for a network providing basic data services such as e-mail and Internet access.) Determining whether any downtime is allowable—and if so, how much—is important because cost to repair is usually directly related to response time.

As networks evolve and provide more critical services, the need for 99.999 percent uptime (the proverbial "five nines") will become the norm. Likewise, as more and more school networks are tied together, the need for that 99.999 percent uptime becomes even more critical. If one classroom loses connectivity for an hour, that may be deemed a tolerable inconvenience. If the same network supports administrative functions such as attendance or payroll, however, the need to strictly control or eliminate downtime becomes more critical.

Currently, most school systems deal with operations and maintenance issues through some combination of IT staff, spare-parts inventory, contracts with local third-party integrators, and manufacturers' warranties. Most probably also have some form of network monitoring software in place, which sends out alarms when problems occur. As more school systems create their own private WANs and put critical 24/7 services such as phone and voicemail onto these networks, monitoring will become an essential part of the operating process. (Consider, for example, the importance of *always* being able to dial 911 in the event of a serious emergency.)

In the future, schools may decide to outsource monitoring services to third-party vendors. This is already happening now in many areas of the private sector, and the costs of such services are declining. The school's actual support needs must be documented to determine the service levels required. All contracts with monitoring-service vendors incorporate a service-level agreement (SLA) that specifies not only the number of devices and concurrent users but also the quality level of the service provided. As school systems become more and more connected and their networks become larger and larger, outsourcing may extend not only to monitoring services but also to maintenance of the entire network.

This trend toward outsourcing can be taken a step further: as schools create their own private WANs, it will no longer be necessary for schools to have their own servers (special-purpose computers that perform specific functions such as e-mail, web hosting, etc.). These servers can be consolidated into one location and—as is happening in the private sector—outsourced to a third-party company in the business of providing secure server-farm facilities. This can translate into space and cost savings for schools. Care must be taken to ensure that needs are thoroughly understood before long-term agreements are entered into. The principal cause for failure in outsourcing agreements is poorly measured expectations. Anticipated cost savings are often negated, and costs tend to increase exponentially if after-the-fact, unanticipated changes must be negotiated.

The best means of determining when and how to use internal IT staff, local contractor support, or comprehensive outsourcing (assuming each can meet functional needs) is to perform total cost of ownership (TCO) calculations for each option. If needs aren't well enough understood while a new facility is being designed and constructed, an interim operations plan can be used for the first year or so, during which a history can be compiled that will allow for more accurate TCO calculation. Then longer-term support needs can be defined and the most appropriate contracts can be finalized.

DATA WAREHOUSING/DATA MINING

Until very recently, questions regarding which kinds of educational approaches really work to improve performance and which do not haven't lent themselves to scientifically based answers. That's because these questions are inherently extremely complex. More often than not, the question isn't whether one particular approach (a traditional lecture-based format, say) works better than another particular approach (for example, small-group activities). Rather, we need to know which combinations of a wide variety of approaches might best improve performance over time. Since so many factors might influence performance—the degree to which a school implements block scheduling, the amount of time students spend in self-directed study, and even the time of day at which an examination is taken—the task of finding the right balance has largely been left to educators' intuition, informed by anecdotal evidence.

The technique known as *data mining* promises to change this—to enable us to use hard, verifiable data to determine which kinds of educational practices, in which kinds of combinations, are the most likely to produce desired results.

Until a few years ago, the data-gathering capability and interpretive tools for making such judgments weren't even thinkable. But computer systems' memory capacity and processing speed have grown exponentially over the past decade, and new programming techniques now allow information gathered from disparate sources (and stored and organized by different kinds of software) to be effectively combined and searched, creating a very promising resource: the data warehouse. A data warehouse is an electronic repository containing vast amounts of information—information that can be effectively mined to answer questions that, by their nature, are extremely complicated. Philip A. Streifer (2000), an educational consultant and authority on data warehousing/mining technology, lists some of the kinds of questions for which this new technique might help us find scientific, evidence-based answers:

- What is the impact of attendance on student achievement (test scores, class grades, etc.)?
- What is the relation between achievement test scores and course-taking trends (and class grades)?
- What is the relation between state mastery tests, norm-referenced tests, SAT scores, etc., over time?
- How do various groups (by gender, ethnicity, race, etc.) perform on class grades and standardized tests? Are results equitable across groups?
- What is the relationship between class grades and standardized test scores for matched subject-matter areas?

Data warehousing/mining even has the potential to change the *kinds* of questions we ask, by enabling us to include an incredibly wide variety of variables in our assessments of performance. For instance, if school cafeteria records—including the menus for specific days—were included in the data warehouse, it might be possible to ask whether particular kinds of food influence test scores. Does pizza make kids better or worse at math? The question may sound silly, but it's becoming obvious that nutritional factors influence learning. In the future, data warehousing and mining might help us measure those effects.

The effective use of a data warehouse or data-mining system, however, depends on the integrity or quality of the data supplied to it. More complex systems (= more data sources mined) require the support of a specialized technical resource known as a database administrator. Such a resource might be shared among schools or with a municipality, or might be provided by a private firm. This is one of the many technology-related areas in which local school districts could use help and guidance from state departments of education, which in general have been too lax about providing strong leadership in the technology arena. The responsibility of state DOEs should go beyond providing assistance (for example, in the development of technology plans); it should also embrace the implementation of technologies, like data warehousing/mining, that few if any districts could afford on their own.

USING TECHNOLOGY TO *REDUCE* FACILITY-RELATED COSTS

Sometimes it seems as if advances in educational and other technologies do nothing but increase the financial burden on our public schools. But isn't there something wrong with that picture? After all, it seems that technology can also help control or reduce costs in virtually every other area of human endeavor. Why isn't this also true of education? The too-well-kept secret is that it *is* also true of education.

Granted, the costs of in-school technologies will continue to mount as schools come to rely even more heavily on even more sophisticated systems and networks. By the same token, however, the judicious implementation of technology can, we're convinced, significantly reduce educational space needs and thus aid in controlling construction costs. This chapter mentions in passing a few of the cost-saving consequences of technological development. Mobile computer labs utilizing wireless technology, for example, may well eliminate the need to incorporate permanent, dedicated (and expensive!) computer labs into school buildings. And schools might well save on space (and associated costs) by giving up their own servers—which not only take up room but have special power, air conditioning, and security requirements as well—and relying instead on third-party firms that operate server farms. But there are other ways, too, that technology can cut facility-related costs:

- The proliferation of electronic information resources (the Internet, e-books, etc.) can dramatically reduce the amount of stack space required by school media centers.
- Virtual labs—in which experiments are conducted on the computer screen rather than at a lab bench—can replace at least some of a middle or high school's fully (and expensively) equipped lab spaces. (Virtual labs are, we think, especially appropriate for basic science courses.)
- Individualized instructional programs will have the ultimate effect, we believe, of reducing learning-space needs throughout the school. Since so much individualized schoolwork can be done at home (or anywhere, for that matter), it becomes much less important for children to pursue all—or even most—of their learning activities at school. That means that the purposes of school buildings can become more specialized (accommodating group learning activities and cer-

tain kinds of hands-on learning, for example)—and therefore that schools may well grow *smaller* over time.

- Individualized, computer-based learning also has the potential to affect the length and structure of the school day. Why should we remain stuck on the idea of a fixed seven-, eight-, or nine-hour school day—during which every school-child is required to be on site—if so many learning activities can be accomplished elsewhere? Obviously, a school's physical size could shrink, perhaps substantially, if only a portion of enrolled students had to be at school at any given time. But reconceiving the school day could have other space-related effects. For example, individualized schedules, combined with sophisticated scheduling software and the enhanced navigational capabilities enabled by the global positioning system (GPS), might well make it possible to reduce the size of school-bus fleets. (Each bus would be used throughout the day, picking students up and dropping them off on an as-needed basis.) That, in turn, would lessen the amount of school-site space given over to bus queuing. (Since individualized scheduling would lessen or eliminate *all* morning and afternoon traffic congestion, parent dropoff/pickup areas could also be less extensive than they now are.)

Of course, there's likely to be a great deal of resistance to altering school buildings' purpose or the structure of the school day, and such changes will occur very gradually, if at all. But we certainly ought to be thinking about them as we contemplate our schools' technological future. And space- and cost-saving measures like reducing media-center stack space and replacing some fully equipped lab spaces with virtual labs can be accomplished right now.

THE LONGER VIEW

In talking about schools' use of data warehousing/data mining, we begin to step into territory that's largely uncharted. It's time, then, to speculate about the future of educational and education-related technologies—not just over the next couple of years but over the next couple of decades.

It's obvious that America's public school classrooms are changing. True, too many educators still use the computer as little more than an occasional substitute for "sage on a stage" instruction and who continue to think of the relationship between the computer and the learner in terms derived from that old-fashioned model in which the computer is the active deliverer of knowledge and the student, its passive recipient.

At the same time, however, a different way of relating to educational technology—a much fuller and more nuanced response to its varied possibilities—is definitely beginning to take hold. As we point out near the beginning of this chapter, many American schools today are making very good use of technologies such as e-mail, websites, electronic bulletin boards, interactive whiteboards, and distance learning. Moreover, the move is definitely on toward the widespread adoption of innovative forms of what Stallard and Cocker call "distributed learning." Distributed learning ups the ante on old-style distance learning in that it can hook together learners from numerous remote sites, all of whom can together engage in synchronous learning experiences.

But these developments exploit available technologies. What about *future* technologies? What will they look like and how will they be used? For one thing, we're certainly going to witness an immense proliferation in both the number and kinds of electronic devices used in educational settings. In part (and in the near term), this means a proliferation of computers (especially laptops) and PDAs—the result, in part, of the constantly falling cost of IT components. As Stallard and Cocker put it,

> It seems reasonable to expect that the price of IT components will reach a level at which they can be widely deployed in K–12 education by 2005. "Widely deployed" means that each learner in the system will probably have multiple devices at his or her disposal for personal use. Whereas today we count ratios of students to one computer, we very well may be counting the number of computing devices to one student as soon as 2007. (2001, p. 8)

We should know in a very few years whether Stallard and Cocker were on target regarding when this change will occur. But, that said, it's not the "population explosion" of computers and handheld computing devices that will cause the most far-reaching alteration of the educational environment. *That* transformation is portended by developments in the fields of microtechnology (or nanotechnology), robotics, and artificial intelligence (AI). It seems quite possible that within a few short decades, the technological environment will be radically unlike the one we inhabit today. The computer—as a discrete, recognizable device—may be consigned to history's scrap heap, to be replaced by a world of intelligent (or intelligent-seeming) devices with which we casually interact on an ongoing basis. Sound far-fetched? It shouldn't. Already, our cars talk to us—and, with the help of the global positioning system, navigate for us as we travel from place to place.

The coming transformation of the technological environment has to do with what might be called the increasing *transparency* of technology. Sooner than we think, our interactions with virtual realities won't be mediated through devices that seem separate from the reality being communicated. What that means, in concrete terms, is this: an interactive whiteboard—that is, a specific, separate device for communicating information—won't be needed when it becomes possible for an "ordinary" wall to serve the same function. (Imagine interactive technology being an integral part of the fabric of the wall.) Separate computers may likewise become a thing of the past when virtually all components of the environment are interactive. Nanotechnology, robotics, and AI will alter the physical character of our interaction with technology. In medicine, for example, the operating room and all the surgical paraphernalia it contains (including laser surgery devices) may vanish from the scene when it becomes possible to accomplish complex surgical interventions through the injection of microscopic surgical robots—"nanobots"—directly into a patient's bloodstream.

The growing transparency of technology will inevitably affect education as well, and science fiction has already given us some clues as to what a transparent, interactive educational environment might look like. Take, for example, the 2002 remake of *The Time Machine*. In this latest film version of the H. G. Wells sci-fi classic, the hero (who hails from the late 19th century) visits New York City in 2030 and wanders into the New York Public Library. There, he encounters a pedagogical "device" that confuses and astounds him. This is Vox, a holographic "human being" who is the repository, it seems, of all human knowledge. Ask Vox for any piece of information, and he'll give you the answer—complete with cross-references to related topics. He not only walks and talks, but (as played by actor Orlando Jones) he's also witty, charming, engaging, and has a decent singing voice. Although it's true that Vox doesn't have complete freedom of movement—his 3-D image appears within a series of glass-like panels that bisect a library corridor—he is nevertheless disconcertingly lifelike. But he's unlike a real human in that he never tires, doesn't get cranky, and—as the movie eventually reveals—is virtually indestructible.

When the time traveler first encounters him, Vox is busy entertaining (and teaching) a group of schoolchildren. Watching his interaction with them, you can't help but wonder whether this digitally engendered apparition might not be the teacher of the future. He certainly has subject-matter expertise down cold. But, just as important, he's emotionally warm, emotionally *there* for the children in the way that any good teacher would be. And his salary demands couldn't be very high . . .

THINKING CRITICALLY ABOUT TECHNOLOGY

. . . and that, of course, is the rub. A technology like Vox would threaten the livelihoods of actual human beings. (Beyond that, he'd do quite a number on human beings' high opinion of themselves.) Of course, fears of technology's job-stealing, dehumanizing effects have been around since the beginning of the Industrial Revolution, but that doesn't mean such fears are unfounded. As this book was being written, newspapers and TV news programs were full of stories about how the end of the early-2000s economic recession was not—to many people's surprise—being accompanied by much growth in jobs, especially in the manufacturing sector. Why not? The answer seems to be that computerized automation has so enhanced productivity that factory production can jump without a concomitant rise in the number of factory workers. You don't need more human beings to "man" machines that are essentially unmanned.

The point we want to make, however, is a larger one—and one with direct bearing on the relationship between technology and education. Technological advances always, it seems, have their downsides—sometimes obvious, sometimes hidden. For example, the Internet, for all its wonders, has had some less-than-desirable consequences. It has made the theft of intellectual property infinitely easier than it used to be—to the enormous consternation of record company executives, among others. And the ease with which plagiarism can now be accomplished, electronically, is making educators' jobs harder: How is it possible to fairly and accurately assess students' work when it's likely that some students are downloading written materials from the Internet and passing them off as their own original compositions? How can we responsibly filter Internet content to block children's access to pornography and other age-inappropriate material while ensuring reasonably free access to information? Who controls the filtering technology? And what about students' ability to critically evaluate the information they read? Much of the information dispensed by millions (billions?) of websites is suspect—biased, partisan, or out-and-out false. So how is a young person—or anyone, for that matter—to sift through this increasingly huge barrage of information to determine what's factual and what's not, which sources are trustworthy and which aren't? (As it turns out, curriculums are already being written to help students develop Internet-savvy critical-thinking skills; for one such example, see Dalton and Grisham 2001.)

As technology becomes more and more integral to the education process, there's a crying need to help students develop the critical faculties needed to maintain an even keel in this stormy sea of information. There's also the correlative need to instill in students, from an early age, a critical attitude toward high technology and its many impacts on our society and culture. By *critical attitude* we don't mean a condemning, "Luddite" posture that rejects any and all technological advances out of hand. (We are, after all, strong proponents of learning technology.) Rather, we mean a thoughtful, discerning attitude that enables a person to understand the far-reaching moral, economic, and political repercussions that technological advances so often carry—and to develop informed opinions about a very wide variety of issues. Here's just a brief sampling of the kinds of issues with which our society is now grappling:

- Privacy (What kinds of information ought and ought not to be gathered? Who should and should not have access to that information?)
- Medicine and health (What are the ethical implications of medical advances ranging from reproductive technology—including cloning—to stem-cell research and genetic mapping?)
- Environment (What environmental dangers are associated with genetically modified foods? Do developments in nanotechnology threaten disastrous environmental consequences, and, if so, how do we guard against them?)

These aren't just abstract, speculative matters. In fact, many such questions will come to the fore within the school environment itself. Will school security systems begin to employ biometric access-control devices, and, if so, what are the privacy issues involved? What kinds of information about students should a school system's data warehouse contain, and how can that information be safeguarded? How involved ought schools be in the dispensing of psychopharmaceuticals and other drugs whose long-term effects may be poorly understood? As the years go on, these kinds of technology-related questions will grow more pressing and complex.

Inspiring our public school systems to make fuller, better, and more creative use of the technological tools at our disposal while simultaneously helping students develop the critical-thinking skills needed to address the profound questions that technology raises—this is a very tall order indeed. But it's urgently necessary, we believe, to energetically pursue both aspects of this agenda. We've got to prepare our children to function successfully in a high-tech world. And we've got to equip them with the intellectual tools needed to participate, in an informed way, in the democratic decision-making that, we hope, will shape our technological future.

For more on how advanced technology may transform public education and the educational environment over the coming decades, see the introduction to this book. A list of organizations contributing to educational standards for use in new schools, and their web addresses, appears in an appendix to this volume.

NOTES

1. The eRate program is part of the Universal Service Fund created by Congress in the Telecommunications Act of 1996 and is paid for through telephone-bill surcharges. The USF's purpose is to lower the

"digital divide" by providing money to help schools offset the costs of purchasing and installing telecommunications systems.

2. The Ocoee Middle School is featured in the previous book in this series. See Edwin T. Merritt et al., *The Middle School of the Future: A Focus on Exploration* (ScarecrowEducation, 2004).

3. Many schools are entering into regional cooperative partnerships to access one another's curricular content. Some schools work with private providers that charge a fee to access their content, some work with affiliated universities and foundations, and others work with local corporations that make some of their research content available to schools. Some of this content carries restrictions on its use—not everything is made available for open distribution on the Internet. Increasing concern about the need to protect intellectual property rights is raising the need for formal agreements with these kinds of content partners.

4. It should be noted that wireless networks increasingly support a wide variety of devices—not just laptops but also projectors; PDAs (or handheld computers), some with cell phone capability; and tablet computers.

5. Interactive whiteboards are often referred to generically as "SMART Boards," but SMART Board is a brand name for the interactive whiteboards made by SMART Technologies, Inc. Interactive whiteboards are produced by a number of manufacturers, including major electronics companies like Panasonic as well as smaller, more specialized firms such as the U.K.-based Promethean, Inc., whose ACTIVboard technology has been adopted by numerous schools and districts.

Site Design and Landscape Architecture for Urban Magnet Schools

Marcia T. Palluzzi, LA

The magnet school movement is directing many school designers' attention back to the city. For decades, the prevailing model of public school design—and therefore of approaches to site and landscape design—has been a suburban model. True, approaches to site design and landscape architecture for suburban schools have undergone substantial changes in recent years because of a number of factors, including (to name a few) a reduction in the amount and quality of suitable, buildable land in many communities; a heightened demand for regulation-size playing fields for a variety of sports; an increasing tendency of suburban-district students to travel to and from school by private automobile; and a growing awareness—supported by federal, state, and local laws and regulations—of the need to design school sites in ways that respect local ecologies and the environment as a whole. Even so, the suburban model is in many ways inapplicable to—and inadequate to the challenges of—the densely built and often somewhat tattered urban fabric that serves as the locale for most new magnet schools.

Site designers and landscape architects struggling to define functional, aesthetic, and sustainable exterior environments for urban magnet schools face a range of challenges that are either unfamiliar to those who work solely on suburban schools or—as in the case of issues related to traffic flow, parking, bus queuing, and the like—substantially raise the ante beyond anything that a suburban school landscape architect is likely to face.[1]

Unsurprisingly, it's space—or rather, the *lack* of it—that's the most important of the several factors distinguishing urban site design/landscape architecture from its suburban cousin. The extreme space restrictions that are so common on tight urban school sites affect everything from playground and other outdoor recreation-space design to the delineation of acceptable traffic-flow patterns. What's more, space-related challenges dovetail with other issues that, while not absent in suburbia, are of heightened importance in the urban context—including the need to ensure schoolchildren's physical safety, to protect the school building from vandalism, and to balance the on-site interplay of permeable and impervious surfaces (and thus to reduce environmental heat levels and provide effective means of controlling stormwater runoff). Each of these issues will be touched on in the remainder of this chapter. To start with, though, let's look at a set of broader issues that provide—or *should* provide—the overall framework for all the site and landscape design–related decisions that will be made for a given urban magnet school.

Figure 10.1. A series of 14 planters—one for each of the school's classrooms—enhances the courtyard garden at Hartford, Connecticut's Montessori Magnet Elementary; landscape design is by TO Design. *Photograph by Charles R. Cassidy.*

THE BIG PICTURE: NEIGHBORHOOD REVITALIZATION

As is emphasized elsewhere in this book, to be and remain successful, magnet schools must be *magnetic*. Because they compete for students, magnets must attract a target population, or populations, of potential enrollees and their parents. This doesn't just mean that such schools should "look good" (though there is, of course, a lot to be said for a beautifully designed facility on a beautifully landscaped site). It also—and just as importantly—means that they must be designed in ways that attract families from outside the magnet school's urban neighborhood, as well as in ways that will convince those who live and work in the immediate vicinity (parents, other residents, and local businesses) that the new school's presence should be welcomed. Since the mission of so many magnets is to bring communities together, these two seemingly different goals go hand in hand.

The attraction to an urban magnet school must be powerful enough to overcome the ease that families feel in having their children educated in a local setting. Thus, from a site design/landscape architecture perspective, the task of calming parental anxieties begins with creating an aesthetically pleasing environment. Additionally, parents from more affluent neighborhoods or districts, in order to entertain what they may perceive as the risk of sending their children to a school in a poor or minority neighborhood, will need to feel that their children will be safe while in school, as well as on their way to and from school. Especially where travel distances are long, parents from remote neighborhoods or districts will also have to be convinced that it will be convenient—to their own lives and those of their children—for their kids to attend a given magnet school.

As may already be obvious, these two needs—safety and convenience—have implications that extend beyond the school itself to the surrounding streets. Even if beautifully designed, a magnet school that seems an island (or fortress!) in the middle of a neighborhood that's perceived as chaotic, hostile, treacherous, or depressing is saddled with a *big* image problem to overcome. That's not to say that such a school *can't* succeed—the strength of its program may be enough to convince parents to bracket their other concerns—but such a school faces a very real public relations hurdle.

The need for a magnet to be welcomed by the surrounding neighborhood is the other side of the same coin. Although it's true that the prospect of a new school promising enhanced educational opportunity will probably be viewed as a very positive development by most residents of most city neighborhoods, it's also the case that some new magnets have encountered community opposition. It's easy to imagine situations where plans for a new magnet might inspire resistance on the part of neighbors. If, for example, a magnet will be pulling in a large number of students from a variety of neighborhoods or districts, it's likely that vehicular traffic—school buses and private cars—will increase sharply on surrounding streets at certain times of day. If that jump in traffic isn't ameliorated somehow—or if the inconvenience it causes isn't offset by other benefits—local residents may grumble or growl.

Of course, being on good terms with your neighbors always makes life easier, but the issue isn't just one of good PR. The larger point is that in the best of worlds, new magnet schools *should* participate in—should be viewed as just one dimension of—the comprehensive revitalization of the city neighborhoods in which they're located. Undoubtedly, there are as many ways to achieve a successful integration of school and neighborhood as there are individual magnet schools. A magnet occupying a larger urban site, for example, might incorporate a plaza—similar to the plazas of some urban business areas—that creates a dynamic, open, public space; provides a place for parents and local residents to meet and socialize; and aids in the building of community. Or a magnet might be planned as just one aspect of a larger scheme that also includes housing revitalization, the development of a local business district, or the creation of a local center for the arts. In such cases, site and landscape design strategies would necessarily extend well beyond the borders of the school's lot.

Of course, such multidimensional revitalization efforts require coordinating the work of many different city agencies. We're not saying that such coordination is easy, or that every magnet need be part of a larger, more comprehensive plan to succeed or fulfill its mission. What we *are* saying is that the magnet school concept can provide a springboard for the exploration of opportunities for cross-fertilization and interagency cooperation that enhance the urban environment as a whole.

In small ways, that's already happening. If a magnet school's site, for example, is too tight to allow much in the way of outdoor recreational space, schoolchildren may travel (under their teachers' supervision) to a nearby public park for sports and outdoor play. This kind of school use of public space requires, of course, the cooperation and coordination—including budgetary coordination to share any additional maintenance costs such use may engender—of the school district and the municipal parks and recreation department. Likewise, adapting neighborhood traffic patterns and developing dropoff/pickup areas for buses and private cars will require the participation of school officials, city planners, and personnel from the municipal department of transportation.

The results of such interagency cooperation, if approached in the right spirit, can improve life for the neighborhood as a whole. The regular presence of schoolchildren and supervisory school personnel may transform an underused or neglected park into a desirable greenspace the entire community takes pleasure in using. The manipulation of local traffic patterns, the imposition of various "traffic calming" techniques (e.g., chicanes, bumpouts, raised crosswalks), and the addition of streetscape improvements (e.g., landscaping, lighting, ornamented walkways, and street furniture such as benches, trash receptacles, and bus-stop shelters) can together significantly improve the outdoor environment throughout a neighborhood, raising quality of life for everyone. (Interagency alliances can also be helpful when pursuing grant money for park and streetscape improvements.)

PLAYSCAPES AND OUTDOOR CLASSROOMS

Themed magnet elementary schools invite designers of outdoor play areas to give free rein to their imaginations. Today, playground equipment is manufactured by a number of competitive companies that specialize in the creation of updated, elaborate variations of the jungle gyms, swing sets, and sliding boards of yore. There's an immense range of products on the market—the number of different products is growing all the time—and many of these playscapes incorporate visual themes that can be matched to the academic focus of a magnet school. (An environmental-themed magnet elementary might select a jungle- or treehouse-themed playscape, for example; a science-themed magnet might opt for a rocketship- or nautical-themed playscape.) Moreover, these complex, sometimes wildly inventive "play environments" are typically modular, and among the components offered are activity boards that integrate cognitive learning into the experience of physical play. These activity boards—sometimes placed at ground level, sometimes forming protective barriers attached to the playscape's raised platforms—can be as simple as tic-tac-toe games or as complex as models of the solar system that incorporate movable, manipulable parts. The activity boards, too, can be chosen to underscore a magnet school's theme.

But playground design doesn't stop with the equipment. As we say, playground equipment is now solely the province of manufacturers that test and guarantee their products for safety and durability (the days of unique, architect-designed playscapes are long gone). But there's still plenty of opportunity for the landscape architect to design a school's outdoor recreational environment in ways that extend or enhance a playscape's theme. For example, at one planned multicultural magnet elementary school, the surface of the outdoor play space will incorporate a boldly colored image of a globe (done in durable color-seal coating) that not only will visually transform what would otherwise be a drably homogenous blacktopped area but will also "bring the classroom outdoors" by giving children at play a graphic reminder of the school's mission.

Of course, carrying the academic exploration that goes on inside the classroom into the outdoor spaces surrounding a school can entail much more than simply applying a visual cue to an exterior surface. The outdoor classroom concept has, over the past decade, been pioneered by suburban schools—particularly those whose sites include wetlands or other environmentally significant features. The idea is to utilize those features of a school's landscape for genuine academic purposes—for example, by incorporating observation, study, or even cleanup/remediation of a wetlands area into a middle or high school earth sciences curriculum. But there's no reason that such uses of school sites should be restricted to the suburbs. Cityscapes are habitats, too. Often, of course, urban ecological systems are severely degraded, but this in itself can present an educational opportunity, since designers can devise ways of ameliorating the degradation that can also be used to teach students about the interplay of environmental systems.

For instance, cityscapes are marked by an abundance—an *over*abundance—of impervious surfaces. As we now understand all too well, impervious surfaces, when they are not interrupted by permeable areas that permit the working of natural biofiltration processes, can be environmentally destructive. Rain falling onto impervious surfaces is carried directly into storm drains and sewers, picking up contaminants—surface oils and particulates—as it goes. Under overflow conditions, stormwater may bypass water treatment facilities, emptying directly into local waterways, whose ecology is degraded by the contaminants it carries.

Playground areas and other outdoor spaces, however, can be designed in ways that mix and balance impervious and permeable surfaces. Obviously, a ball court's surface must be hard and impervious, but there's no reason that, given the right site conditions, portions of a surrounding space can't be paved with cobbles set in gravel that allows stormwater to percolate through to the ground below—or that "hardscape" paved areas can't be alternated with "softscape" planted areas to achieve the same environmentally beneficial effect. (Strategies for capturing runoff and using stormwater for the "graywater" irrigation of planted beds could be incorporated into such a scheme.) In the same way that architectural and engineering elements of a school building's interior—for instance, exposed piping, ductwork, and other ceiling-hung infrastructure—can be used to teach children about the way a building works, these and other landscaping strategies can provide a visible, sensory, real-world means for instructing students about the interplay of natural systems and environmentally conscious design.

In fact, the use of outdoor play space for learning can be even more straightforward. For example, at the Montessori Magnet Elementary School on the campus of Hartford, Connecticut's Learning Corridor (see page 172), the ingeniously designed play area incorporates a series of raised planters, each assigned to one of the school's classrooms. These planters serve as little gardens in which children can plant and grow flowers, vegetables, or herbs—and thereby learn basic lessons in botany, horticulture, and agriculture in a hands-on way.

Problems related to stormwater runoff—which include the potential for flooding as well as the impact on natural water systems mentioned above—can also be lessened through appropriate and inventive grading strategies. Many urban school sites are on relatively level terrain (this depends on the city, of course). Still, water flowing downhill must be directed away from buildings and into controlled systems. This does not mean, however, that water must travel a direct route from rooftop to piped system. Although the water will always find the most direct route, this need not occur in a straight line. Grading therefore provides an opportunity to heighten visual interest through the creation of landforms, earth walls, and steeply or gently sloping planes—while ensuring that water gets to where it needs to go.

THINKING GREEN—LITERALLY AND FIGURATIVELY

Besides their potential negative impact on nearby rivers, lakes, and other bodies of water, the impervious surfaces that cover our cities have another deleterious effect on the environment: the large expanses of horizontal impervious surfaces that dominate the cityscape—especially heat-absorbent dark-colored surfaces such as asphalted streets and parking lots, flat tarred roofs, and blacktopped playgrounds—cause a dramatic buildup of heat in the ambient environment. Calling this buildup "dramatic" is, in fact, almost an understatement: studies have shown that on sunny summer days, the temperature in urban "hot spots" can exceed that of nearby suburban or rural areas by as much as 10° to 12° F. Not only does the preponderance of such surfaces turn our cities into sweltering infernos, but the heat buildup they cause also leads to increases in ozone—a prime constituent of urban smog—in the lower atmosphere. (Ozone, whose presence in the upper atmosphere provides a desirable shield against ultraviolet radiation, is a pollutant when it occurs near ground level.)

Reductions in urban heat levels can be achieved in a number of ways, including replacing dark surfaces with light-colored paving and reflective roofing materials. But the most effective way of making our cities cooler (and improving air quality in the bargain) is to maximize the green. Trees, of course, provide much-needed shade, but plants and planted areas of all sorts—trees, shrubbery, flower beds, and lawns—act to lower ambient temperatures. Not only does the water vapor released by plants help cool the atmosphere, but the exchange of carbon dioxide (CO_2) for oxygen (O_2) that occurs during plant respiration reduces air pollution in the lower atmosphere. Planted softscapes aren't just literally green; they're also essential constituents of environmental-sustainable ("green") site and landscape design.

Of course, finding space for wide expanses of green can be a difficult task in a densely built urban setting. But there is one place—mostly ignored by designers until relatively recently—

capable of accommodating the large planted areas needed to significantly lower city temperatures and improve air quality: the roof. The greening of America's city rooftops is a trend that's just begun, but it's a strategy that, we believe, will be employed more and more often in the years ahead. (Green roofs—which have the added benefit of lessening the volume of water that will end up in stormwater drainage systems—are one of the techniques that can help a building earn LEED certification from the U.S. Green Building Council.)

The roofs of new school buildings provide—if readers will forgive the pun—exceptionally fertile ground for furthering this trend, because green roofs can serve a dual purpose: benefiting the environment while providing additional outdoor recreational space (so long as appropriate safety measures are taken). To put it boldly: rooftop gardens and lawns convert school roofs into much-needed, premium real estate.[2]

Beyond their environmental value, of course, plantings—whether on rooftops or at ground level—vary the design palette available to the landscape architect/site designer. Vegetation visually softens the cityscape, providing interesting color and textural opportunities and assisting in the articulation of space. (Plantings can even enhance security, as the specification of what's known as "hostile shrubbery"—thorny bushes that make for very uncomfortable hiding places—can help protect vulnerable areas on a school's site.) It should be mentioned, though, that designers of city school sites must take great care to select trees, shrubs, and other plants capable of surviving and flourishing under conditions that are likely to be much more stressful than those encountered on suburban sites. Planning for irrigation is especially important. Moreover, the long-term cost of maintaining plantings must also be figured into any landscape-design decisions.

NOTES

1. For a detailed look at the kinds of challenges typically encountered in suburban school site and landscape design, see the relevant chapters in two earlier books in this series: Merritt et al., *The Elementary School of the Future: A Focus on Community* (ScarecrowEducation, 2004), and Merritt et al., *The Middle School of the Future: A Focus on Exploration* (ScarecrowEducation, 2004).

2. For more on the use of rooftop lawns on school buildings, see the award-winning K–8 school designed for the Chicago Public School by Marble Fairbanks Architects featured in *The Elementary School of the Future*, pp. 24–27.

Improving School Acoustics: A Systems Approach

Try reading the following paragraph:

> Many educators feel is important to acoustics in classrooms by children with problems but unnecessary do so in used by students normal hearing. Yet populations of students normal hearing also from better classroom.

Difficult (or impossible) to understand, yes? Why? Because every fourth word—25 percent of the text—has been removed. That's the visual equivalent of a speech intelligibility rating of 75 percent, which the Acoustical Society of America says is the acoustical condition that prevails in many American classrooms today (Seep et al. 2000). A look at this unintelligible paragraph illustrates the direct correlation between speech intelligibility and student performance. The actual paragraph quoted above reads as follows:

> Many educators feel it is important to improve acoustics in classrooms used by children with hearing problems but unnecessary to do so in those used by students with normal hearing. Yet many populations of students with normal hearing also benefit from better classroom acoustics. (Seep et al. 2000)

Reinstating the ten missing words makes it clear, demonstrating both the critical importance of speech intelligibility and the meaninglessness of a statement not fully communicated. Granted, there are other clues to understanding the spoken word, including body language, gestures, lip movement, and voice modulation. These clues are most effective during a live, in-person presentation. But today's instructional methods include many prerecorded presentations, as well as live, distance-learning interactions, and these and other high-tech instructional methods will come into even greater use in the years to come. A 75 percent intelligibility rating in the classroom of the future is therefore unacceptable, especially when one considers that raising the level of intelligibility is, with some thoughtful planning and design, a fairly simple matter.

WHY DOES THE PROBLEM PERSIST?

One of the major reasons behind the poor acoustics in today's classrooms is a simple lack of awareness of the problem, despite a recent U.S. General Accounting Office (GAO) report that ranks noisy classrooms high on the list of educators' frustrations. Poor acoustics is not always a glaringly obvious problem; it cannot be recognized simply by walking into a room. Only the users of the space can discern it, and then only when actively engaged in the educational process. The GAO's *Condition of America's Schools, February 1995* survey reports that more than 28 percent of schools have unsatisfactory or very unsatisfactory acoustics for noise control (GAO 1995). That is worse than the results for other environmental problems, including ventilation, security, indoor air quality, heating, and lighting.

Given the total school-age population in the United States of about 50 million, poor acoustics affects the learning process of millions of American students. And the effects of poor speech intelligibility fall disproportionately on already underserved populations. Overcrowding, which has a negative effect on classroom acoustics, is much more prevalent in large, urban schools and in schools that serve minority populations (Lewis et al. 1999). Magnet schools with racial-balance incentives are likely to include a high percentage of students for whom English is a second (or third) language—and whose learning and performance are likely to suffer most from poor speech intelligibility.

Designs for magnet schools largely ignore the issue of classroom acoustics. True, new or renovated classrooms do typically include some acoustical treatments, such as carpeting, acoustical ceiling tiles, gypsum wallboard partitions, and batt insulation in the wall cavities between classrooms, and renovated spaces benefit to some extent from the addition of new finishes. But these are minimal measures. Many school buildings built before 1950 may have masonry demising walls, high ceilings, or hard plaster surfaces on ceilings and walls. These surfaces are highly reflective for sound, extending its reverberation time by bouncing sound waves around the room and muddling intelligibility. Such surfaces demand remedial solutions, such as acoustically absorptive finishes. For budget-conscious schools, these may include lay-in acoustical ceilings and acoustical wall panels.

Classrooms are usually acoustically separated from adjacent spaces, but this typically represents the extent of acoustical design. Specific acoustical criteria, such as speech levels, background noise, reverberation times, or speech-to-noise ratios, are often not even considered. And classrooms are designed iteratively: if there are no complaints, a design is considered acceptable and is used for other schools. In this way, an important psychological reality is ignored: users of a new facility are usually so grateful for the opportunity to teach and learn in a brand new space that they are often hesitant to complain about perceived trivialities such as classroom acoustics. After all, the thinking goes, the building was designed by experts. Assured that they have state-of-the-art learning spaces, teachers (and students) remain unaware that classrooms might be even better, acoustically speaking.

The problem persists for two other reasons. Until recently, there have been no acoustical performance and testing standards for classrooms, leaving designers with limited data on which to base their designs. A building code change, proposed to the International Code Commission (ICC) on November 14, 2001, would add a classroom acoustics section to the International Building Code. The proposed code is closely based on a draft American National Standards Institute (ANSI) standard (S12.60-20X). With ICC approval, classroom acoustic provisions would become requirements in all states adopting the International Building Code. Although every school design is unique, and each school has different programmatic needs, the careful application of guidelines to a well-considered plan would go a long way toward solving the technical acoustical problems that are now so widespread.

The perceived cost of specialized design for acoustics or of remediating existing problems also contributes to the persistence of the problem. But these costs should be considered as integral to the unit costs of a new school building or renovation, and acoustical design should not be subject to value-engineering cuts. The value of acoustical improvements far outweighs the long-term costs of acoustically disadvantaged learning.

POOR SPEECH INTELLIGIBILITY: THE PROBLEM'S ORIGIN

Speech intelligibility can be impaired by unintentional noise or intentional sound that is inadequate for conveying meaning effectively or that interferes with other, intentional sound.

Unintended Noise. Unwanted background noise from a number of sources can compete with desired or intended sounds. Most commonly, background noise arises from building systems or from a lack of acoustical separation between occupied spaces. Here are some sources of the unintended noises that commonly afflict school buildings:

- *Partial-height partitions:* Partitions that extend from the floor to a hung ceiling (rather than the structure above) allow crossover sounds from room to room above the ceiling.
- *Impact noise from the floor above*: This includes the movement of furniture or equipment on the floor above and footfall sounds.
- *Mechanical systems:* The need for ventilation and temperature control in modern schools requires that a large volume of air constantly be moved in and out of classrooms. That movement—the rush of air through ducts, grilles, and diffusers—can create background noise, which is often compounded by sounds generated by the fans and motors used to drive the air. In some older school buildings, the hissing radiators and banging pipes of steam heat cause problems during the heating season. Classrooms located directly below the roof are subject to low-frequency vibrations created by rooftop-mounted mechanical equipment such as air-handling units, chillers, and exhaust fans.
- *Crossover noise:* Sounds that come through ducts and pass from one room to another are not uncommon.
- *Lighting and electrical systems:* Because of its economy and efficiency, fluorescent lighting has become the standard for virtually all buildings except residences. This type of lighting requires electronic ballasts, and these ballasts create a distinct drone. Electrical transformers that step down voltage, usually located in electrical closets throughout a building, also emit a constant hum. Even though this noise is of a fairly low frequency and volume, it nonetheless contributes to background noise in adjacent areas. Boiler rooms, electrical switchgear, and receiving areas are all sources of such equipment-generated noise.
- *People:* Background noise often results from people going about their everyday activities—moving around, talking, interacting, and working. One often hears teachers complain about the noise created by the shuffling of desks and chairs. (In rooms with tile floors, one frequently finds an ad hoc solution to this problem: tennis balls stuck on the bottoms of desk and chair legs.) Other occupant-generated noise is often an acoustical separation prob-

lem. Any movement through corridors outside a classroom (not to mention the banging of lockers) generates noise. If classroom doors are left ajar to improve ventilation, sounds can migrate into the corridor and infiltrate nearby spaces. Food service areas can be particularly troublesome: the movement and conversations of workers, product deliveries, and the ordinary use of utensils and equipment in food preparation can produce quite a racket. Though kitchen areas are typically back-of-the-house spaces, the noise can easily carry through reverberant corridors, as can the din produced in the cafeteria at mealtimes. Crossover noise emanating from gymnasiums or caused by custodial activities, especially when combined with sounds from other sources, can create a significant background noise level.

- *Reverberation:* Large spaces like cafeterias and gyms are generally noisy spaces—not by planning but by default. Ask any teacher assigned lunch duty about the din in the cafeteria. These spaces are outfitted (appropriately) with washable surfaces that are hard and smooth: exactly the kind of surfaces that reflect sound. In such a space, reverberation time is extended, and sound is constantly being regenerated, producing the din: a constant, elevated, background noise level. Too often, the cost of providing acoustical treatment to control such noise is perceived as prohibitive. If a gymnasium is noisy, the thinking goes, that's okay; after all, a gym is meant to house noisy activities. A gymnasium, however, isn't just a basketball court with bleachers: it's also an instructional space, and the fact that physical education teachers, like all teachers, need to communicate information verbally should be considered when designing gyms and other high-occupancy spaces.

- *Exterior noise:* Noises from the surrounding area—from vehicular or pedestrian traffic, nearby manufacturing facilities and construction sites, or buildings and grounds maintenance equipment—can infiltrate the school building. The sounds of students engaged in sports activities or recess play (especially where outdoor athletic fields and play areas are located very close to the building) and of school buses queuing up for the afternoon trip home occur every school day.

Intentional Sounds. Intelligibility problems are sometimes created by the desired sound source itself. For example, if that source is weak, it may not be able to overcome background noises described above. Here are some of the intelligibility problems related to intentional sounds:

- *Teachers' voices:* Every individual has a different voice pattern. Some people project well, with plenty of volume and clear articulation; others are very soft-spoken. There is an endless range in between. Some teachers have speech impairment issues; others have foreign or regional accents that may make it difficult for students to understand them. Everyone occasionally suffers from an illness—a cold, sore throat, or laryngitis—that affects speech. Those teachers who have difficulty overcoming background noise levels are those who suffer the most from poor acoustics. They must strain to be heard, which may color their presentation and even put them at risk for stress-related health problems.

- *Audiovisual sound systems:* The audiovisual equipment used in schools is sometimes not as good, or in as good repair, as it might be. Intelligibility problems can occur if the speaker system in a video monitor used for presenting a prerecorded program is inadequate or damaged, or if the equipment used in live distance-learning is malfunctioning. In fact, if a video system is not a state-of-the-art product designed specifically for the space, it will almost certainly be inadequate. We've come a long way from the shaky-voiced, 16-millimeter instructional movies of yesteryear. Vast improvements have been made in the content and production values of audiovisual presentations. But sound quality can still be a problem, and designers still struggle with the question of how best to distribute a clear and properly attenuated signal to each individual, especially in spaces in which seating is not fixed. Turning up the volume leads to greater distortion of the signal and does not necessarily improve intelligibility. High-volume sound may even bleed into other spaces, adding to the background noise level and disrupting activities in adjacent classrooms.

- *Public address sound systems:* Schools are required to have public address (PA) systems as part of a their emergency response plans. PA systems are also communication tools for disseminating broadcast messages. Unfortunately, PA systems are subject to cost cutting: good ones are value engineered and replaced with systems barely capable of the minimum requirements for code compliance. For the most part, such systems produce poor-quality, nearly unintelligible sound.

- *Learning activities:* The clatter of keyboards in a computer lab, the chatter of students working in small groups, and other classroom activities all create background noise. The noises from the activities of multiple small groups blend together, magnifying the problem.

- *Gyms as performance spaces:* If you've ever attended a school band concert in a gymnasium, you probably understand what bad acoustics are. Gymnasiums simply don't work well as performance halls. Schools that have the funds to build an auditorium usually build it correctly, consulting an expert in acoustics. Such auditoriums are generally acoustically separated from surrounding spaces and do not present crossover acoustical problems.

Whatever its source, when the background sound level approaches the level of the intended sounds in a classroom or other learning space, any message will be partially masked, resulting in poor intelligibility.

THE SYSTEMS APPROACH TO ACOUSTICAL DESIGN

The solution to poor speech intelligibility rests in a systems approach to acoustical design. Two basic principles underlie the systems approach:

1. *The users and occupants of the building are an integral part of the system.* They are often the generators of the sounds, and they are always the receptors of the sounds. Decision makers must be convinced of the importance of good acoustical design and that it has a positive cost-benefit ratio. Student performance is enhanced by the proper acoustical design of instructional spaces. Good acoustics diminishes the stress that teachers experience, and there is a corollary reduction in stress-related health problems.

2. *All of a building's problems are in some way related to each another.* Addressing one problem without considering the overall system may cause or exacerbate another problem. An acoustical problem may be solved by adding a soft surface to a room, but that solution might provide an environment for mold growth. (Because mold spores can be distributed by the ventilating system, this may cause a problem for the whole building.) Turning up the volume in one room may cause additional background noise in an adjacent room because of noise crossover through

the ventilating system's ductwork. Adding acoustical duct liners to reduce the crossover noise might, in turn, have a negative effect on indoor air quality.

SOME DESIGN GUIDELINES

The following guidelines exemplify a systems approach to the design of school acoustics.

Programming. In the programming phase, acoustically critical spaces, like the core teaching/learning spaces, are identified, and adjacency criteria are established. To ensure good building acoustics, acoustical adjacencies should be carefully considered, and adjacency studies should be part of the programming task. These matrix-type studies have long been part of the programming phase of all kinds of projects, but as the design profession has become increasingly specialized, many programming tasks have become second nature, no longer receiving the focused attention they once did. Such studies will reveal problem areas that need special attention or treatment.

Site Selection. In choosing a site for a new magnet school, diligent consideration should be given to the surrounding area in order to identify both noise generators and sensitive receptors (because the school itself will be a noise generator). If at all possible, schools should be located far away from the following noise generators: manufacturing and industrial processing plants, warehouses or shipping facilities, retail facilities with frequent deliveries, landfills, emergency-vehicle stations (such as police, fire, and ambulance stations), and municipal public works yards. Also to be avoided are sites near construction company yards where equipment is stored, and sites that are close to other sites where construction is scheduled or likely to occur. (Construction noise is temporary, but construction on major projects can last for years.) Sites that are close to transportation infrastructure—railroads, light rail systems, airports, heliports, and highways (especially limited-access roads or major truck routes)—should also be avoided. In fact, many of these noise generators can have a deleterious effect on other aspects of the school environment. For example, vehicular exhaust from a nearby highway might have a negative impact on air quality inside and outside the school.

Site Design. Site designers need to consider the acoustical impact of areas where buses will queue and where parents will wait in cars (with motors running) to pick up their children. When deciding on the location of outdoor activity areas, consideration should be given to the way sound from those areas may affect activities within the building. Instructional areas inside the building should be located away from loading docks (which may have frequent truck traffic) and receiving areas.

Building and Learning Space Design. All spaces in the building, especially instructional spaces, should be designed to specific criteria in order to enhance those spaces' acoustical properties. While design generally proceeds from the macro- to the microlevel, the acoustics of classrooms and other learning spaces need to be considered early in the overall building program to ensure that they are acoustically appropriate.

While there are multiple criteria for measuring and analyzing sound and the acoustical performance of spaces, most are too esoteric to be of practical value to educators. There are three acoustical criteria, however, that the decision-makers involved in school construction projects should be aware of:

- *Speech sound level*, perceived as loudness.
- *Speech-to-noise* (or *signal-to-noise*) and *speech-to-reverberation ratios*.
- *Reverberation time.* (Sound waves, much like the waves created by a pebble dropped in still water, reflect off hard surfaces and bounce around until their energy dissipates.)

These criteria are all expressed as dB(A), which is a measurement of sound pressure. The *dB* designates decibels. The suffix *(A)* denotes the bandwidth of the measurement that closely approximates the normal range of human hearing: 20 to 20,000 hertz, the unit of measure for sound-wave length. Reverberation time is measured in the number of seconds it takes for the reverberant sound to decay (or fade out) by 60 decibels. The criteria are as follows:

Speech sound level = 65 dB(A) at all points in the room. This level can be attained through normal speech (without amplification) in a classroom of 600–900 square feet that includes some acoustical treatments, such as carpeting and acoustical ceilings.

Speech-to-noise and speech-to-reverberation ratios = +15 dB(A) at all points in the room (background noise levels not to exceed 35 dB(A) as measured in an unoccupied room). Speech-to-noise (S/N) ratios compare the difference between the sound levels of the speech and the noise. Since both speech and noise are measured in dB(A), the S/N ratio, a relative measure, is simply the difference, in decibels, between the sound level of the signal (the speech) and the sound level of any competing noise. Speech-to-reverberation (S/R) ratios are defined in the same manner as S/N ratios, with the A-weighted sound level of the reverberant sound substituted for the A-weighted sound level of the noise. A good S/N ratio for speech intelligibility is a minimum of +15 dB greater than the background noise, or a minimum of 50 dB(A): 35 dB(A) background noise + 15 dB(A) speech sound level. If background levels are at 35 dB(A) and the speech sound level is at 65 dB(A), 65 − 35 = 30 dB(A), or two times the recommended minimum of 60 dB(A).

Reverberation time = RT60 of 0.4–0.6 seconds. Reverberation times are defined as the time in seconds required for the reverberant sound to decay 60 dB.

Meeting these criteria will ensure acoustical properties that enhance communication within the classroom for the vast majority of students, including those with some hearing impairment.

Building Systems Design. Integrated systems reduce overall noise. As advances in design move buildings toward greater environmental sustainability, building systems will become more and more integrated. As thermal efficiencies of building materials increase, mechanical systems will be downsized to maximize efficiency. Mechanical systems will integrate with lighting systems to better control heat and cooling loads; natural daylighting systems will integrate with artificial lighting. Lighting systems will link with security systems, which, in turn, will form part of the overall intelligent building. This integration will continue until each new building—including every new school building—is a single, intelligent system supporting the needs and desires of its users. Much of this technology is already available and in use today, bringing us closer and closer to the time when completely integrated, intelligent, environmentally oriented buildings are the norm.

LISTENING TO THE FUTURE

What will magnet schools of the future sound like? Acoustically, these spaces will suit their purposes, with furniture and finishes that enhance their acoustical properties. Acoustical treatments will include a mixture of reflective and absorptive surfaces that can be adjusted, or "tuned," to the needs of particular users and activities.

Designers will continue to specify acoustical ceilings, which will have enhanced noise-reduction coefficients. As in today's classrooms, floor coverings will mix hard surfaces (such as tile) with soft, acoustically absorbent materials (such as carpet, cork-based products, and other renewable resources). Heating, cooling, and ventilating systems will be acoustically transparent, as will lighting systems.

REFLECTION, DISPERSION, AND ABSORPTION

The flexibility required in typical classrooms confounds most attempts to design an acoustically perfect classroom. Engineers and acoustical consultants rely on some constant to which they can apply variables in order to make and test assumptions about how a space's acoustics will actually work. In typical school classrooms, the only constants are the physical dimensions of the space: the height, length, and width of a room do not change (except where movable partitions are used). But classroom acoustical design that uses only fixed sound reflectors will be ineffective if the sound source is relocated (by moving the teacher's desk from the front to the side of the room, for example). If, however, the designer places adjustable sound reflectors and absorbers on the walls—treatments that can be easily manipulated by the users—the room can be acoustically tuned to changing configurations using reflection, dispersion, and absorption.

A ceiling that combines soft and hard surfaces by alternating soft, noise-reducing tiles with hard, gypsum-type panels can distribute sound effectively to the entire room without excessive reverberation times. (This concept is now being utilized in corporate conference rooms to help contain the sounds around a large conference table.) The right mixture of hard and soft surfaces in the ceiling grid will reflect the sound of the teacher's voice to the opposite end of the classroom while reducing the reverberation time, preventing reflected sound from muddling the primary source. The same principle can be used for the wall surfaces: adjustable reflectors can be placed on the center sections of the walls, while corners are treated with absorptive surfaces.

Like today's classrooms, those in the future will be located along exterior walls to take advantage of natural ventilation and daylight. In such an arrangement, at least one wall has windows—and glass is a sound-reflective material. Some sort of window shade or blind is generally employed to control the amount of daylight entering the room. The opportunity for acoustic control that these shading devices provide is too often overlooked. If fabric curtains or fabric-based blinds are used, the room will also have an adjustable acoustical control device, much as one might see in a theater or auditorium.

Furniture should also play a role in enhancing room acoustics, and doors and partitions should be thoughtfully staggered and constructed to reduce sound transmission from one learning space to another, or from one side of a corridor to the other. Increasing the mass of a wall not only helps control lower-frequency sounds, it also augments the wall's value as a fire separation.

The long-term goal of switching to renewable energy sources will have a beneficial acoustic side effect. Solar, geothermal, and fuel-cell systems, because they are relatively passive, are much less noisy than the systems traditionally relied on, and thereby enhance speech intelligibility.

ACOUSTICS VERSUS INDOOR AIR QUALITY

No discussion of school-building acoustics would be complete without mentioning the ongoing debate between proponents of improved classroom acoustics and advocates of improved indoor air quality (IAQ). IAQ advocates would like to eliminate materials that can support the growth of molds, mildew, fungi, and other microorganisms, as well as those that contribute volatile organic compounds (VOCs) to the indoor environment. Unfortunately, these are typically the same materials used to enhance the acoustics in classrooms.

Carpet, for example, has some acoustical benefits. It absorbs higher-frequency noise and provides a buffer between the furniture and the floor, reducing the noise created when furniture is moved. But carpet can be a source of various biological and chemical contaminants that negatively impact a classroom's air quality. If not meticulously maintained, carpet has the potential to become host to various molds, dust mites, and other biological contaminants. There is also an association between new carpets and VOCs, either in the carpets themselves or the adhesives used to install them. The Carpet and Rug Institute, an industry organization, has led the way in establishing stringent guidelines for safely off-gassing carpets, as well as for their maintenance. If carpet is properly maintained, it can provide acoustical benefits without health risks.

Sound attenuation treatments inside ductwork are also controversial. Sound attenuation is usually achieved through the use of glass-fiber duct lining. This insulation, however, provides an environment for the growth of molds, mildew, and fungi that contaminate the air stream. The exposed glass fibers can also break off and float into the breathing-air zone. By properly sizing and routing ducts and terminals, and through the strategic placement of sound attenuators throughout the system, air distribution systems can be designed to keep noise at an acceptable level without the use of duct lining. In cases where some sort of duct lining is unavoidable, one of the alternatives to exposed glass-fiber duct liners should be used.

Starch and cellulose, the materials used in typical lay-in acoustical ceiling tile, can also provide a medium for the growth of molds, mildew, and fungi. Even when the tiles are made of glass fiber with an organic binder in the glass matrix, exposure to moisture or excessive humidity can foster the growth of molds. Manufacturers do offer antimicrobial treatments, but their long-term effectiveness remains untested. The solution is to control moisture, which requires a properly designed, balanced, and maintained heating, ventilating, and air conditioning (HVAC) system. Once again, a systems approach provides the best solution.

Some schools will also want to factor in the possibility of using sound field amplification systems, which can be adjusted to meet each room's specific acoustical requirements. These systems add another layer of equipment to an increasingly complex technology environment. They require knowledge to operate and maintain at optimal performance.

12

Indoor Air Quality: Problems and Solutions

Magnet schools of the future will be housed in buildings both new and old, and indoor air quality (IAQ) problems show no preference for old or new construction. The fundamental issue in all IAQ problems is the pollutant source. Air quality pollutants generally fall into three categories: microbial, gaseous, and particulate. This chapter examines the various sources of indoor air contamination and describes some basic principles for improving IAQ in future schools.

VOLATILE ORGANIC COMPOUNDS

In new buildings, IAQ problems often involve either chemical off-gassing or inadequate ventilation. Finishing materials used in new construction (e.g., paints, wall coverings, and flooring materials) go through a curing process during which some of the chemicals used in their manufacture are emitted, yielding volatile organic compounds, or VOCs. (*Volatile* in this case refers to the material's instability in its natural state—solid or liquid—and its tendency to change into a vaporous state at room temperature.) These chemical compounds, some artificially created and some naturally occurring, evaporate at varying rates, after which they are present in the air. Some compounds, like alcohol or acetone, evaporate very rapidly; others, like the oily substances used to create residues in spray pesticides or smoothness in alkyd-based paints, evaporate so slowly that they are referred to as SVOCs, or semivolatile organic compounds. People usually experience VOCs as odors, but they don't always have a smell. VOCs are not necessarily dangerous; toxicity depends on the compound itself and the level of someone's exposure to it. Chemical compounds like benzene (carcinogenic) or formaldehyde (reasonably anticipated to be carcinogenic) are hazardous to human health, but perfumes, air fresheners, and citrus fruit oils are also considered VOCs.

There are many potential product sources of these chemicals in new and renovated buildings. The most common are paints, adhesives, sealants and caulking, resilient flooring materials, carpet, and some furniture components. Some indoor air pollutants—for example, fumes and odors from consumable materials such as magic markers, cleaning fluids, and chemicals used in office machines and printers—originate in everyday activities.

Careful and knowledgeable specification of finishing materials can reduce VOCs. Project specs should require that sheet-type materials, such as carpeting, be aired out prior to installation. This airing process allows the majority of chemical residues to evaporate outside the new facility.

The amount of off-gassing in most materials decreases very quickly after a few days, but each material has its own requirements. Another effective way to improve air quality is to air out the building itself by setting the mechanical systems to maximum ventilation for a specified period of time prior to occupancy. (The heating system should never be used to "bake out" the building; this can drive VOCs into other materials. These materials, in turn, may begin to release the VOCs after occupancy.) Airing out a building sometimes presents scheduling problems, because school projects usually adhere to very tight deadlines, utilizing each and every day prior to the beginning of a school year. Early planning and a schedule that treats the airing-out period as an essential step in the construction process can help prevent IAQ problems.

OTHER GASEOUS POLLUTANTS

Other gaseous pollutants may originate from the site itself. Radon gas, a naturally occurring, colorless, odorless, radioactive element, is a common problem in some areas of the United States. Radon is easily mitigated with simple exhaust systems that use fans to pull the gas from the adjacent soil and vent it into the atmosphere above the occupied level. Other soil gases may leach from leaking underground fuel tanks or originate in previous site uses, such as landfill or other waste disposal. The initial preselection site assessment work should uncover these possibilities, and such land should usually be eliminated as a potential site for a school. Additional site-related pollutants include exhaust fumes from buses and delivery vehicles and odors from trash containers.

Before a building is renovated for school use, particular attention must be paid to its ventilating system. Guidelines for the amount of fresh air that must be supplied to occupied spaces vary with the use for which a building was originally designed. For example, an office building has a much lower occupancy level than a school. In fact, schools have some of the highest occupancy levels (measured by square feet per occupant). A ventilating system designed for an office building will likely not be adequate for a school, and replacing a heating, ventilating, and air conditioning (HVAC) system is difficult and expensive.

COMFORT SYSTEM PROBLEMS

A school's HVAC systems, also known as the indoor comfort systems, are designed to specific criteria for ventilation rates and heating and cooling loads. When working as designed, these systems create well-balanced conditions in an occupied space. An appropriate amount of fresh (outdoor) air is supplied to the space and balanced with a certain amount of air exhausted from the same space to avoid a buildup of carbon dioxide (CO_2). The fresh air brought into the space is conditioned to a certain temperature and humidity. The fans that move the air, the air volume dampers in the ductwork, and all the grilles and diffusers are adjusted for proper air distribution. Temperature and humidity controls are calibrated and set to normal comfort ranges.

Ideally, after the systems are balanced, an independent contractor commissions the building systems. This involves activating all the systems in normal operating mode under normal operating conditions, and verifying that all system components are in proper working condition. The systems are then fine-tuned, and any substantial remedial work is completed before the occupants move in.

Even then, some additional adjustments may be needed, as CO_2, humidity, and heat levels fluctuate with occupancy.

Older ventilating systems were typically designed for economy as well as efficiency. They recycle a certain amount of indoor air; mix this tempered air with fresh, outdoor air; and redistribute the blended air to the breathing zone. While this saves on heating and cooling, recycled air can become contaminated with pollutants or compromised by the presence of too much CO_2. (Although CO_2 is not lethal, an overabundance can cause fatigue, lethargy, inattention, headache, irritability, and drowsiness.) The mechanical system then becomes the distribution pathway for gaseous or particulate indoor air pollutants. Gaseous pollutants, such as VOCs, are chemical based. Particulate pollutants can be biological (molds, mildews, and fungi) or inorganic (silica dust, asbestos, and fiberglass). Newer systems that include energy recovery systems retain the heat of the exhaust air without mixing old and new air streams.

OPERABLE WINDOWS: THE DOWNSIDE

There is nearly universal insistence on having operable windows in school buildings, but it is impossible for design engineers or HVAC system balancers to accurately predict their use. The school's occupants can become a significant factor in operational problems. Conservative planners design for a building in which all windows and doors are shut. Problems then arise when windows or doors are opened, upsetting the balance of mechanically induced air ventilation. For example, open windows can reverse the airflow from a lavatory that has been designed with negative air pressure, causing odors to be forced back into a corridor. Open windows can also create localized ventilation loops that disrupt normal air distribution or cause a buildup of CO_2 in spaces occupied by groups of students.

Even though the object of opening windows is to bring fresh air indoors, open windows can, ironically, engender indoor air quality problems. When fertilizers and spray pesticides are applied to spaces outside open windows, these chemicals can easily make their way into a building. Open windows can also allow the entrance of insects and other pests, as well as pollen and other plant-based allergens, all of which can impact the quality of the indoor environment. Dust and debris from adjacent areas can infiltrate, as can odors and fumes from outdoor activities. The problems are as variable as the use of the windows. Despite the greater mechanical efficiency of sealed buildings, however, most people still prefer the option of being able to open windows.

Typical ventilating systems for schools do not include filtration systems other than nuisance dust filters that affect only visible particulates. In the absence of such systems, the indoor air is only as clean as the outdoor air. While a variety of air purification systems have been developed, their efficacy and reliability remain largely untested. Systems such as ultraviolet sterilization, bipolar ionization, or photocatalytic cleansing of the ventilation air stream are available, but their upfront costs are usually prohibitive.

BIOLOGICAL POLLUTANTS

While biological pollution is more common in older buildings, given the right conditions, molds, mildews, and fungi can grow just as readily in a new building. Mold spores are ubiquitous, though at normal concentrations do not pose problems for most people. But when the right conditions are present, the spores can settle, the mold can multiply and release more spores, and, in just a matter of days, concentrations in the air can become significant enough to require remediation. In order to grow, mold and fungus need darkness (or, more accurately, the absence of ultraviolet light), moderate temperature, high humidity or moisture (at the surface), and a food source such as cellulose or some other organic material. These conditions are not uncommon inside wall or ceiling cavities—hidden areas where mold growth may be difficult to identify until it is so extensive it becomes visible on exposed surfaces, at which point the problem is acute.

People's reactions to mold and fungus exposure vary. Some people may merely perceive a nuisance odor, while others react with life-threatening illness; the intensity of reactions and symptoms are unpredictable. Susceptibility depends on age, health, genetic predisposition, exposure levels, and the type of mold or fungus. School-age children are, as a group, more vulnerable to exposure than adults, making this a critical issue for schools.

Certain types of molds and fungi are particularly toxic and require immediate attention. Experts in the field of industrial hygiene should be consulted if a mold or fungus problem is suspected. They can identify the species, assess the scope of the contamination and risk, and make recommendations for a course of action. It is important to note that killing the mold or fungus only stops its amplification. Dead spores contain the same mycotoxins as viable spores. And dead spores are easily aerosolized if disturbed, entering the breathing zone and even the building's ventilating system. Remediation therefore often requires extensive site cleanup, with area containment similar to an asbestos remediation project.

The single most significant factor in the growth of biological pollutants is moisture, which can derive from many sources commonly found in schools. In summer, warm, moist air will condense on cool surfaces, such as pipes and air conditioning ducts. Moisture can come from leaking plumbing or roofs, from liquid spills, or from rain infiltration through windows or walls. Significant moisture is tracked into a building on rainy days by people entering the space. Routine cleaning procedures typically use water.

The best way to control biological pollutants is to control moisture. Repair leaks immediately and clean up spills as they happen. Use dry cleaning techniques where possible, and force-dry areas where water is used. Quickly mop up rainwater tracked into a building. Do not let moisture collect anywhere for more than a few hours. If the local climate dictates, install humidity controls to keep the interior relative humidity to 45 percent or less, and insulate pipes and ducts against condensation. If the building is kept dry, molds, mildews, and fungi will not propagate.

INORGANIC PARTICULATE POLLUTANTS

Particulate pollutants also derive from building materials. Buildings constructed prior to the early 1970s likely contain asbestos insulation. Most school districts have cleaned up their buildings in accordance with the federal Asbestos Hazard Emergency Response Act of 1986. Remaining asbestos-containing materials should be catalogued and strictly managed so that they pose no threat to air quality. While asbestos is no longer used in construction, fiberglass, mineral wool, fiber-type thermal and acoustic insulation, and some spray-on fireproofing materials used on structural steel can still contribute to airborne dust problems if not properly specified, installed, and maintained.

IAQ IN THE FUTURE MAGNET SCHOOL

How do we go about ensuring good IAQ in the magnet school of the future? For new buildings, the solution is straightforward. Install a ventilating system that uses exclusively fresh air tempered to a temperature and humidity that suits the occupants and their activities, rather than designing to minimum codes or guidelines. (Displacement ventilating systems that provide this volume of fresh air have proved successful.) Never recycle exhaust air into the breathing zone. If the outdoor air is fouled by smog, dust, or other industrial pollution, the building should include air-cleaning filtration within the ventilating system, and the number and control of operable windows should be limited. Through the use of sensors and controllers, the ventilating system should compensate for temporary pressure imbalances caused by operable windows.

Adapting systems to fit existing building parameters is, by its nature, custom work that will increase the design and construction costs of a project. The physical constraints of the building or the cost of adapting the systems may even disqualify a building for school use. Educational planners need to be aware of IAQ issues, and IAQ must be considered in the early planning stages of a project to help make this very difficult programmatic decision.

A few final cautions are necessary. Keeping a building clean and dry is the formula for keeping it healthy. But the goal of a clean and dry building must be attained through the thoughtful and judicious use of environmentally sensitive cleaning methods and products. Schools are becoming increasingly specialized, high-performance, technical buildings. As such, they require a certain level of expertise to maintain them, much the way a high-performance vehicle demands specialized maintenance. These solutions do not come without added cost, but that cost must be balanced against the need for healthy indoor air, a requirement for good health and improved learning. And educators need to be aware that many factors, including improper lighting, acoustics, excessive noise or vibration, overcrowding, and poor ergonomics can produce symptoms similar to those associated with poor indoor air quality. In addition to ensuring the quality of the indoor air, these other stressors must be controlled for overall indoor environmental comfort.

13

A Sustainable Approach to Specialized-School Design

Architecture worldwide changed forever when the Organization of Petroleum Exporting Countries (OPEC) embargoed the United States and other western countries in 1973, causing widespread shortages of fossil fuels. Energy-efficient design became paramount, and building codes and standards were revised to reflect the need to conserve energy and reduce reliance on oil. This new energy consciousness heightened interest in developing technologies such as solar and wind power. Unfortunately, when the embargo was lifted and OPEC's oil pipelines once again flowed freely, these technologies were marginalized and never became part of mainstream commercial design. The relatively high up-front cost for these systems, and a lack of demonstrable performance reliability, proved to be the Achilles heel of this emerging industry. It faltered and became a special-interest sector relegated to the back-page classifieds of industry periodicals.

The energy crisis of the early 1970s did, however, engender a persistent interest in environmental issues at an academic and popular level. Today, as a generation of environmentally aware people assumes leadership positions in the professions, the idea of utilizing renewable resources and conserving nonrenewable ones is at last becoming mainstream. We find ourselves at the cutting edge of a 30-plus-year-old idea: sustainable, or "green," design—methodologies that tread lightly on the environment and work creatively with renewable resources.

GREEN DESIGN

With this new (or restored) environmental awareness, architects are turning with great fervor to what are called *holistic* building techniques. Because there is general popular agreement about the importance of environmental issues, depletable resources are being conserved and renewable resources utilized. Schools are now designed with specific functional areas for recycling programs. Going one step further, adaptive reuse, or the consideration of what a building might become after its initial function passes, is now part of the initial design process, with some components designed to be recycled rather than demolished after a building is dismantled. Even building materials are designed and manufactured to be recycled into the same or different products. Carpet used to be torn out, hauled off to a landfill, and replaced. Today, recyclable carpets can be leased: the worn material is removed for recycling whenever new carpet is required. Though not always practiced, conservation of resources has become a mainstream idea.

Julie A. Kim contributed to this chapter.

In fact, capturing energy resources from the environment is now standard practice. Geothermal heating and cooling—tapping into the constant ground temperature for indoor climate control—is increasingly being used in school construction. Passive solar energy collection for hot-water heating is common. The industry growing up around the production of electrical power through the use of photovoltaic collection devices, or solar energy cells, is maturing. Environmentally friendly technologies such as fuel cell electrical generation are gaining favor as their initial costs stabilize. Collecting rainwater for plumbing systems is coming to be considered conventional design, as is collecting wastewater for "gray water" irrigation systems. The use of highly reflective materials and colors to avoid heat buildup on large surfaces such as paved parking areas and large, flat roofs is an easy choice. And even more adventurous roofing strategies, like grass-planted roofs, are finding proponents among public-school designers. These are just a few of the green ideas being included in present-day designs.

A life-cycle cost analysis of various building materials and systems should be part of any design process and is often mandated by regulatory agencies. These analyses consider not only the costs to purchase, install, maintain, and eventually replace a material or system, but also the costs of the energy required to collect, process, and transport the raw materials used in the manufacture, packaging, and delivery of the system. Replacement and ultimate disposition costs of materials (through landfills or recycling) are now considered along with construction, installation, and maintenance costs to inform the selection of building components.

Likewise, sustainable design requirements are being met by manufacturers competing for green budget dollars. In fact, companies with generous research and development budgets are often leading the charge with new products. A good example is the carpet industry. With millions of tons of used carpeting filling up landfills, the carpet industry recognized a problem and developed ideas in marketing and manufacturing technologies to reclaim these potential raw-material resources.

Sustainable products are hardly new to the marketplace. Some of the most sustainable materials are those that have been used in school construction for the past hundred years, including exterior brick, masonry interior walls, ceramic tile, and terrazzo floors. In older school buildings, these materials have long since paid for themselves in savings on maintenance expenses. But the quantity, variety, and availability of sustainable materials is greater now than ever before. In the long run, the use of such materials can be kind to both the environment *and* the operations budget. While it is the purview of the architect to make the best decisions for the specifics of the individual school program and budget, it is incumbent on him or her to make sure that project decision-makers are informed about life-cycle costs and are not bound by a first-cost-only mindset.

THE FUTURE MEETS THE PRESENT

As sustainable design techniques become fundamentals of design philosophy, a new building prototype is emerging. While the building may not *look* so different from the magnet school of today, it will operate very differently.

Comfort systems will be much more user controlled. As reliance on fossil fuels—and therefore operating cost—declines, the strict controls now placed on building heating and cooling will become more lenient. If an individual room is too cool in the early morning hours, its occupants will be able to adjust the heat to temporarily compensate. If it is overheating in the afternoon, they will be able to cool it down. The central building intelligence system will register these adjustments and incorporate them into the building's day-to-day operating routines. If a classroom develops an overabundance of fumes or odors, sensors will detect the imbalance and purge fans will engage to ventilate the room to proper fresh-air levels.

Advances in lighting technology are already providing balanced illumination and color temperature approximating natural daylight. Other lighting system–related architectural strategies and electronic features, all currently available, will come into greater use in tomorrow's magnet schools. Light shelves (horizontal devices with a reflective surface) will redirect daylight into building interiors, decreasing the need for artificial light and reducing power consumption. The lighting control system will read the level of daylight entering an interior and correct the balance of natural and artificial illumination for the time of day and the solar orientation of the room. Lighting control systems will communicate with the building management system and adjust the HVAC systems to economize on heating or cooling, depending on lighting conditions.

Green design has two equally important aspects: it is good for the environment *and* for the human occupants of a building. That double benefit can be clearly seen in the push to maximize natural daylighting of interior spaces. Natural daylighting not only reduces electricity bills, lessening dependence on the fossil fuels used to generate electricity and reducing a building's contribution to air pollution, but it also improves the interior environment for those who study and work there.

Connecticut recently mandated that school districts consider maximizing natural light in new school buildings as well as those undergoing alteration or renovation. Why? Because natural daylight is a great mood enhancer, which can lead to greater attentiveness, improved attendance, and higher achievement.

In the magnet school of the future, communications systems will be merged. The public address system will no longer be separate from the telephone and intercom system. Communications devices will be part of an integrated voice, data, and video network, which itself will be part of a larger intelligent building system that incorporates security, life safety, and building management systems. Imagine the intimacy of a school in which the principal makes routine announcements to all students in a video conference, rather than through wall-mounted speakers that distort sound. Many of these technologies are available today, although the complexity of programming and operating them will require that the staff of the school of the future include trained network systems managers.

Classroom acoustical problems will be resolved through the strategic use of materials that reflect, diffuse, or absorb sound. (This topic is addressed in detail in Chapter 11, "Improving School Acoustics: A Systems Approach.") Indoor air quality will no longer be an issue, as the building will be infused with conditioned fresh air. Displacement ventilating systems might well replace ducted central air systems fed from rooftop air handlers. As filtration technology advances, the indoor air will be as clean as (and quite possibly cleaner than) the outdoor air. (For more on this topic, see Chapter 12, "Indoor Air Quality: Problems and Solutions.")

A SUSTAINABLE APPROACH TO SITING AND SITE DESIGN

The individual school's specific requirements and the character of the surrounding environment must drive the site-selection process. Urban schools usually have a vertical orientation because of the shortage of suitable real estate in cities. Suburban schools face transportation-related issues. Where can buses queue? Where can parents, driving their own cars, drop off kids in the morning and wait to pick them up in the afternoon? Regional schools generally require large athletic fields and facilities. All schools have to deal with deliveries and services.

While site selection is project specific, certain sustainable criteria ought to be considered during any magnet school's site-selection process. For example, sites where mass transportation is both available and likely to be used will reduce the number of trips in private motor vehicles, thereby cutting down on localized pollution. Proximity to population centers encourages the use of nonpolluting modes of transportation such as bicycles and walking. Schools should not be located near major industrial facilities or near trucking routes or other heavily traveled highways.

Other sustainable design ideas include capitalizing on what might otherwise be considered site problems. In a suburban setting, wetlands and animal habitat issues frequently become problematic. In a sustainably designed school, these will become on-site educational assets—tools for teaching about ecology and conservation. Geological problems with bedrock or poorly draining soils can lead to a sanitary waste disposal problem. A sustainable approach would involve on-site processing, whether by a packaged sewage disposal processing plant or some other alternative processing technique. This, too, might serve as an educational asset, acquainting students with recycling and biomechanical processes. (For more on the use of urban school sites as "outdoor classrooms," see Chapter 10, "Site Design and Landscape Architecture for Urban Magnet Schools.")

FUTURE USE OF THE SCHOOL BUILDING

Sustainable design includes thinking about the future. Near-term concerns address the building construction costs and schedule, operating costs, and environmental impact. Long-term considerations include the possibility that the building may become obsolete as a school because of pedagogical changes or demographic shifts. Could it someday be utilized for municipal offices, housing, business, manufacturing, or warehousing, without major reconstruction or a needless waste of resources? If these changes can be planned for, the life of a building can be extended by decades.

If major reconstruction would be required to convert the building to some other function, could the materials removed from the building be reused or recycled? The recycling potential of all of a building's materials needs to be considered. Metal, including steel, cast iron, aluminum, and copper, is easily recycled. Many plastics can be recycled to provide raw materials for other products. Non-pressure-treated wood products can be recycled into other wood- or cellulose-based products. Some single-ply-membrane roofing products can be reclaimed. Although the building itself cannot exist forever, its components may exist as sustainable resources for other buildings or as other products for decades to come.

One-Stop Shopping? The Perils and Promise of Design-Build Project Delivery

Patricia A. Myler, AIA, and James A. Keaney Jr.

Pursued in the conventional way, the process of building a new public school can be an extremely lengthy one, and the total cost of construction can often far exceed original budgetary projections. To bring new schools online more quickly while reining in construction costs, several states have passed legislation encouraging the use of an alternative delivery method—design-build—for school design and construction. The trend is gathering steam: Florida pioneered the use of design-build for school construction beginning in 1989, and in recent years has been joined by Arizona, California, Texas, and other states.

For those unfamiliar with delivery-method terminology, some nutshell definitions may be in order:

- Under the conventional *design-bid-build* delivery method (also known as the "hard bid" method), the owner[1] first retains the services of a design professional. At this point the owner also has the option of retaining a construction manager (CM) to work with the design professional during the design and documentation phases and to administer the construction phase. Only after the completion of the design and documentation phase does the project get put out to bid, either to trade contractors through the CM or directly to general contractors (GCs), in the absence of a CM. In either scenario, contracts are awarded to the lowest qualified bidder.
- Under *design-build*, the owner awards one contract covering both design and construction to a single team—either a relationship between a design firm and a CM/GC or a design-build firm with in-house design *and* construction capabilities. In the former arrangement, the relationship can be led by either the design entity or the CM/GC entity, but most are led by the constructor.

Some states are aggressively pushing the adoption of the design-build model; others—like our firms' home state, Connecticut—are taking a more cautious approach. States that have dived headlong into design-build tend to be in the South and Southwest, where skyrocketing school-age populations have created a pressing need to build lots of new school buildings as quickly as possible. By contrast, Connecticut's law (effective 2003) merely creates a pilot program allowing the use of design-build for up to two school buildings within the state each year. (As of this writing there had been no school construction in Connecticut under this pilot program legislation.)

Whether more widespread adoption comes quickly or slowly, however, design-build is clearly a wave of the future, and we believe it's high time to closely examine this delivery method and to analyze its merits and disadvantages when employed for school design and construction. Switching to design-build does hold real promise for certain kinds of public school buildings and for certain kinds of school districts, but a few strong cautions are in order.

CONVENTIONAL PROJECT DELIVERY VERSUS DESIGN-BUILD

Design-build isn't really a brand-new idea—in fact, by placing the responsibility for both design and construction in the hands of a single entity, it hearkens back to the ancient, worldwide tradition of the master builder. Many of the great architectural monuments of the past were the work of master builders who planned, designed, engineered, and oversaw construction of the buildings they created. But as buildings grew more technically complex and as the architectural, engineering, and construction professions became more specialized, the master-builder tradition waned, to be replaced by a system in which designers and constructors performed their jobs separately, under separate contractual agreements with building owners.

For more decades than any of us can remember, virtually all American public schools—in fact, most public- and private-sector buildings of whatever sort in the United States—have been designed and built using the now conventional design-bid-build delivery method. As we'll see, however, this model possesses certain inefficiencies that are ameliorated or eliminated when the design-build method is chosen instead.

Unsurprisingly, given the industry's constant desire for low cost and speedy delivery, some private businesses began turning to the alternative design-build method much earlier than did the public sector. But by the 1980s a number of federal and state governmental agencies were also choosing design-build delivery for certain public works projects. And by the early 2000s, the vast majority of states allowed, encouraged, or mandated the use of design-build for at least some kinds of construction—especially transportation-related projects (Design-Build Institute of America 2002). Nevertheless, design-bid-build today remains the predominant method for new school construction in most places in the United States—even in states that have approved design-build for other kinds of facilities.

There's no question that the conventional design-bid-build method can be cumbersome. The following is a step-by-step synopsis of the design-bid-build process in Connecticut; it resembles the process in other states, though there are variations in state funding and approval mechanisms.

1. Educators (including the local board of education and superintendent) develop educational specifications for a proposed project. This "ed spec" is the means by which the educators describe the educational activities that will go on in the school and the spaces that need to be incorporated into the proposed new or renovated facility.
2. The ed spec is translated into space and site requirements and a cost is developed reflecting the defined scope of work. Local public approval is sought through a referendum proc-

ess or some other form of authorization. Once local funding is secured, an application is filed with the state requesting state funding.

3. After receiving local and state authorization, the owner selects a design professional (an architect) through a traditional request-for-qualifications (RFQ), request-for-proposals (RFP), and interviewing process.

4. The architect—working with the owner, with other design consultants, and (often) with committees representing facility "stakeholders"—designs the project. If retained early enough in the process, the CM works with other team members to provide certain services (e.g., estimating, constructability reviews, value engineering) throughout the design phase.

5. At the conclusion of the design phase, the design documents—which must be 100-percent complete—are submitted to the appropriate state agencies for review and approval.

6. Upon approval of the documents, the owner approves the project and authorizes it to go out for competitive bidding, selecting the lowest qualified bidder or bidders.

7. The construction process ensues.

But merely outlining the process in this way doesn't really convey just how slow and (sometimes) contentious the conventional delivery method can be. In Connecticut, for example, state authorization of funding can take eight to ten months after submitting an application, and the review of final design documents can take three months or even longer if the state reviewing agencies have a backlog. The process of choosing a design firm might take two to three months. The design phase itself can take upwards of a year. The bidding period is generally two to three months long. And all these things must happen *before* construction, which depending on the type and size of the project can take anywhere from 18 to 36 months.[2] The whole process is one of starting and stopping and starting again, and school planning/design/construction schedules are typically rendered even more complex because it's so often necessary to time the project so that construction is completed before the beginning of the school year. (Scheduling complexities ramify in the case of additions to or partial renovations of existing school buildings, which may be occupied during construction. Such projects must be phased to interfere as little as possible with ongoing activities.)

All told, the "adventure" of bringing a new school into physical being can easily consume three, four, five years—or longer. Change orders due to unforeseen site or environmental conditions or to problems in coordinating trades can lead to construction delays and cost overruns. Moreover, in the design-bid-build system, it's almost inevitable that conflicts will arise when architects are intent on seeing their designs fully realized and contractors are focused on delivering the scope of work defined in the contract documents in a cost-effective manner. The owner will be drawn into these issues, because any agreed-upon resolution will ultimately affect the quality and cost of the project. This process requires the owner or owner's representative to be involved in the project in a hands-on way—a time-consuming commitment. It's no wonder that people have searched for a faster and smoother way of doing things.

But let's stop for a moment before taking a closer look at the relatively streamlined design-build alternative. Despite its cumbersomeness, the conventional design-bid-build process does possess several features that, on examination, turn out not to be so bad. For one thing, state reviews of design documents—in Connecticut and, we're sure, other states as well—tend to be extremely rigorous in testing code compliance, which is helpful in eliminating costly code-driven changes during the construction period and which helps facilitate local review. For another, there are real advantages—which we'll return to below—to allowing the design phase to proceed on a sequential schedule. Doing so can ensure, for example, that there's adequate time and opportunity for all project stakeholders to creatively participate in fashioning the facility's design.

Even admitting these positive aspects, however, it appears at first glance that the conventional method can't hold a candle to design-build when it comes to cutting time and expense. Design-build proponents forcefully argue that their delivery method can shave months or years off a school construction schedule and ensure that a project will remain on budget because:

- The owner awards a *single contract* covering design and construction services, allowing for a fast-track approach in which design and construction can proceed simultaneously.
- Design-build is typically a *fixed-price arrangement*. Because the design-build team must produce the facility at the agreed-upon price, the chance of budget overruns is greatly reduced.

Here, then, is a step-by-step description of how the school construction process typically works when the design-build delivery method is employed.

1. The owner issues a request for qualifications (RFQ) to solicit qualifications packages from interested design-build teams (either CM-architect partners or stand-alone design-build firms).
2. The owner shortlists the best-qualified teams and issues a request for proposals (RFP) to those teams.
3. The owner evaluates the proposals submitted based on quality of design *and* price, selects the best, and awards a fixed-price design-build contract to the winning team. (Occasionally, the owner presents conceptual designs to the shortlisted teams, but most design-build projects allow the successful candidate to perform some level of design development.)
4. Design and construction ensue.

By following this method, the owner might be in possession of a new, completed school building within as little as two years (or even less) after the contract is awarded, depending on the project's size and complexity. What's more, the owner will be spared involvement in disagreements between designers and contractors, since these will of necessity be resolved by the design-build team. And because errors must be corrected by the design-build team, the need for change orders during construction is eliminated. Figure 14.1 graphically illustrates the time savings that can be realized with the design-build method as compared with the conventional design-bid-build process.

Sounds like a snap, yes? So if design-build is really so much simpler and faster than the design-bid-build method, why hasn't everyone abandoned the inefficient conventional model? The answer to this question has to do, in part, with *what's left out* of the step-by-step summary above.

A FRONT-LOADED PROCESS

The synopsis of the design-build process just given disguises the fact that design-build requires much more in the way of up-front preparation on the part of the owner than does the conventional

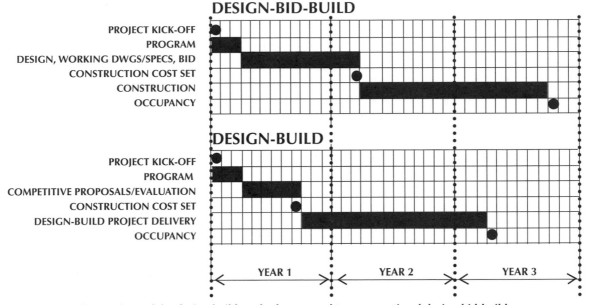

Figure 14.1. Time savings of the design-build method compared to a conventional design-bid-build process.

design-bid-build method. Design-build is heavily front-loaded, and the preaward responsibilities that design-build places on the owner can be burdensome, especially in the case of programmatically complex buildings such as schools.

It's critical to remember that once a design-build contract has been awarded, everything is more or less set in stone. Because construction can begin soon after initial design tasks are completed—perhaps as soon as a few months after the contract's award—there's little or no opportunity to modify a facility's design once work has begun. Therefore, to ensure the quality of the design and construction and to make certain that the owner really ends up with the facility it wants, the RFP must be extraordinarily thorough and detailed—much more so than a typical RFP issued to competing architectural firms as part of the conventional design-bid-build process. Whereas a typical design-services-only RFP might consist of little more than an educational specification, a design-build RFP for a school construction project must also include the following:

- Detailed site information, including the property survey, environmental report, geotechnical report, wetlands flagging, and traffic studies.
- Detailed product and performance guidelines for all materials and equipment (everything from doorknobs to carpet to whiteboards) to be used in the school.
- Detailed design standards covering typical classroom and specialty-room configurations, furniture and equipment layouts, and building and site program flow and adjacencies. (In some cases fully developed conceptual drawings may be required.)

Developing this documentation is obviously a tall order, requiring substantial expertise and a large expenditure of time and money. In fact, the depth of expertise required to put together the needed RFP documents will no doubt exceed the in-house capabilities of many smaller public school districts—necessitating the hiring of a consultant.

When this preaward workload is figured in, it becomes clear that any claim to the effect that the design-build approach *always* saves time and money would be suspect. To its credit, the Design-Build Institute of America (DBIA)—the design-build industry's professional association—carefully steers clear of making such an indefensible claim in its promotional materials, and DBIA advises owners with limited in-house resources to hire consultants to guide them through the RFP process (DBIA 2002, p. 5). By the same token, however, DBIA's otherwise helpful publications stop short of explaining why design-build might in some cases be just as time-consuming and expensive as the conventional design-bid-build approach—and even more difficult.

Can the design-build approach to school-construction project delivery really be more difficult than the conventional design-bid-build procedure? In certain cases, the answer is definitely yes. For small districts without appropriate in-house resources, the design-build approach might well be more complicated than design-bid-build and might produce very little in the way of time and cost savings when all the owner's up-front work is calculated in. Design-build is especially problematic for very small districts that undertake school-construction projects only very rarely—and where building committees are assembled on an ad hoc basis and dissolved when a project is completed.

Extrapolating from this, it probably makes little sense for *any* district (small or large) to switch to design-build if it is not undertaking a reasonably extensive, multibuilding school construction program, since preparation of RFP documents only becomes truly cost-effective when those documents (or significant portions of them) can be reused for a number of projects. And the wisdom of the design-build approach is at least questionable in districts with little undeveloped land or with highly varied terrain. In such cases, site surveys and site preparation work (e.g., demolition of existing structures, rock removal, environmental remediation procedures) are likely to be unusually extensive and to differ dramatically from project to project—meaning that a great deal of the documentation accompanying any particular RFP will be unique to that project.

OTHER CAUTIONS

Besides the potential difficulties connected with RFP preparation, there are a number of other reasons to be cautious about across-the-board adoption of the design-build delivery method:

- *The design-build approach limits or eliminates user/community participation in design.* If a district's approach to school construction is to produce cookie-cutter facilities—and the reasons for such an approach may be very good ones, including the need to erect numerous school facilities in a hurry—stakeholder participation in the school design process may be relatively unimportant. But it's a different story in districts concerned to provide each school building's stakeholders (faculty, staff, parents, students, and members of community groups eager to use the facility after school hours) with a facility that's as closely customized to their needs as possible. The very speed of the design-build process tends to shrink the opportunity for such a complexly iterative design process.
- *Relatedly, the design-build approach may inhibit or prevent a local community's "buy-in" on a new school project.* Community buy-in—the development of real enthusiasm for the project by local residents, businesses, and institutions—can be especially important to

school construction projects in urban neighborhoods (1) where community members may be understandably suspicious of government interventions that do not take community members' wishes into account, and (2) where property crimes, including vandalism, are endemic. This is not an inconsequential consideration. It's a truth of human nature that people will care about—and take efforts to care for and protect—buildings in whose "ownership" they feel they share.

• *The design-build model can replace thorough and comprehensive state-level review (of design documents) with potentially less-effective review of proposals.* As with the preparation of RFP documents, there's a potential problem here if the owner doesn't have appropriate in-house expertise. It might be necessary to retain an outside consultant to review proposals as well as to assist in RFP preparation, but in any case some mechanism must be established to ensure that technical aspects of proposals are expertly evaluated, lest the district lose control over the actual design quality of the facility. Obviously, this would not be an issue for states where all school construction procurement, statewide, is conducted by a single, centralized agency, but it could be a big problem in a state like Connecticut, which is divided into scores of mostly small, more or less autonomous districts and where the pilot-program legislation simply does not address the matter of how design-build proposals are to be reviewed.

• *The design-build method is inappropriate in cases where site conditions cannot be determined ahead of time with a high degree of exactitude.* Design-build RFPs must stipulate the scope of work very precisely. Design-build is probably inappropriate for most school renovation projects, because it's likely that site conditions requiring additional work (e.g., structural problems, presence of hazardous materials) will only be revealed during the demolition phase of construction.

THE UPSIDE OF DESIGN-BUILD

The design-build approach to school construction shows undeniable promise for certain kinds of school districts and for certain types of school buildings. Let's look first at the kinds of districts that may well benefit from the adoption of the design-build method.

• Certain large districts (some big-city districts, large suburban districts, unified school districts) with standing building committees and in-house expertise that is well-rounded and deep enough to handle much of the work of preparing RFPs and evaluating proposals.

• Districts planning extensive, multiyear and multibuilding construction programs, where it is likely that much of the work performed to develop an RFP can serve as a boilerplate for subsequent RFPs.

• Districts where a highly standardized, cookie-cutter approach to school construction makes sense, because (1) a fast-growing school-age population is creating a great demand to build several schools in the shortest possible time, and/or (2) the district contains a large amount of buildable, undeveloped land whose terrain is basically similar from site to site.

Regarding facility types that lend themselves to design-build, a general rule might be that the design-build method is more appropriate for simpler school building types, *especially* if a district's building plan calls for the creation of multiple buildings of a given kind. For example, many urban districts across the country are turning to a K–8 model for elementary and middle grades education. If a district's capital plan involves the construction of several new K–8 facilities over, say, a five- or ten-year period, using design-build for those projects may make sense—assuming, of course, that state law allows its use, and also assuming that site conditions are somewhat similar across the district.

By contrast, not only are comprehensive high schools more complex, programmatically, than facilities for the lower grades, but it's also the case that, in most districts, the building of a new comprehensive high school is a relatively infrequent event. Too, comprehensive high schools often possess the kinds of features and amenities—large gyms, fieldhouses and extensive athletics fields, well-equipped auditoriums—that make them more attractive than less-elaborate, lower-grade schools to community users whose needs should be taken into account during design. For these reasons, design-build is probably less appropriate for the delivery of a new comprehensive high school—*except*, perhaps, in those comparatively rare districts where a lack of existing facilities and an exploding school-age population combine to necessitate the rapid creation of numerous comprehensive highs.

Regarding the use of the design-build method for new magnet schools (of whatever grade configuration), we're divided. On one hand, magnet schools—especially career-based magnets—tend to be more programmatically complicated than traditional elementary, middle, or high schools. On the other hand, magnets are generally intended to bring together students from diverse, often geographically distant communities. Since a magnet doesn't "belong" to a specific community, there may be less need to achieve community buy-in from the neighborhood in which the school is located.

USING DESIGN-BUILD SUCCESSFULLY

If a district is contemplating using design-build for at least some of its school-construction projects, there are a few strategies that may help the process run more smoothly—and that will increase its chances for success. Several of these have already been alluded to, including the advisability of retaining consultants to assist in the development of RFP documents and the establishment of some mechanism to ensure that the technical aspects of proposals receive adequate review. But a number of other strategies should also be kept in mind:

- *Make sure the educational objectives of the new school are clear—and that they're clearly communicated in the design-build RFP.* Under the conventional method, educational goals can be tweaked and modified through the design phase, but that can't happen with design-build.
- *Strictly limit the number of shortlisted design-build teams.* The design-build process requires a large, up-front commitment of time and money from competing design-build teams as well as from the owner issuing the RFP. Design-build teams are much less likely to dedicate adequate staff time and money to the task of creating a truly responsive proposal if they think they have too slender a chance of winning the job. The DBIA recommends that, for most design-build projects, owners should shortlist no more than three of

the teams that submit qualifications packages—and we strongly agree. The longer a short-list is, the less likely it is that the district's RFP will elicit high-quality proposals. In fact, if the qualified design-build teams think competition will be too stiff, they may well decline even to submit a proposal.

- *Carefully balance the weight given to quality of design with that given to price when evaluating proposals.* It's a bad idea to choose a design-build firm solely on the basis of price. (By contrast, selecting the lowest qualified bidder makes sense under the design-bid-build process, because the quality of design is defined by the detailed contract documents developed by independent design professionals.) Several sensible strategies for balancing quality and price considerations in the evaluation of proposals are outlined in *The Design-Bid Process: Utilizing Competitive Selection*, an extremely useful document produced by the DBIA. These include the weighted criteria, adjusted low-bid, equivalent design/low-bid, fixed budget/best design, and meets criteria/low-bid methods for choosing the winning design-build team. Their specifics differ, but each method is designed to ensure that price will not be the sole (or even the most important) criterion guiding the selection.

As we hope we have shown, design-build can offer a promising alternative to the conventional delivery method. But design-build is not a panacea for correcting every inefficiency, nor is it the best method for addressing every school district's new-facility needs. Furthermore, we are convinced that design-build legislation must be carefully crafted to ensure, for example, that districts receive sufficient funding to cover the significant upfront costs and that design-build proposals receive thorough technical review. Vaguely worded, open-ended design-build legislation—however well-intentioned—may end up creating more problems than it solves. Superintendents and school business officials in states whose legislatures are currently considering or writing legislation permitting the use of design-build for school construction would therefore be well advised to become as educated as possible about design-build's pros and cons, and to make their own recommendations known to their state legislators.

NOTES

1. Throughout this chapter, the term *owner* is used to designate the contracting and decision-making body leading the construction project. Depending on how the school system of a given city, town, or region is organized, the owner could be a permanent town building committee, an ad hoc building committee assembled for one specific project, or a local or regional board of education (or subcommittee thereof).

2. A typical K–8 school (100,000 square feet of new construction) would typically take 18 to 22 months to build; the construction period for a typical high school might last 36 months or longer, depending on the issues.

Epilogue

The Future of Magnet Schools

Edwin T. Merritt, Ed.D.

This book is about designing specialized schools to improve educational opportunity, change the educational process, and—we hope—give American school systems more bang for their buck. As we focus on making change, we understand full well that, as influential architect/theorist Christopher Alexander has written,

> When you build a thing, you cannot merely build that thing in isolation, but must also repair the world around it and within it, so that the larger world at that one place becomes more coherent, and worthwhile; and the thing which you make takes its place in the web of nature, as you make it. (Alexander, Ishikawa, and Silverstein 1977, p. xiii)

Or—to reverse the coin—the entire society must be involved in change if it is to be effective.

WHY CHANGE?

Throughout this book, we've spoken about the need for educational change and the importance of families having a hand in choosing how their children are educated. The main purpose of pre-K–12 public education is to help students acquire basic reading, writing, and computational skills within a framework of learning that will ultimately help them earn a living, be effective parents, and become responsible citizens. Study after study finds us coming up short in meeting this goal. Change is clearly needed.

The magnet school concept seems to do best in moving toward this goal of change. Magnet schools are good laboratories for studying educational change and, by extension, helping all pre-K–12 institutions to improve. Many charter schools, by contrast, are underfunded, lack programmatic support, and have less-than-adequate facilities, so—despite the arguments of charter proponents—they're generally not in as good a position to serve as change-oriented laboratories. (There are certainly exceptions, such as Philadelphia's Charter High for Architecture + Design; see pages 57–62.)

Although they are also interested in promoting change, other kinds of specialized public schools—for example, schools for special-needs students—don't focus as squarely as do magnets

209

on the basic, common, core challenges all public schools face. It's certainly true that these kinds of schools have made real progress, especially in individualizing learning, but data derived from their programs are often focused on special needs and are therefore less useful than data from mainstream-oriented magnet schools. (The intensive, one-on-one work between teacher and student, for example, that has proved so effective in autism education is mostly inapplicable in other public school contexts simply because of the enormous expense involved.)

Besides testing and promoting better strategies for learning, magnets can also be a means for actualizing the democratic principles of educational equality and parity. We see this all over the country: in the schools that are part of Hartford, Connecticut's Learning Corridor (see pages 31–33); in Florida, where widespread use of magnet schools has helped achieve national integration goals and now helps deal with socioeconomic disadvantage; and in Clark County, Nevada, where an active magnet program brings much-needed diversity to schools in ethnically homogenous neighborhoods.

But while it is critically important to foster equality of educational opportunity, it is just as important for public education to fuel economic development. Without an educated workforce, the nation's economy will surely wither. Meaningful, relevant education is necessary to keep the American workforce productive and the gross national product growing. Unfortunately, it's our experience that the educational community in this country has traditionally paid too little attention to the relationship between education and economic development. Overall, American educators have been reluctant or unable to make this connection, to adapt their schools quickly to meet local economic needs, or to keep up with other educational systems around the world, which pay more attention to training workers.

MAGNET SCHOOLS TODAY—SOME PROBLEMS

Magnet schools are still in their infancy. Though it is true that many are making great strides in improving the educational experience, it's also true that some magnet programs and individual magnet schools are exploring blind alleys—and that those who create and operate magnets don't always do an adequate job when planning and running these "alternative" institutions. By their very definition, magnets are supposed to *attract* students, pulling them toward a highly productive and worthwhile educational experience. In all frankness, however, many magnets don't live up to their PR—shying away, for example, from instituting truly interdisciplinary approaches to education and relying instead on students' ability to "put it all together" by themselves. Such schools continue to separate art from science, when in fact art is science and science is art. And even where magnets do try to introduce cross-disciplinary learning, their strategies are all too often half-baked or disorganized.

Moreover, magnets too often seem to develop their "attractiveness" on a somewhat willy-nilly basis. Often, educational leaders propose magnet programs based more on whim than on national or—more important—local economic and educational needs. But as Charles Cassidy, who directed magnet programs in both New York State and Connecticut, explains so cogently in the essay he contributed to this volume (see Chapter 3, "Planning, Creating, and Funding New Magnet Schools"), this cart-before-the-horse way of creating magnet schools is a mistake that may doom a magnet to failure.

Granted, guidance on developing magnets in ways that truly meet needs is very limited at present. There is no national think-tank whose purpose would be to help local school systems create and organize magnet programs. That's a shame, because it's our belief that some standards and controls are definitely needed.

In many cases, magnet schools are created intuitively, with local, seat-of-the-pants guidance. A superintendent of schools, for example, might decide that a fine arts/performing arts magnet would be nice and so will set about beating the political drums for support. If the community likes the idea, state legislators will support the concept and, in many cases, federal funding will follow. On one hand, this kind of process is good because it generates local motivation to make change. On the other hand, however, the process is flawed because no systematic thought is given to meeting the community's real common core of learning needs.

Without naming names, let us mention a good example of this not-so-good trend that we happened upon while researching this book. This particular magnet school—a new urban, interdistrict magnet—is an International Baccalaureate (IB) program high school. It is designed to serve about 200 students and is open to enrollment by students from throughout its region, both urban and suburban districts.

Admission to this school is by lottery—for good reason, since in this school's state the law prohibits magnet schools from employing achievement- or examination-based selection processes. However, there's a problem. The actual academic demands of the International Baccalaureate program are extremely rigorous. The school's creators/administrators give lip service, of course, to the benefits of an IB program, but in reality the school appears to be sliding toward failure. Many of the students entering the program are vastly underprepared for this kind of high-powered academic environment. Those who cannot make the grade drop out, and after two years of operation, the school is facing major retention problems. Moreover, very few graduating seniors are able to pass the International Baccalaureate degree completion tests. Witnessing this school's problems, we have to ask how well suited it is to its community. Was it even a good idea to think about creating an IB magnet program when the school would have no real control over admissions?

"Build it and they will come" may be a good enough rationale for constructing a baseball stadium (at least in Hollywood fantasy), but it's certainly an off-base method for creating successful magnets. A magnet's theme and instructional method really matter—and if these don't suit a community's needs and capacities, trouble is on the way.

Magnets' problems aren't limited to the planning/development process. They also concern the ways in which the educational process is carried out. For example, too few of these "schools of choice" invest enough time and attention in the training of the faculty who teach in them. Comprehensive, rigorous, specialized training of magnet school teachers is rare.

In the case of interdistrict magnets, long-term funding is often a problem. If they are asked to contribute more than a token amount toward tuition, sending districts often balk, for understandable budgetary reasons. And magnet school tuition is often used as a political pawn in budgetary battles, with districts leveraging parents' enthusiasm for magnet schools to ensure that overall budgets are passed. Many host districts are supposed to receive municipal per-student revenue that, for local political reasons, they have trouble getting their hands on—though some are able to fill the gaps with federal funding. The net result is a seesaw funding process that is characterized by high instability and is generally inadequate in scope. Successful magnets have learned to cope with this shifting array of funding sources, but it takes a lot of time, energy, and, yes, money to do so—resources that would be better spent on truly educational purposes.

NAVIGATING THE WATERS OF CHANGE

To repeat: magnet schools show enormous potential to produce positive change in American education. Magnets of the future will work with detailed, well-defined student profiles to provide meaningful individualized programming. The learning process as promoted by future magnet schools will be a "24/7/365" process, involving the entire family and society in general. Magnet schools will recognize that education can gradually leave the classroom and enter the global arena, where questions can be answered as they are raised, where information can be gathered at two o'clock in the morning or at four in the afternoon. Magnet teachers will spend more time being facilitators, counselors, and researchers instead of merely presenters of canned information. They'll be better trained in handling information and making appropriate referrals. Magnet schools of the future will recognize that while all students must have equal educational opportunity, individuals differ in their abilities and capacities—and magnet schools will design their programs to accommodate these differences.

In short, the magnet school, created as a special educational entity, has a mandate to make change. It has the best chance of leading the way—if the magnet school movement is given the help to overcome some real problems.

The patchwork-quilt picture of magnet school planning and funding and of magnet faculty training leaves much to be desired, so we suggest a tightening of the planning process, an increase of required training, together with an accountability component and a coordination of revenue streams on local, state, and federal levels. Allocation of operational expenditures requires more sophisticated legislative oversight and a more focused administrative effort at all levels. The magnet school "ship," while of good design, needs to be more carefully built, and much more attention needs to be paid to navigating it through the waters of change. This book has been an attempt to help in that endeavor.

Appendix

Educational Technology Standards

The following organizations are contributing to educational technology standards for use in new schools (in some cases, the URLs given direct you to specific articles of interest).

Building Industry Consulting Services International (BICSI): www.bicsi.org

Construction Specification Institute (CSI): www.csinet.org/s_csi/index.asp

Educational Technology Resources: http://ifets.massey.ac.nz/links/pages/Educational_technology_resources/

Educational Technology Review: www.aace.org/pubs/etr/issue4/current.cfm

Institute for Electrical and Electronic Engineers (IEEE): www.ieee.org/portal/index.jsp

Internet Society: www.isoc.org

Milken Family Foundation: www.mff.org/edtech

National Education Technology Plan: www.nationaledtechplan.org/

National Educational Technology Standards Project: http://cnets.iste.org/

References

Alexander, Christopher, Sara Ishikawa, and Murray Silverstein. 1977. *A Pattern Language: Towns, Buildings, Construction.* New York: Oxford University Press.

Barr, Robert D., and William H. Parrett. 1997. *How to Create Alternative, Magnet, and Charter Schools That Work.* Bloomington, Ind.: National Education Service.

Bottoms, Gene, Betty Creech, and Mary Johnson. 1997. "Academic and Vocational Teachers Working Together Contribute to Higher Levels of Student Achievement." High Schools That Work Research Brief 9. Accessible online at www.sreb.org/programs/hstw/publications/briefs/97brief9.asp.

Brooks, Robert G., Judith Stein, Donald R. Waldrip, and Phale D. Hale, eds. 1999. *Definitive Studies of Magnet Schools: Voices of Public School Choice.* The Woodlands, Tex.: Magnet Schools of America.

Charter Friends National Network (CFNN). 1999. "Paying for the Charter Schoolhouse: A Policy Agenda for Charter School Facilities Financing." Accessible online at www.charterfriends.org/facilities.html.

Csikszentmihalyi, Mihaly, and Barbara Schneider. 2000. *Becoming Adult: How Teenagers Prepare for the World of Work.* New York: Basic Books.

Dalton, Bridget, and Dana L. Grisham. 2001. "Teaching Students to Evaluate Internet Information Critically." Accessible at the Reading Online website at www.readingonline.org/past/past_index.asp?HREF=/editorial/december2001/ind ex.html.

Design-Build Institute of America (DBIA). 2002. *Survey of State Procurement Laws Affecting Design-Build (Combined Design and Construction Contracting)*, 2nd ed. Washington, D.C.: DBIA.

Dillon, Sam. 2002. "Heft of Students' Backpacks Turns Into Textbook Battle." *New York Times,* December 24.

Dillon, Sam. 2003. "In Some Schools, It's One Teacher, One Student." *New York Times,* January 19, A1, A10.

Educational Development Center (EDC). 2000. *IT Pathway Pipeline Model: Rethinking Information Technology Learning in Schools.* Newton, Mass.: EDC.

Fisher, Kimball, and Mareen Fisher. 2000. *The Distance Manager: A Hands On Guide to Managing Off-Site Employees and Virtual Teams.* New York: McGraw-Hill.

Florida, Richard. 2002. *The Rise of the Creative Class.* New York: Basic Books.

Gormley, Michael. 2003. "Charter Schools Scoring Bigger Gains Than Traditional Schools." *Stamford Advocate,* November 12.

Grandin, Temple. 1995. *Thinking in Pictures and Other Reports From My Life With Autism.* Foreword by Oliver Sacks. New York: Doubleday.

Gross, Jane. 2003. "What's Big, Yellow and Humiliating? Full Lot at Greenwich High Means New Reality: The Bus." *New York Times*, January 27.

Herszenhorn, David M. 2004. "Report Faults New York's First 3 Charter Schools." *New York Times,* January 13, A1, B2.

215

Kay, Jane Holtz. 2003. "Trinity Corridor Shows How to Stop School Sprawl." *Hartford Courant,* March 23.

Kretchmer, Mark R. 1999. "The Do-It-Yourself Approach to Interbuilding Networks." *School Planning and Management,* November.

Lewin, Tamara. 2003. "Last Chance High: A School for the Unwanted; At School for Hardest Cases, Perseverance, Night and Day." *New York Times,* July 3.

Lewis, L., et al. 1999. "Condition of America's Public Schools." *Education Statistics Quarterly*, Fall.

Malyn-Smith, J., J. Donaldson, V. Spera, J. Wong, R. Kimboko, C. Llorente, M. Miller, S. Bredin, and V. Guilfoy. N.d. *IT Pathway Pipeline Model: Rethinking Information Technology in Schools.* Newton, Mass.: Educational Development Center.

Pinker, Steven. 2003. "How to Get Inside a Student's Head." *New York Times*, January 31.

Schorr, Jonathan. 2002. *Hard Lessons: The Promise of an Inner-City Charter School.* New York: Ballantine.

Seep, Benjamin, et al. 2000. *Classroom Acoustics: A Resource for Creating Learning Environments With Desirable Listening Conditions.* Melville, N.Y.: Acoustical Society of America, Technical Committee on Architectural Acoustics.

Stallard, Charles H., and Julie S. Cocker. 2001. *The Promise of Technology in Schools: The Next 20 Years.* Lanham, Md.: ScarecrowEducation.

Star Tribune (Minneapolis–St. Paul). 2002. "School Choice: Widely Embraced, Beneficial . . . But More Oversight Is Needed." Editorial. June 6, A22.

Sterling, Bruce. 2002. *Tomorrow Now: Envisioning the Next Fifty Years.* New York: Random House.

Stern, Robert A. M. 2000. "Schools Too Grand to Turn Into Trash." *New York Times,* January 22, A15.

Stone, James R., III. 1995. "Cooperative Vocational Education in the Urban School: Towards a Systems Approach." *Education and Urban Society* 27(3): 328–52.

Streifer, Philip A. 2000. "Decision Support Systems for School Improvement." Unpublished essay.

U.S. General Accounting Office (GAO). 1995. *School Facilities: Condition of America's Schools, February 1995.* GAO/HEHS-95-61. Accessible online at www.access.gpo.gov/su_docs/aces/aces160.shtml.

Visher, Mary, Doug Lauen, Linda Merola, and Elliott Medrich. 1998. *School to Work in the 1990s: A Look at Programs and Practices in American High Schools.* Berkeley, Calif.: MPR Associates.

Visher, Mary G., Peter Teitelbaum, and David Emanuel. 1999. *Key High School Reform Strategies: An Overview of Research Findings.* Berkeley, Calif.: MPR Associates.

White, Emily. 2003. "School Away From School." *New York Times Magazine,* December 7, 34–44.

Winter, Greg. 2003. "Gates Foundation Providing $31 Million for Small Schools." *New York Times*, February 26.

Index

About the Authors and Contributors

AUTHORS

Edwin T. Merritt, Ed.D., is director of educational planning and research for Fletcher-Thompson, Inc. Over his 29-year career as a school superintendent (in three different districts), he was involved in more than 25 new construction, renovation, and major maintenance projects. A futurist, educator, and expert on educational technology, Merritt has received many awards, including the Connecticut State Superintendents' Golden Shield Award for Exemplary Service (1999), the General Connecticut Coast YMCA "Strong Kids Builder" Award (1999), the Bridgeport Regional Leader of the Year Award (1998), and the Rotary Club's Paul Harris Fellowship (1998), and he has been a National and State Parent/Teachers' Association Honoree (1993, 1999). In 2004, Merritt was the recipient of the Connecticut Association of Public School Superintendents' Emeritus Award. He has written for *American School & University* and *School Business Affairs*, among other publications.

James A. Beaudin, AIA, is the principal of Fletcher-Thompson, Inc.'s Education Practice Group. Over his career, he has been involved in the design of almost 100 schools in 45 communities—for a total of more than 10 million square feet of public and private school construction. Besides new construction projects, he has directed renovations, code-compliance improvements, system-wide studies, and educational programming and specification development. Under his leadership, Fletcher-Thompson's Educational Studio has received numerous awards and other recognition. Articles authored or coauthored by Beaudin have appeared in *American School & University*, *Facilities Design & Management*, *School Business Affairs*, and *School Planning & Management* magazines.

Charles R. Cassidy is director of planning specialized educational facilities for Fletcher-Thompson, Inc. Prior to joining the firm, he served for more than ten years as administrator of Connecticut's Interdistrict Magnet Schools and Interdistrict Cooperative Grant Programs. Earlier in his career, he held a similar position in the New York State Department of Education. Cassidy also serves as secretary of Magnet Schools of America (MSA).

Patricia A. Myler, AIA, is director of pre-K–12 facilities and a senior associate at Fletcher-Thompson, Inc. Since joining the firm in 1995, she has served as a studio leader and project manager and is currently director of the Hartford, Connecticut, office, focusing on educational projects that have ranged from feasibility studies for elementary, middle, high, and magnet schools; to additions and renovations; to new primary, magnet, middle, and high schools. She has also provided prereferendum consulting services to several Connecticut school districts. Myler also serves as commissioner of government affairs, is a member of the board of directors, and is president-elect of the Connecticut chapter of the American Institute of Architects (AIA). Her published writings include several articles for *School Business Affairs* and *American School & University.*

CONTRIBUTORS

Donald Bodnar has more than 20 years of experience in the communications industry. In 1993, he founded D&D Systems for the purpose of providing "best of breed" telecommunications engineering, design, and project management services to its clients. In 1998, he founded Trading Support Solutions (TSS) to provide technical engineering, support, and project management services to financial trading floors. In 2001, these entities merged, becoming Axiom Group.

Christine M. Casey, Ed.D., is an independent consultant working for the improvement of technology education in schools and colleges. Over her long career in public education, she has held leadership roles in the school systems of New York City, Westchester County (N.Y.), New York State, Stamford (Conn.), and the State of Connecticut. Casey helped found El Puente, now a thriving youth program in Brooklyn. She chaired the Advisory Board for the New York Public Library Early Childhood Resource and Information Center. For two years, she was a regional associate for the New York State Department of Education. She has served as a district director of special education, as an assistant superintendent, and, for the Stamford Public Schools, as an assistant superintendent for curriculum and instruction. She led the team that formed the Academy of Information Technology and Engineering, a nationally acclaimed technology-based high school in Stamford. In 2002, she researched a report for the Connecticut Office for Workforce Competitiveness that proposed ways to reform education to produce a pipeline of future employees with the necessary skills to be productive in a highly technical, knowledge-based economy. Its recommendations have been implemented in a pilot initiative called Connecticut Career Choices.

Timothy P. Cohen has more than 15 years of experience in the architectural field. Before joining Fletcher-Thompson he served as a designer at a Hartford, Connecticut–based architectural firm, where his primary responsibilities included master planning, programming, and design. As a project designer for Fletcher-Thompson, he is responsible for project design quality and for ensuring that owners' expectations and project budgets are appropriately reflected in the design solutions.

Daniel Davis, AIA, a senior design architect with Fletcher-Thompson, Inc., has more than 20 years of experience designing a broad range of project types, including educational, institutional, commercial, corporate and industrial facilities. He is a professor in the University of Hartford's Department of Architecture, where he teaches architectural history and design. His architectural writings have appeared in a variety of publications, ranging from local newspapers to national professional journals. His projects have been published in leading architectural magazines and have won prestigious design awards.

Robert Dixon is a nationally recognized leader in telecommunications. With Gary Therrien, he founded Advantech Group, LLC, in June 2003 with a small team of information technology professionals who have public- and private-sector experience across a broad range of IT environments, including planning, project implementation, change management, and operating support. Previously, Dixon worked for more than 30 years with central service agencies of the State of Connecticut, planning and delivering IT services and solutions across state and local government and many affiliated not-for-profit agencies. He specialized in developing and implementing networks using leading-edge optical technologies, especially for the Connecticut Education Network, which serves 1,150 public K–12 schools, 450 libraries, and 70 public and private colleges and universities. He was director of operations for Connecticut's Department of Information Technology, managing a staff of more than 100 professionals who consolidated several data centers into a new facility housing large mainframe computers, several hundred web-servers, storage networks, and a sophisticated network operations center supporting 1,600 government sites. Dixon has led several user associations to improve their use of emerging technologies, measure their investments, and obtain regulatory relief. Advantech Group specializes in developing strategies for implementing the most appropriate technology for meeting the needs of a particular business, and the firm helps organizations develop processes that routinely reprioritize IT efforts to meet current needs.

L. Gerald Dunn, R.A., a senior design architect with Fletcher-Thompson, Inc., has extensive experience in designing schools, performance centers, retail/entertainment facilities, hotels, and mixed-use projects, as well as in master planning large-scale developments worldwide. He served as director of urban design for the Disney Development Company in Paris and as principal concept architect for Disney's Animal Kingdom in Disney World, Florida. Educational projects on which he has worked include high schools, vo-tech schools, middle grade and elementary schools, and higher education facilities.

Thomas A. Fantacone, AIA, is principal of the College and University Practice Group of RJF Fletcher-Thompson Architects, LLC, with offices in East Brunswick, New Jersey. Over his long association with the firm, he has served as senior designer on a wide range of projects, including more than 1 million square feet of educational, research, and laboratory facilities. He has designed a variety of facilities for colleges and universities throughout New Jersey, and his experience extends to the design of specialized educational facilities, such as the award-winning Norman A. Bleshman Regional Day School for the Multiply Handicapped; the Middlesex County Academy for Science, Mathematics, and Engineering Technologies; and the new Eden Family of Services autism education/treatment center in Princeton, now awaiting construction.

Mark S. Hesselgrave, AIA, a project designer for Fletcher-Thompson, Inc., has extensive experience in the design of educational facilities, including high schools and a full range of building types for institutions of higher education across the United States.

James A. Keaney Jr. joined Diggs Construction, LLC, in 2003 as a program manager for the Hartford, Connecticut, Public Schools. Phase 1 of the program consists of five schools with a total combined budget of more than $200 million and is scheduled to be completed in the second quarter of 2006. Prior to joining Diggs Construction, Keaney provided program management services to Edison Schools, the nation's leading and largest education management company. For Edison, he managed the preconstruction and construction efforts for multiple sites in the Northeast.

Julie A. Kim, AIA, a project manager with Fletcher-Thompson, Inc., has 20 years of professional experience in commercial, institutional, and educational design. Recent work includes programming three K–8 facilities in New Jersey, as well as a design-build project for the Breakthrough Academy in Hartford, Connecticut. She has prepared districtwide design guidelines for new pre-K–8 schools in Hartford and New Haven, Connecticut.

LEARN is a Regional Educational Service Center (RESC) serving 24 school districts in southeastern/shoreline Connecticut. Established in 1967 by local districts, LEARN is one of six RESCs in the state. The purpose of each RESC is to enhance the quality of education and provide solutions to identified needs through a wide range of programs and services. LEARN currently serves 25 towns and communities with a combined student population of nearly 53,000. Through its leadership and resources and by working with schools, students, families, and community agencies, LEARN promotes regional and statewide cooperation and provides a framework for districts to achieve their goals.

Jeffrey M. Leavenworth, P.E., is Fletcher-Thompson, Inc.'s chief electrical engineer. He has more than 30 years of experience in all aspects of electrical design, working on a wide range of projects that have included educational, aviation, office, industrial, municipal, medical, military, retail, and extended-care facilities.

Richard S. Oja, AIA, was a senior project manager at Fletcher-Thompson, Inc.

John C. Oliveto, P.E., is principal of Fletcher-Thompson's Government Practice Group. His education-related work includes construction support services for a number of Connecticut school projects, including additions and renovations to the Eleanor B. Kennelly School in Hartford and renovations to the 6 to 6 Magnet School in Bridgeport. Long active in the Connecticut Building Congress, he is now serving his second term as that organization's president.

Marcia T. Palluzzi, L.A., is a registered landscape architect in Connecticut, Massachusetts, and Rhode Island with wide experience in the planning, design, and implementation of educational, recreational, and commercial design projects. She has performed districtwide option and feasibility studies for several Connecticut school districts and has served as landscape architect for both K–12 and higher education projects.

Chester A. Salit, AIA, is a managing principal of Fletcher-Thompson, Inc., and the firm's chief operating officer. Over his more than 25 years as an architect, he has overseen the planning and design of more than 2 million square feet of educational facilities, both new construction and renovations.

Michael E. Schrier is a project manager for Fletcher-Thompson, Inc. Since joining the firm, he has been involved in numerous education-related projects, including preparation of required state-funding proposals, feasibility studies, programming, and the design of additions and renovations to the Brien McMahon High School in Norwalk, Connecticut.

Jeffrey A. Sells, AIA, is the design leader of Fletcher-Thompson, Inc.'s Education Practice Group, responsible for the design approach on all of the firm's educational projects. He has designed new elementary and high school buildings, as well as additions and renovations of elementary, middle, high, and magnet schools in districts throughout Connecticut. He has also designed college and university facilities, including the Thomas Dodd Archives and Research Center at the University of Connecticut—the subject of a front-page story in the *New York Times*'s Connecticut section. His work has been featured in professional publications and has won numerous awards and special recognition. His written work has appeared in numerous design and construction industry trade publications, as well as in the popular media. He has often been quoted in newspaper and television reports focusing on Fletcher-Thompson projects in Connecticut.

Gary Therrien is cofounder, with Robert Dixon, of Advantech Group, LLC. He has more than 27 years of information technology experience, with more than 6 years in the private sector (Travelers Insurance Co. and Hartford Insurance Group) working in computer science and telecommunications, and 21 years working for the State of Connecticut developing programs that promote the efficient use of new technology across agencies with similar needs. He has been responsible for the development of business solutions that meet current needs while leveraging current applications and databases to keep the costs of new systems down. Before founding Advantech, Therrien led the team that implemented a comprehensive technical architecture process that defines IT standards, best practices, and policies for all state agencies in Connecticut.

James Waller is the editor of Fletcher-Thompson's Schools of the Future series. He has more than 15 years' experience as a public relations representative for architecture, engineering, construction management, and other firms in the building design and construction industry. He has ghostwritten hundreds of articles for the building industries trade press. A longtime freelance editor and journalist, Waller is now the principal of a Brooklyn, New York–based editorial, graphic design, and book-packaging firm, Thumb Print New York, Inc. He is the author of several books packaged by Thumb Print and published by Stewart, Tabori and Chang. He also teaches writing, most recently at Polytechnic University in Brooklyn.